Merry Christmas 1990
All my love.

Rudoly.

DERBYSHIRE

The King's England

A New Domesday Book of
10,000 Towns and Villages

Edited by Arthur Mee

The First Eight Volumes

Enchanted Land
London
Derbyshire
Kent
Lake Counties
Lancashire
Sussex
Warwickshire

NOTHING like these books has ever been presented to the English people. Every place has been visited. The compilers have travelled half-a-million miles and have prepared a unique picture of our countryside as it has come down through the ages, a census of all that is enduring and worthy of record.

THE King's England is not greatly concerned with private or inaccessible places, but it gives all that can be seen by all. It should be observed that the mention of a century means the century in time and not in style of architecture, though often the two agree.

HODDER & STOUGHTON

The Dove Winds its way through the Hills

THE KING'S ENGLAND

DERBYSHIRE

THE PEAK COUNTRY

EDITED BY
ARTHUR MEE

With 226 Places
and 134 Pictures

THE KING'S ENGLAND PRESS
1990

First Published 1937 by
Hodder & Stoughton Ltd

This edition published 1990 by
The King's England Press
37 Crookes Lane, Carlton
Nr Barnsley, S. Yorks

ISBN 1 872438 01 6

Printed and bound by
SMITH SETTLE
Ilkley Road, Otley, West Yorkshire LS21 3JP

TRIBUTE

*To Claude and Lois Scanlon for their invaluable
services in producing this book*

for the pictures to
Sidney Tranter, Art Editor,
and to the following photographers:
*Messrs. E. Bastard, Brian Clayton, Fred Crossley, Country
Life, J. Dixon-Scott, W. P. Frith, F. A. Holmes, Newtonian
Press Service, H. P. Nunn, John Stone, E. W. Tattersall,
W. F. Taylor, Valentine & Sons, F. Deaville Walker, W.
Winter, and to the L M S Railway and the National Trust*

PICTURES OF DERBYSHIRE

*Where the picture is not on or facing the page given
it is in the set of pictures beginning on that page*

PICTURES OF DERBYSHIRE

PICTURES OF DERBYSHIRE

Traveller's Delight

IT is one of the delightful counties, not overpowering with history but filled with Nature's lovely places, packed with natural beauty in infinite variety, from magnificent Peakland heights to caverns deep in the heart of the rock.

It teems with interest for those who seek the story of the past in mineral and stone, in stone circles and barrows. It is watered by charming rivers spanned by lovely bridges, and has fine parks where historic families have lived for centuries. A place for everybody is Derbyshire, with more than a thousand square miles of wonderland almost in the heart of England, with about 750,000 people on 650,000 acres, and as fine a group of villages as any of our inland counties.

The oldest tale of Stone Age Derbyshire is told by Cresswell Crags, where was found the first example of pictorial art in England. The great stones take up the tale of the prehistoric past, with Arbor Low Stone Circle second only to Stonehenge, fortresses like Carl Wark and Markland Grips, ruined chambers, and barrows where pottery and bronze have been found with the people who used them. There are traces of stations and roads made by the Romans who mined the lead they found in Derbyshire, and Saxon crosses among the finest in the land. Of feudal castles and keeps the most outstanding is Peverel Castle, crowning a high precipice at Castleton, the centre of government in Norman times for the High Peak Forest, and the setting for the submission of Malcolm, King of Scotland, to Henry the Second. The foundations of Duffield's massive keep are laid bare.

There are monastic ruins at Repton and Dale Abbey, and Haddon Hall is the finest medieval house for a hundred miles, or perhaps in England. South Wingfield manor house, which held captive Mary Queen of Scots, is the splendid ruin of the finest fortified house of the 15th century. Chatsworth, the Palace of the Peak, is one of the stateliest homes of England, set in a glorious park and filled with treasure; it was another of the prisons of the tragic queen. Halls like stately Kedleston, or Barlborough and Melbourne, the charming halls of Tissington and Sudbury, Elvaston Castle, and many an ancient manor (among them the delightful Eyam Hall) carry on the tale of the domestic architecture of this homely countryside. Lea Hurst at Holloway is 19th century, but it is a fine place, and was the home of Florence Nightingale.

Here and there the old market-houses stand, as at Bakewell and Winster, and there are old village crosses—charming ones at Repton, Bonsall, and Higham, and a rare one at Wheston. Some of the old villages keep green the spirit of the past with picturesque customs and famous events—the ringing of the curfew and the pancake bell at Ashford-in-the-Water, the great Well-Dressing Day at Tissington, the Garland Day festival at Castleton, the sheep-dog trials in the valleys and the pastures, and the remarkable Shrove Tuesday football match at Ashbourne. There is a pilgrimage in June to Padley Chapel in memory of two martyrs, and a service every August at Cucklet Delf in memory of the heroes of Eyam. We come upon the memory of Robin Hood, and Little John who buried his friend with a green sod under his head and another at his feet is said to sleep at Hathersage. Fishermen follow the wake of Izaak Walton and Charles Cotton, and walkers tread the haunts beloved by John Ruskin, Charlotte Brontë, George Eliot, and Dr Johnson.

A marvellous place it is to walk or ride in, with the glories of Derbyshire scenery working up to its climax in 56 miles from south to north. The golden meadows of the south, watered by the Trent and the Dove, and the richly pastured farms, give way to a charming countryside of green hills and dales, and then comes a world of stone-walled fields and treeless moors, white roads and the sky, bringing us to the wild grandeur of the

Kinder Range with its great heights, its moorland and trackless wastes, its cloughs and waterfalls.

There are broad and beautiful dales where we may ride, looking up to heights all round; and exquisite dales where only feet may walk and no wheels run, dales like gems of rock and wood and water adorning the feet of the hills. There are dry dales like stark ravines, gaunt mountain passes and delightful dells, rocks in fantastic formation, and cliff-like edges overhanging the valleys. There are highways and views as surprising as they are entrancing—the Via Gellia riding along a lovely ravine shut in by cliffs mantled in green, the cornice road above Ashwood Dale with its views of the Wye, and the grand stretch of a dozen miles between Ashopton and Glossop, climbing to nearly 1700 feet, with one of the wildest tracts in the country on one hand, and on the other the Kinderscout Plateau. Steeply edged by bold rocks, this high land, extending for miles over 2000 feet above sea level, gives the name of the Peak to the most distinctive mass of the Pennine Chain before it sinks gradually into the Midland plain.

One unforgettable Derbyshire view is from Headstone Head, where the Wye is seen swinging sharply round into Monsal Dale, a paradise into which the railway came in Ruskin's day, stirring him to mighty wrath. Another is the magnificent panorama from the summit of Win Hill, into which come the valleys of the Derwent, the Ashop, and the Noe, and the peaceful Vale of Hope. A third is from Mam Tor above the Vales of Hope and Edale; and a fourth the famous Surprise from Millstone Edge Nick above Hathersage, where we see the Vale of Hope and the Derwent Valley framed in a fine array of moors and hills. For those who wander through the valleys and climb the hills there are a thousand kinds of wild flowers.

Derbyshire's unique beauty lies in the track of its streams, and must often be sought on foot. As every lover of the county knows, there is no other way by which we can make its full acquaintance. In this it is like the Lakes. Nearly the whole of it is in the basin of the Trent, for, though this river crosses only the rich southern meadows, it takes to itself the three chief rivers and their countless tributaries gathered on their way. The Dove falls into the Trent at Newton Solney, and the Derwent (swelled by the Wye at Rowsley) at Wilne near Sawley.

The Derwent, dominant river of Derbyshire, rises on the lofty pathless moorlands culminating in Bleaklow at a height of 2000 feet and Barrow Stones a little less, its head waters for about five miles forming the boundary with Yorkshire. Then it flows down the middle of the county through scenes of great beauty, its moorland tributaries, the Westend, the Abbey Brook, the Alport, and the Noe, coming from wilds as remote in feeling as any in the British Isles. Engineering feats in our own day are transforming the Upper Derwent Valley above Bamford into Derbyshire's Lake Country, by damming the river into a chain of reservoirs for our water supply. Below its junction with the Noe, at the end of the green Hope Vale, the Derwent is escorted by ridges between 1200 and 1500 feet high on each side; then it winds through Chatsworth Park and receives the Wye at Rowsley. Beyond Darley Dale it reaches the rocky gorge of the Matlocks, the valley continuing wooded and picturesque by Cromford to Ambergate, where it is joined by the Amber. It flows through Belper and Derby to the wide vale of the Trent, saying goodbye to its last mill-wheel at Wilne after collecting the waters of nearly 300,000 acres.

Charming as is the Derwent Valley, the Wye Valley equals it in beauty, though it lacks the broader views and the finer grouping of the hills around the Derwent's course. Impetuous and hurrying, it helps in the making of delightful pictures in its short journey, which we can follow in the length of a summer's day. It flows in a deeply cut channel through narrow, steep, wooded dales; only here and there can they be seen well from above. Rising near Buxton, one of its springs on the slopes of Axe Edge, one in the neighbourhood of Combs Moss, another coming to life in the depths of Poole's Cavern, the Wye leaves the town through Ashwood Dale, and threads Wye Dale, the limestone ravine of Chee Dale, Miller's Dale, Cressbrook Dale, and Monsal Dale where it winds round the foot of Fin Cop. Here it is joined again by the highway which left Wye Dale to climb to Taddington and has come down Taddington Dale, and the river and the road go on as companions for the rest of the way. After passing through Ashford-in-the-Water (the Garden of the Peak) and through Bakewell, the valley opens out a little into meadowy sweetness; the river passes Haddon Hall with its grey towers, receives the waters from exquisite little dales, and falls into the Derwent.

We are not alone in thinking that there is no river in England to compare with the Dove, which rises on the slopes of Axe Edge and becomes the county boundary with Staffordshire till it reaches the Trent. In spite of its peerless beauty it is the most modest of rivers, hiding itself, where it is at its best, in a deeply-cleft passage of which the whereabouts cannot readily be perceived. Dovedale, its most exquisite part, is matchless in delicate loveliness. It lurks unseen. No highway quite reaches it. It can be more easily missed than found by those who casually pass, and when it is found it can only be seen by walking.

For the first part of its course the river is shut in on each side by a limestone plateau which rises now and then to greater heights. Its first patch of great beauty comes with Beresford Dale, where the clear stream runs between green margins and limestone rocks, plentifully wooded and decked with flowers in due season, and the charming little fishing house Charles Cotton built for Izaak Walton still stands on the Staffordshire side. Then the river runs through a sombre ravine, and into this at its southern end comes the dry windswept gorge of Biggin Dale. The river winds on to the remote hamlet of Milldale and the quaint little Viator's Bridge, and quite suddenly rocky portals are reached, and the Dovedale which enchants the world begins. We are now at one of the loveliest spots in the loveliest countryside in the land, and it continues for over two miles as the crow flies.

It is a succession of scenes of dainty beauty set in a frame of rocky wildness. The sides of the sheer narrow gorge are constantly varying in outline, and are thickly wooded and clad with green, with wild flowers in every crevice. The stream runs clear with little windings giving the view a perpetual freshness. It foams in shallows over the stony bed, and its still deep trout pools make it a veritable Angler's Paradise. The footpath rises and falls. There is no monotony. The whole scene is a rarity, complete, with no discordant feature. Seen in quietude, it is the choicest scrap of England, and has laid its charm on every sensitive traveller who ever trod its slender path. We should see it both ways. At the end of the gorge come the stepping-stones, the grassy Thorpe Cloud rising like a cone to block the expanding view, and Bunster Hill, Guardian of the Dale on the Staffordshire side. The Dove slips past to meet its first tributary, the River Manifold, beyond an open glade, and we have lost our beautiful companion.

It is a heartening thing to remember that most of this enchanted vale belongs to the English people, and that soon the whole of it may belong to them. Perhaps the most exquisitely English piece of England, it has great claim to be one of our National Parks, for though so hidden away it is in the very heart of the land, within reach of thousands who live in crowded industrial towns.

No higher praise is needed of the old Derbyshire bridges than that they are worthy of the rivers they span. Among the outstanding ones are the two at Ashford-in-the-Water, two at Bakewell, those of Baslow, Beeley, Rowsley, Cromford, Conksbury Bridge over the Lathkill, the Monk's Bridge at Egginton, and the romantic and partly medieval Swarkeston Bridge which crosses the Trent and strides for most of a mile over meadows like the Field of the Cloth of Gold in spring. The Young Pretender's advance guard came to this bridge in 1745, but, instead of crossing it, went back to Derby to join in the retreat which ended at Culloden. At Froggatt, Haddon, and over the Bradford near Youlgreave are three of the little pack-horse bridges still left in the county, and another is at Bakewell.

From the point of view of industry and business it is the

eastern mineral belt of Derbyshire and the agriculture of the south, with the influence of Derby, that in the main makes the county prosperous; but it is the call of northern Derbyshire to lovers of Nature that appeals to the world most strongly. Next to the Lake District, it is the part of England that has attracted the greatest number of enthusiastic ramblers during the last half-century. Sheffield, on the one hand, built on the spurs from the Pennine range, and Manchester and its neighbouring towns on the other hand, pour them forth in thousands.

For those who want caves Derbyshire has some genuine ones, such as the Peak Cavern at Castleton and the Bagshaw Cavern at Bradwell, with glittering arrays of stalactites and crystals all skilfully shown; and there are mines well worth a visit, with miles of underground recesses inviting variations from the breezy moorlands.

There are bare grey hilltop villages, like Taddington and Over Haddon, which are keys to beauty close at hand; villages which are delightful green oases such as Hassop and Snelston, and Alport where the Lathkill and the Bradford Brook join hands. There are villages which have come into history. At Whitting-ton the Glorious Revolution was born; here the Whigs got to-gether and decided that the Stuarts must go and that Dutch William should rule in their stead. Pentrich has its pitiful story of the rioters after Waterloo. At Dethick was born a boy who grew up to lose his handsome head for plotting against a queen. In an attic at Blackwell an invention was perfected which revolutionized the hosiery trade. Alabaster from humble Chellaston has found its way into many a fine hall and church, and stone from Darley Dale has helped to make the Thames Embankment. Here at Darley Dale the old Mill Close Mine has revived the prosperity of Derbyshire's lead production.

Derby, the county town, has lost much that was old, but makes up for it in enterprise. It was the home of the first silk mill in England, and has set up the fine iron gates of the old mill, typical of a noted county craft, by its library. Now arti-ficial silk is made on its doorstep, at Spondon. Derby makes

7

some of our loveliest china, our most luxurious motor cars, and aeroplane engines; and it builds the trains for one of our great railway systems. Dr Johnson was married in the chancel of one of its churches. All Saints, now the cathedral church, has one of the finest towers in the land, and shelters the great monument to Derbyshire's great builder, Bess of Hardwick.

In 1773 calico was first made in a mill at Cromford; at Riddings the petroleum industry was born, mother of our great oil industries. Glossop, the northern gateway of the Peak, is the county's little cotton town today, with paper mills as well as cotton mills. Ashbourne, the gateway to green hills and dales, has one of two factories turning out together a million tins of milk a week, half of it going abroad; it comes, of course, from the rich pasture lands, which support many dairies of repute. Buxton, famous like Matlock for its warm springs, is perhaps our highest town in a glorious situation, and has one of the biggest domes in the world in its hospital. Long Eaton, making lace, is near the biggest railway sidings in the world, at Toton.

The story of Derbyshire's churches is one of fine architecture of all the great building centuries, of beauty and many treasures, of rare and unique things. Chesterfield has a famous twisted spire, Mellor has perhaps the oldest wooden pulpit in England. Wilne has one of the two oldest fonts in the land. Youlgreave's Norman font is unique. Lovely Repton, with its fine school, is the site of the first Christian church of the converted Saxons in the Midlands, and has in its church a crypt which has been described as "the most perfect example of Anglo-Saxon architecture on a small scale now extant." Melbourne has one of our finest Norman churches, and modest Steetley has what many believe to be the loveliest example of a small Norman church either in England or in Normandy. Bakewell has one of the finest collections of ancient coffin stones, and groups of faded funeral garlands (rare pathetic relics) are to be seen at Matlock and Trusley and Ashford-in-the-Water.

There is beautiful woodwork old and new, and much old glass at Morley and Norbury. There are brasses of knights and priests

The Wooded Hills and Valley

The River winding through the Gorge

DOVEDALE BEYOND COMPARE

The Beauty of Dovedale

Monsal Dale

A Hillside Farm below Mam Tor

The Winding Road below Mam Tor

and civilians, and fine monuments in alabaster and stone. There is no more dainty tomb than that with the figure of Thomas Cokayne in Youlgreave church; no more lovely figure than Penelope Boothby, who sleeps in Ashbourne church, below the soaring spire known as the Pride of the Peak. Kedleston's old church has a rich modern chapel where the sculptured figures of Lord Curzon and his first wife lie on their tomb. Tideswell church is beautiful enough to be called the Cathedral of the Peak. Dale Church, in the village with the ruins of Dale Abbey, is one of the smallest in the land, and shares its roof with a farmhouse.

Some of the loveliest trees in the country are in the churchyards. Darley Dale has one of England's oldest yews, and Doveridge has another ancient veteran. Rowsley has a grand old elm, and Ashbourne a cedar it would be hard to beat. Bretby, the place Disraeli loved to stay at, has one of the oldest known cedars of Lebanon in England.

Into Derbyshire's roll of honour for men who won national distinction come John Flamsteed, our first Astronomer Royal, Samuel Richardson the novelist, William Howitt the poet, Herbert Spencer the philosopher, Joseph Wright the painter, Chantrey the sculptor (who will always belong to Derbyshire though Yorkshire has lately seized his native village), Jedediah Strutt who invented the ribbed stocking frame, Sir James Outram, the Bayard of India, William Bagshawe, Apostle of the Peak, William Newton, the Peak Minstrel, Anthony Fitzherbert the great judge, William Hutton, historian, Thomas Linacre, physician, Aston Cokayne, the poet, and Sir John Chandos of Radbourne, who saved the Black Prince at Poitiers. Here lies Erasmus Darwin, born in Notts but buried at Breadsall; and at Ault Hucknall sleeps Thomas Hobbes, closely connected with the county as tutor in the Cavendish family. George Stephenson lies at Chesterfield, where he settled down when his work was done; the town owes its rise very largely to him. Florence Nightingale belongs to the county too, for though she was born in Florence it was her childhood home at Holloway that came to her mind in the quiet hours when she was far away.

Take it for all in all, the traveller who has seen his last of Derbyshire will never see its like again, for it is unique in its beauty, as changing as a flower in spring, with a freshness and a tenderness which seem to hang about its hills and dales, and a haunting loveliness which rises to enchantment at its greatest heights and in its deepest solitudes.

Proud Knight of the Peak

ABNEY. It stands with Abney Grange, two hamlets a mile apart, set in a solitary world of moor and hill and wooded vale. From a thousand feet above the sea Abney looks out to Shatton Moor nearly half as high again, and to that proud knight of Derbyshire Sir William Hill, 1408 feet high on Eyam Moor.

A lovely green hill is Abney Low, with two brooks flowing round it on their way to join the Derwent through rocky woodland and a charming glen. Whether we come to Abney or leave it the road is sheer delight. One way we come by deep plantations to where the ancient Highlow Hall stands near the road, a battlemented manor house now a farm, with a quaint ball-topped gateway and a stone dovecot.

On Eyam Moor, presided over by Sir William Hill, are the remains of the Wet Withens, one of the country's most important stone circles.

In a Hollow of the Moors

ALDERWASLEY. It lies in a hollow of the moors, high above fine woodland slopes rising from the lovely valley of the Derwent. With a glorious hill all aglow in rhododendron time, and flowers abounding everywhere that need but Nature's tending, it has views as fair as eye could wish to see in a landscape full of story.

We see Crich's monument to 11,400 men who died for Peace; the woods of Lea Hurst, home of Florence Nightingale; and Dethick's ancient tower, which Anthony Babington knew before he prayed in vain that Elizabeth would save him from the scaffold. Less than two miles away rises Alport Height, the loftiest ground in the south of the county, nine acres of it belonging to the National Trust. Here the great crag called Alport Stone challenges climbers, rewarding the successful with a grand view.

Sorrowing for a tenant was the great house in the park when we called. It has been the home of the Lowes and the Hurts until not long ago; it was Thomas Lowe who built the old church, now all forlorn, when Henry the Eighth was king, and Francis Hurt who built the new one in the middle of the last century. A simple building now used for funerals, the Tudor church has a doorway carved in somewhat crazy fashion under a hoodmould with stone heads.

Francis Hurt's church (he died the year after he built it) is just within the gates of the park, where stand two majestic trees. A splendid cedar throws its shadow on the walls, while just below a sparkling stream runs with little waterfalls and clear trout pools.

Five Memories

ALFRETON. It was mining coal in Chaucer's day, but it has kept some beauty and much interest. Close to the stir of the busy little market town, but peacefully set at the end of a road which opens out to a path across the deer park of the great house, is the church with a story going back to the last days of the Normans when Robert Fitz Ranulph gave it to Beauchief Abbey. Its oldest fragment is the lofty pointed tower arch of about 1200, with cable and nail-head in its capitals, the rest of the tower being 200 years younger. As old as the tower arch is part of a coffin lid carved with the head of a cross; now under glass, it may have marked the grave of the first priest of this place.

The fine 14th-century porch is guarded by a modern figure of St Martin in an elaborate niche, below which projects a cornice carved with flowers and shields. The doorway through which we enter the church is as old as the porch. So too are the nave arcades, though each was given an east-end bay last century, when the north arcade was rebuilt stone for stone. From the 15th century comes the vestry with its stone-vaulted roof.

Faces on windows and porch smile on us as we come and go, and on the old steps of a vanished cross a sundial counts the hours.

We found five memories here which touch the chords of human sympathy. Three of them are in the church—one an altar to a curate who gave his life in France while trying to save the wounded; one a window to a father and the son he vainly tried to save in Lincolnshire, both being drowned; the third a window to a schoolboy who gave his life in trying to save a little child. His window shows an angel lifting the boy from the water and another angel holding the girl he tried to save.

In memory of those who did not come back Alfreton has set up in the marketplace a bronze figure of a soldier with a little maid. The fifth memorial we came upon is a little wayside garden at the foot of a hill, with a chapel, a manse, and a school across the way. They are the gift to the village of an old Alfreton boy who lived here as a child and went to America and made a fortune, He was Robert Watchorn, who came back to his village, laid out this garden, built the chapel on the site of his old home, and opened it on the day his mother would have been 100 years old.

The Brave Old Parson

Here lies a brave old parson whom none could stop preaching, with a story well worth remembering.

BORN near Chesterfield in 1627, and educated at Bromfield grammar school, Cumberland, John Oldfield was appointed, when 22, rector of Carsington. Although his parishioners were difficult to please, he refused a much richer living to serve them.

For 15 years he conducted the meetings of church elders held at Wirksworth, and it was at their instigation that he preached a series of sermons against the errors of the Socinians, disciples of two 16th-century Italians who held that unless a doctrine was reasonable it should be rejected. The Act of Uniformity of 1662 drove him from his parish, and for the last 20 years of his life he was mainly a wanderer.

He was caught up in the toils of a system which made it a criminal offence for more than five people, in addition to the members of the family, to meet for worship not according to the Church. From that age of persecution came a shoemaker's man named George Fox and a tinker named John Bunyan, and Oldfield, sound mathematician and scholar, quietly plodded on through it all, risking fine, penal servitude, and transportation, always in peril, and once in grave danger from the false testimony of perjurers, who were afterwards pilloried for swearing what was untrue.

His closing years were passed here, and he ventured, in spite of threat of pains and penalties, to hold fortnightly services at the house of a friend. He died in 1682, leaving four clergyman sons, of whom Joshua Oldfield was a notable Presbyterian minister who won a considerable reputation at Oxford University, where scoffing undergraduates found him a man of high character and great ability.

Roman Road to a Norman Font

ALKMONTON. We find it at the end of a five-mile stretch of Roman road that is all up and down but as straight as an arrow, with glorious views reaching into Staffordshire. Its church, with lancet windows and a bell-turret with a leaded spire, was hardly a centenarian when we called, a neat and trim little place unusual in the neighbourhood for its outside walls of flint and stone. In the east window are scenes of the Birth, the Ascension, and the Resurrection; in the west wall are windows of Paul and Lydia.

The new church has one ancient possession, a fine Norman font like part of a massive pillar. It is all that is left of an ancient chapel, and after being lost for three centuries was dug up on a farm.

Old Yew

ALLESTREE. It is growing new in pleasant fashion, but it keeps its fine view over the valley of the Derwent, and what is old clings to its little hilltop in company with the church, the old cross set on a wall between the churchyard and the vicarage, and two fine old yews, one of which the villagers will tell you is as old as the story of the church. Its gnarled and twisted trunk looks as if it had grown out of a fairy tale. Very fine it looks from the lychgate, and the lychgate itself, with its shingled roof, fits into a charming picture seen from under the yew, with a splendid Norman doorway inside the timber porch.

It is this doorway with its curious carvings which is the chief possession of a church made almost new last century. It keeps its low 13th-century tower and part of the east wall of the chancel built at the same time; and under a 14th-century founder's arch is a stone engraved with a cross which may have covered the grave of the builder of the first church here. Part of a piscina is 700 years old.

Here are many memorials of the families of Allestree Hall, set in a park now given up to building and golf. One is to a schoolboy drowned by jumping into the foam of the weir when the River Wharf was in flood; to the Johnson family are windows with the Annunciation, the Nativity, and the Presentation in the Temple, and in memory of one of them is a beautiful silver lamp for ever burning in the chancel.

Still going on here when we called was a labour of love making this small church beautiful with oak stalls, the altar in the lady chapel, and oak seats in the nave, all by a village craftsman.

The Little Brook Makes a Great Stir

ALPORT. Derbyshire delight, with grey houses in gay gardens, and a mill by the bridge where stream runs into stream and dale meets dale.

We may come to it along the dale that bears its name, the river flowing with many little waterfalls over a rocky bed, and the road fair with flowers; or we may come from Youlgreave, glorying in the sight of two of Derbyshire's loveliest valleys drawing closer to each other till their waters, the Lathkill River and the Bradford Brook, meet at the foot of the hill.

The little Bradford Brook made a stir in the world last century by disappearing and running six miles underground and into the Derwent at Darley Dale, instead of joining the Lathkill at Alport as usual. It seems that heavy floods and disused mines were responsible for its adventure, but happily it found its way home again.

On a slope of Priest's hill, a mile away, is a farmhouse with a gable of Old Harthill Hall, the home of Edmund Cokayne, whose figure lies with his father's in such a noble setting in Ashbourne church. It was probably from the old house that he rode out to fight at Shrewsbury against Hotspur. He was knighted on the field and died that morning, a knight for an hour.

In the fine view from the old Hall across the valley, a queer mass of rock called Tuppenny Loaf stands out conspicuously.

John Alsop's Welcome

ALSOP-EN-LE-DALE. Set in lovely country, a mile from the River Dove and the Staffordshire border, is this cluster of homes, an ancient chapel, and a great house with gables and windows telling us it is from the 16th century.

To this secluded spot a wanderer found his way 400 years ago. He was Thomas Becon, chaplain to Cranmer and Protector Somerset, a preacher who preached himself from Canterbury Cathedral into the tower. Free once more, he sought obscurity in travel and found shelter here for a year with John Alsop, writing of his welcome:

Coming into a little village called Alsop-en-le-Dale I chanced upon a certain gentleman named Alsop, lord of the village, a man not only ancient in years but also ripe in the knowledge of Christ's doctrine. After we had saluted one another, and taken a sufficient repast, he showed me certain books which he called his jewels. I found there very good wits and apt unto learning.

15

The Alsops were lords of the manor for 500 years till 1688, and 200 years later their descendants were again in the old home.

The tiny chapel with a 19th-century tower has a Norman doorway with unusual moulding like two rows of zigzag. There is a little Norman window in the south wall. The sides of the pointed chancel arch, and the crudely-shaped piscina niche, are perhaps Norman too.

Old Friends Lost and Found

ALVASTON. Almost lost in Derby's 20th-century fringe, it goes back a thousand years. A few of its old houses are older than the church, yet the church has something in it which men would look at curiously before the days of Agincourt, before Magna Carta.

The church has a 14th-century piscina, and a font rather oddly given as a thankoffering for the capture of Sebastopol; but it is notable for three other things in iron and stone.

One is a piece of beaten ironwork, now against a wall, with an angel trumpeting the song of the Shepherds. Once a reredos and now preserved as a fine piece of craftsmanship, it may have been the work of the famous Nottingham blacksmith Huntingdon Shaw, who made for William the Third the fine gates which used to be at Hampton Court.

The oldest things in Alvaston are two coffin stones, old friends indeed if stones are friends. They were together for centuries in the Norman church which once stood here; they were buried for centuries under the old tower, and were found together in 1856 when the church was made new. Now they are companions in the porch, a greeting from the ancient world as we come into this modern place. One from the 12th century has a cross with a round head; the other, perhaps from Saxon England, is a truly remarkable tapering stone (with the lower end missing) with a cross of unusual design, having 11 rings about it.

Gateway to Romance

AMBERGATE. A fine stretch of road brings us from Belper to this gateway of the romantic country of the Peak, now a workaday village where roads, rivers, and rails meet, keeping the lovely setting Nature gave it in the sweeping valley of the Derwent, with the splendid woods of Alderwasley and the slopes of Crich Chase rising on each side. Here the Amber joins the Derwent, flowing with it under a bridge to a bower of trees.

Ashbourne   Pride of the Peak

Norbury

Wirksworth

Tideswell

Alsop-en-le-Dale

Penelope Boothby

Sir Humphrey Bradbourne and his wife

Edmund Cokayne

Capital in South Arcade

Sir John Cokayne and his wife

Children on Bradbourne Tomb

The 13th century Font

THE SPLENDID CARVINGS OF ASHBOURNE CHURCH

Its church is new, but in two small windows of the porch is old glass found in a box in a cottage, some of it English and some Flemish; some quarries are 500 years old, a panel of the Ascension is 16th century, one of the Crucifixion is 18th century, and a small roundel came from Shrewsbury Abbey.

Three things here recall the Great War. In three windows in memory of heroes who did not come back are figures of St Alban, St Martin, and St George. The figures above the chancel screen were given by five of the Johnson family who came home safely. The marble figure of an angel protecting a child from a serpent is the work of a Belgian sculptor who sought refuge here in war-time. He was carving the statue for a church in Belgium, but, the church being destroyed by the war, he brought the statue with him to Fritchley close by. There he finished it, and the Ambergate people bought it, setting it up on a base of Derbyshire marble, in memory of those who served and those who died. On it is a brass plate made from shells picked up in Belgium, and among the names upon it are those of a mother and her children who went down in the Persia, sunk by a German submarine in the Great War.

The Place of a Great and Famous Company

ASHBOURNE. All roads find this little place among green hills and lovely dales, and a great and famous company of people all these roads have seen. King Charles himself and Prince Charles Edward, and men with fame outlasting kings and princes; John Wesley and Samuel Johnson, the poet Thomas Moore and the novelist George Eliot, the happy angler Izaak Walton, Congreve the dramatist, Canning the statesman, and that most astounding Frenchman Jean Jacques Rousseau—all these knew the lovely roads to Ashbourne, for all of them lived or stayed here, and these writers wrote here or put this country in their books.

Ashbourne Hall has lost its greatness, though still it stands, and facing it is a fine little garden in memory of the war which brought so many great houses to their doom. On one of the pillars of the gateway is the name of one of our soldier poets who did not come home again, Francis St Vincent Morris.

Here still is the old inn by the marketplace where Dr Johnson came with Boswell, where the landlady, "a mighty civil gentlewoman," gave Boswell a low curtsy and an engraved sign of her house—the sign of a sitting man in green still swinging across the road with his gun. There are fine little groups of old almshouses: two rows by the wayside separated by a delightful patch of lawn and shrubs and water-tubs, and a little block by the church.

The Elizabethan grammar school is unaltered as we see it, its gables all in a row, its windows with their leaded panes; it has become the headmaster's house. Facing it is the old brick house to which Dr Johnson came for many a holiday with his old schoolfellow John Taylor. Dr Taylor was rector of Market Bosworth and of St Margaret's at Westminster, and was also a prebendary of the Abbey, but he loved his farm and his garden here, and, though winter found him in London, summer brought him home again. Boswell tells us that he was like a hearty English squire with the parson added, and he took notice of "his upper servant, Mr Peters, a decent good man in purple clothes and a large white wig, like the major-domo of a bishop." We have a peep of the gabled front of Dr Taylor's house, with its projecting room, from the bridge over the brook flowing at the bottom of the garden. The coming of the railway has changed the grounds very much since the days when the Duke of Devonshire arrived to dine with the doctor, and the coachman was ordered to drive twice round the grounds to give him a good impression of their size.

Of the two friends Dr Johnson was the first to die, three weeks after leaving Ashbourne in 1784, and it was Dr Taylor who read his burial service in the Abbey. Four years later they laid Dr Taylor to rest in his own churchyard at Ashbourne, where he lies in a grave unknown, somewhere in the shadow of the magnificent steeple which abundantly deserves its title of the Pride of the Peak. It is a noble spectacle rising above a churchyard magnificent with yews and cedars, and with a splendid avenue of 50 trimmed limes on each side. One of these cedars spreads its branches over a patch of ground 80 yards round.

Thousands come to Ashbourne for its monuments, but even without them it would be a place of pilgrimage. It has a few Saxon and Norman stones, but the church as we see it is the work of our three great building centuries, a place of gracious charm without and within. A tiny brass plate in the vestry recording its consecration is believed to be 13th-century, as old as the church. A large and luminous place indeed it is, as Boswell tells us in his Life of

Johnson. It is built in the shape of a cross, with chancel, transepts, nave, and aisle gathered about its central tower, and it has magnificent arcades of lofty bays.

The glorious tower with its spire, rising 212 feet, has been looking down on this countryside since the 14th century. The tower has fine belfry windows and an open parapet; the elegant spire has 20 windows in five tiers, and strings of ballflower running up its eight angles; there must be about 1700 flowers in all. The turret staircase at one angle of the tower is crowned by a pinnacle and is reached from inside the church by a doorway with a sculptured head. In this doorway hangs a fine 14th-century door, cut from a solid block of oak and black with age; it is divided lengthways into two panels and has wrought-iron bands and hinges. The fine arcades are 14th century, their pointed arches resting on clustered pillars, and some of their capitals finely carved. The font is 13th century.

In the chancel is a recessed tomb said to be of Robert Kniveton, who died in 1471; and near it is a tomb with sculptures of Christ on the cross, rising from the tomb, and ascending to Heaven, in memory of Christopher Harland, who died in 1839 and was the last representative of the Knivetons. Battered and worse for much moving about are the 15th-century figures of John Bradbourne and his wife, who must have known Robert Kniveton; they lie in the north transept with the great array of monuments to the Cokaynes and the Boothbys. Enclosing them all is a lofty screen with open tracery about 500 years old, but the splendour of all this sculpture, one of the most remarkable medieval exhibitions in the country, is spoilt by overcrowding.

High on an alabaster tomb lies Sir Humphrey Bradbourne with his wife, he in armour of the days before the Armada, with his sword and dagger, ruffs at his neck and on his wrists, feet on a lion, gauntlets close by and a double chain round his neck. She has a short cloak over a long gown and wears a ruff and a close-fitting cap. The tomb is adorned with heraldic display and the figures of 15 children, three in christening robes.

The monuments of the Cokaynes are with one exception complete with the heads of the family from 1372 to 1592. John of 1372 wears a short tunic and long hose with a purse hanging from his belt, his long mantle reaching to the lion at his feet. His son Edmund is with him, clad as a knight. Edmund's son Sir John lies in armour with an SS collar, his wife in a mantle held with a cord and tassels. Sir John's son John has but a piece of alabaster stone for his memorial, and the next of the line has a beautiful alabaster tomb at Youlgreave. Sir Thomas of 1537 is here at Ashbourne with his wife Dame Barbara, their figures engraved in Purbeck marble; he was with Henry the Eighth on the Field of the Cloth of Gold. His son Francis has his portrait in brass with that of his wife in a long gown with a jewelled girdle, but the brasses were renewed last century. Their son Thomas, who died in 1592, has a fine marble monument on the wall of the transept, showing him kneeling with his wife at a desk, their children and display of arms.

But it is not for these great folk we come to this great place; it is rather for a little child, Penelope Boothby.

Who that has seen her can forget her, the little white figure of a child of six summers set here in marble so that we wait for her to wake from sleep? Her figure, which won for Thomas Banks lasting fame among sculptors, shows Penelope lying on a mattress in a simple frock with a sash, her hands clasped, her feet one upon another. Her delicate and fragile form has never ceased to be counted among the gems of English art.

Penelope was the only child of Sir Brooke Boothby and Lady Susannah, and it is said that her stricken parents parted at her grave, a little tragedy which perhaps explains the epitaph by Edmund Burke:

> *She was in form and intellect most exquisite.*
> *The unfortunate parents ventured their all on*
> *this frail bark, and the wreck was total.*

There are other inscriptions in three languages, one telling of her curling locks of shining gold and the lightning of her smile, which made a paradise on earth.

The church has beautiful glass, old and new. About 20 shields of ancient heraldic glass fill the tracery of the east window, and in the clerestory of the north transept are what is left of about 60 coats-of-arms of old Ashbourne families. Old glass from Fenny Bentley church forms a broad band of shields and odd fragments across a window in this transept with a fragment above it of the Crucifixion, but the priceless treasure of the windows is the 13th-century glass filling the lancet in the same transept. As old as the church and perhaps the earliest glass in the county, it is in five medallions, filled with groups of small figures in scenes from Bethlehem.

Among the modern glass is the story of David and Goliath, which John Ruskin rightly described as a disgrace to a penny edition of Jack the Giant Killer, but much of the modern glass is beautiful. One transept glows with colour from a Benedictus window and the other with scenes of the Te Deum. A nave window shows St Columba of Iona, St Aidan, and St Chad. The great five-light west window has a Jesse tree. The seven lights of the east window, under the old glass in the tracery, has Kempe figures with Christ as King of Kings, and Mary with the Holy Child; it is sometimes called the Mary window because the money for it was collected from the Marys of Ashbourne by Mary Corbet, who gave the little figure of Christ on the pulpit as a thankoffering for the recovery of her sight. She lies in the shade of the majestic cedar in the churchyard.

Arresting in its unusual colouring is the lovely window by Christopher Whall, in memory of the tragedy of two sisters, Monica and Dorothea Turnbull. They were 19 and 21, and they died in 1901 from burns received in rescuing their father from a lighted lamp which exploded in his hands. In the middle of the window St Cecilia has fallen asleep at the organ while a cherub plays upon the keys and a choir of angels takes up the strain. The faces of the two girls are in the figures of two saints at the sides, while below is a garden, a fountain, and a thicket of briar leading to a little gate and a bright pathway to the Golden City.

Here is preserved, its paint remarkably fresh, a fragment of a 14th-century triptych of Calvary; it is on wood and was found under the plaster. By the tower is a tablet in memory of Dean Langton who lies here; it recalls a dramatic little tragedy, for he was riding his horse up a steep track from Dovedale to Tissington when the horse missed its footing and rolled down the bank, killing its master, with whom was a lady, who was saved through her long hair catching in the branch of a tree.

In the lovely country round about Tom Moore lived for about four years. In a cottage at Mayfield, now a farmhouse, he wrote his famous Lalla Rookh, a fantasy of oriental splendour, and it is said that the bells of Ashbourne church inspired his lovely lines:

> *Those evening bells! Those evening bells!*
> *How many a tale their music tells*
> *Of youth and home and that sweet time*
> *When last I heard their soothing chime.*

Those joyous hours are passed away :
And many a heart that then was gay
Within the tomb now darkly dwells
And hears no more those evening bells.

And so 'twill be when I am gone :
That tuneful peal will still ring on
While other bards shall walk these dells,
And sing your praise, sweet evening bells.

Sir Brooke Boothby left Ashbourne Hall to live in one of the stately homes of London, but it was his little Penelope who came to fame, not he.

A Little Lady Comes Into Fame

PENELOPE flitted across the stage of London life a wistful, pathetic little maiden, slowly opening her shy eyes on life, and quite ignorant of what it meant to be the only child and heiress of the seventh baronet of Ashbourne. For over five hundred years there had been English girls running about that ancient house.

This child, the darling of her parents and their friends, became the darling of another lover of children, Sir Joshua Reynolds. If we had no other cause to recognise that great artist's genius in painting child life we should have it in his picture of Penelope. When she was not much more than three this little mite was set on the throne in the studio to have her portrait painted. She was an adorable figure, and sat like a tiny old lady in a huge mob cap and mittens.

It was one of the last portraits Sir Joshua painted. Even then he was peering hard at his work and trying not to face the fact that his sight was becoming affected and that soon he would have to lay down his brush. He was then 66, but his lifelong preoccupation with beauty, with problems of line and tone, had not weakened, and he put into this portrait of the little maid not only his unquenchable ardour as a painter but his own secret grief. This, or the next, and no more canvases would stand on his easel.

There grew up a great friendship between the two, the one at the beginning of life, the other nearing its close, and both were destined, had they known it, to pass into another world almost within sight of each other. Penelope was allowed to enter the painter's studio at all hours. We can imagine her trotting about the room talking to herself about the big canvases leaning against the wall, watching Sir Joshua biting the end of his brush and frowning because he could not see properly, and going quietly out when the carriage came to take her home.

One day there was a great to-do in the Boothby mansion. Penelope was nowhere to be found. Her nurse was ill and could not leave her bed, and the little maid had quietly disappeared. The house was searched from attic to cellar, but Penelope was nowhere.

"She'll have gone to see Sir Joshua," declared the nurse.

A carriage went at once, the horses at a canter, bearing the searchers for Penelope to the painter's studio; and there they found her playing with a palette knife and prattling to Sir Joshua.

A little later, alas, those hands and feet and baby voice were silenced for ever. Penelope sickened and died as the daffodils were opening for her delight on the green banks of Ashbourne Park.

Her father, stricken to the heart, took up his pen and wrote a little book of verse, a few copies of which were published a few years later under the title Sonnets Sacred to the Memory of Penelope. The only child of so much wealth and so many hopes was buried in this old church at Ashbourne, and the years passed by. Presently all who had known Penelope or her story had followed her into the great silence. Her friend Sir Joshua died in the spring following the spring that had wafted Penelope away. But Penelope was not destined to be forgotten.

There came one day to the tomb a young sculptor; he was Francis Chantrey, whom many people had known as a donkey-boy. He pondered on the little figure for a long time, and went away. Not so long afterwards he began to work on his famous figure of the Sleeping Children in Lichfield Cathedral, and it is probable that this work would never have taken its lovely shape had the sculptor not seen Penelope lying on her marble mattress.

Soon after that Penelope's portrait, now generally known as The Mob Cap, was creating a little story and romance of its own. It sold for 1000 guineas and then for £20,000. In 1879 a fancy-dress ball was given in London, and a certain little lady, Miss Edie Talmage, thought she could not do better than dress herself up as The Mob Cap. She must have looked a delightful little figure among the crowd, and Sir John Millais was asked to paint her. He did so, and thus it happened that two men gave of their genius to make immortal the face of a little girl. The difference between the two as sitters was that Penelope was pretending to be a grown-up lady and Edie was pretending to be three-year-old Penelope.

The two pictures of the real and imitation Penelope are now in private collections. Much as we appreciate Cherry Ripe, our thoughts turn most of all to the child in Reynolds's masterpiece, and we ponder on the beauty created directly and indirectly by that tiny speck of life. So much was tiny Penelope loved in the short span of her life, and she can never die, for she belongs to us all.

The Soldier Poet in the Spring of Life

One of Ashbourne's heroes is the soldier poet Francis St Vincent Morris, who died for us in France at 21.

THE vicarage garden was the place he loved, for he had known it since he was two years old, when his father, who was Canon of Southwell, came as vicar here.

He was educated at Chichester and Brighton, and was ready for Oxford at the end of the first year of the war, when he joined the Sherwood Foresters, the regiment for which his father had been chaplain 18 years. Finding the chance of going to France remote, he gave up the Foresters and joined the Royal Flying Corps, and soon he was ready to face the storm of fire and death.

It was in the spring of 1917 that this young man in the spring of life went out, and it was only April, as the daffodils were nodding their heads, that his machine was brought down by a blizzard at Vimy Ridge. He was battered, and his right foot was amputated, and it seemed that he might recover, but while the April showers were falling he slept under an anaesthetic for another operation and did not wake again.

Not for long will his friends forget the poem he wrote to one whose home the war left full of sorrow:

> *Comfort, sad heart! Beyond that little grave*
> *Rests an immortal soul in God's repose.*
> *Others he saved, himself he could not save:*
> *This was the task he chose.*

He was only 18 when the war broke out but in one of his sonnets he tells us how he longed to serve his country:

> *Is this to live?—to cower and stand aside*
> *While others fight and perish day by day?*
> *To see my loved ones slaughtered, and to say:*
> *Bravo! bravo! how nobly you have died!*

Is this to love?—to heed my friends no more,
But watch them perish in a foreign land
Unheeded, and to give no helping hand,
But smile, and say, How terrible is war!

Nay, this is not to love, nor this to live!
I will go forth; I hold no more aloof;
And I will give all that I have to give,
And leave the refuge of my father's roof.
Then, if I live, no man shall say, think I,
He lives, because he did not dare to die!

Alas he was too soon to sleep in the refuge of his Father's roof, the fair blue sky that was looking down on all this worldwide tragedy.

The Maiden Garlands

ASHFORD-IN-THE-WATER. It lies in a lovely valley, Garden of the Peak, where the River Wye flows by mill and weir and placid lake, and under fine old bridges, wooded hills, and rocky heights rising all around.

Of all its joys there is nothing more delightful than the old Sheepwash Bridge and its fold, spanning the tree-shaded stream with three low arches where lusty trout and grayling sport in sparkling shallows. We see from the bridge Great Skacklow Wood, round which the river has come from Monsal Dale; the rough and rugged Kirk Dale begin its steep climb to windblown heights; and a lovely bit of the village with the old pump in its shelter, the old stone dwellings, and the church.

It is an ancient place where old customs linger in the ringing of the Curfew every day and the Pancake Bell on Shrove Tuesday, and where in the church still hang five paper garlands which speak to us with infinite pathos of the past. For the custom was to carry these garlands in the funeral processions of village maidens, and to leave them in the church; sometimes a kerchief, a glove, or a collar would be tucked away among the flowers, and an inscription.

One of the garlands treasured here was made for Ann Swindel, who was 22 when they brought her here in 1798, and the inscription they left on her grave, now faded away, was a prayer that she who had lost her youth might find great joy to come. We have found these garlands also at Matlock and Trusley, and in a score of other churches throughout England; they are pathetic because they bring the touching thought of Shakespeare's Ophelia to mind, for it was these tributes of love, these "crants" as Shakespeare called them, to which the churlish priest objected at Ophelia's burial. She should not be so honoured, whereupon Laertes hurled forth at the priest his proud defiance:

> *I tell thee, churlish priest,*
> *A ministering angel shall my sister be*
> *When thou liest howling.*

Ashford has lost the great house near the church, once the home of the Plantagenets, the Hollands, and the Nevilles, but some of the old church they knew is in the little building which has for company a fine old yew and remains of an ancient cross. It was almost all made new last century, but the tower is mainly 700 years old. Over the south door is the oldest possession of Ashford, a Norman tympanum with two wild creatures, one like a wolf under a tree. The north arcade of the nave and the tower archway are 14th century.

The chancel roof has old stone corbels, one with a head and hands. There are two chairs and a chest of the 17th century, and a splendid Jacobean pulpit with carved panels. The font is 14th century, with the head and tail of a dragon *on opposite sides of the bowl* (as if the creature is creeping through the bowl).

It is good to find here a memorial to Henry Watson of Bakewell, discoverer of the treasures of the village, who not only discovered them but sent them up and down England. His father was Samuel Watson of Heanor, who did much of the splendid old carving at Chatsworth, and Henry invented a machine for cutting and polishing marble. He opened the marble works at Ashford in 1748, and was the first to make ornaments of the beautiful coloured marbles with which Nature enriched this place, lovely things treasured in many homes. How many imposing halls, how many magnificent tombs, owe their glory to this village we do not know, but it is not a few.

Lovely are all the ways about this village. We can climb the delightful road in company with the river till it goes through Monsal Dale, and then uphill through Taddington Dale. We go to Little Longstone for the glorious view from Headstone Head, or with the river through Ashford Dale to Bakewell, getting from the bridge at the eastern end of the village a peep of Ashford Hall in a lovely setting. From the foot of Kirk Dale we see, quaint and pleasing, the house called Ashford Rookery, with its projecting wing, a lawn down to the river, and a two-arch bridge.

The Doomed Village

ASHOPTON. The day is coming when most of it will be drowned, and it is tragic to think that reservoirs which will cover it are beginning to rise. Here the valleys and the rivers meet in the grandeur of Peakland heights and rolling moors, Crook Hill and Win Hill, Bamford Edge and the lovely slopes of Lady Bower, following the compass round.

Down their valleys come the Derwent and the Ashop, the one from the moorlands of the Yorkshire border, the other from the trackless solitudes of Kinderscout, both joining in the village with the brook called Lady Bower, fresh from an exquisite dale.

Ashopton is at the end of one of the finest stretches of road in Derbyshire, a modern highway which climbs 1700 feet and runs a dozen miles from Glossop with hardly a sign of life save at the half-way inn. It is crossed by a Roman road. Could any road stir us more than this, glorying in the wilderness of Kinderscout with lonely hills and windswept summits, and heavenly little dales below?

And who can forget the splendid panorama from Win Hill, with the green vales of the Ashop and the Noe, Lose Hill rising over 1500 feet, the lovely Vale of Hope with Hope and Castleton, Shatton Edge and Abney Moor, and beyond the Derwent Valley the great height of Stannage Edge bounding the county?

John Bunyan's Story

ASHOVER. We are in the lovely valley of the Amber, a land of rocky hills enriching the village with their varied beauty and the wonderful views from their tops, hills that have given abundantly of their riches since the Romans worked them for lead. For long Ashover has lain in their shelter, but into its romance the workaday world has crept with quarries and railway.

But some things are not changed. There is still the Fabric's massive rock-strewn ridge with its magnificent panorama (oddly named Fabric, they say, because it yielded stone for churches). There is Ashover Hay, the rounded hill beyond Milltown hamlet and a little stream; there are still the tree-clothed slopes of Raven's Nest and the height of Cocking Tor, and Overton Hall which was once the home of Sir Joseph Banks, who went round the world with Captain Cook and persuaded Australia to become a nation.

And there is still much charm about the village, in the very happy grouping of the old church with its graceful spire soaring from a bower of trees. The picturesque stone school and ancient inn have something left of the day when Thomas Babington and his Ashover men came home from Agincourt; and still the old men drinking ale in Crispin Inn will tell you how in 1646 the soldiers of the King turned Landlord out while they drank all his ale, and forgot the King and Cromwell too.

The Babingtons of Dethick are said to have built the tower and spire of Ashover church; they are early 15th century and rise 128 feet high, the tower with embattled parapet and three long gargoyles, the spire elegant and lofty, with eight windows.

Of the church which came into the Conqueror's Domesday Book, or of the church his Normans built, nothing remains unless it be the tiny piscina projecting from the chancel wall. But there is a rare Norman relic we would come far to see, for here is a lovely lead font with 20 figures of men in flowing drapery, all holding books and standing under arches raised on tiny pillars. Below these rows of little men is a band of fleur-de-lys. It is believed the font was made about half through the 12th century, and it is one of only about 30 we have seen in England.

The south doorway, with three quaint heads, is 13th century; the north arcade is 14th, as is a fine little doorway with open tracery in the north aisle, and most of the church is 15th century.

The great stone in the chancel floor has the brass portrait of a priest in richly embroidered robes. His head is uncovered, his hands are folded in prayer; he is perhaps Philip Eyre, a 15th-century rector. Another chancel brass has portraits of James Rolleston and his wife; he is in Tudor armour with sword and dagger, she has a flowing robe with tight-fitting bodice, a wide belt from which hangs a pendant, and a headdress with embroidered lappets. With them are their 13 children, girls dressed like the mother and boys in long tunics.

On a fine alabaster tomb lies Thomas Babington of 1518 with his wife, both elaborately carved and painted. He has a long gown with a purse hanging from his girdle, a double chain round his neck and a ring on each hand, his head on a pillow held by an angel each side; her dress is fastened by a tasselled cord, and she has a ring on each hand. The sides of the tomb are carved with handsome canopies under which are little figures of the 15 children and their marriages.

Above this tomb is a brass plate to this same Thomas Babington, interesting for being a palimpsest, with an inscription on the other side to some Robertus Prykke, Sergeant of a queen's pantry. Above the fine open tracery in the bays of the chancel screen Thomas Babington erected is an embattled cresting over a band of quatrefoils.

A tablet in the nave to William Dakeyn, who died in 1630, is interesting because it is thought to be one of the many forgeries of his notorious grandson, whose forgeries of arms and pedigrees sent him to the pillory and lost him an ear.

In the chancel is a tribute to Obadiah Bourne which brings to mind the story of his father Immanuel Bourne, whom he succeeded as rector in 1669, and the fate of their old home, Eastwood Old Hall, whose ivied ruins of a few rooms and part of the tower still stand.

On the outbreak of the Civil War Immanuel Bourne tried to keep out of the struggle by leaning to neither side, but first one party assailed him and then the other. Even when he openly avowed himself on the side of Parliament they did not trust him, but left him with a ruined house and a broken heart.

Immanuel found it vain to plead that he was in the service of Parliament, and when the Roundheads found they could not bring down his house with cannon they set a barrel of gunpowder in the tower, destroying half the Hall and leaving the rest in ruins. Then they sang a hymn, and from the ruins went to the church and did much damage to its fine array of glass.

There are two carved chairs in the sanctuary said to have come from the Old Hall, and an odd tablet on the wall has a quaint memory of David Wall, "whose superior performance on the bassoon endeared him to an extensive musical acquaintance, and whose social life closed in 1796." A small brass plate pays tribute to George Eastwood, who lived for years in the village and did much of the beautiful woodcarving. He carved the panelled reredos over the altar in the north aisle with a wealth of vine leaf and grape, and adorned the ends of the fine benches with fine and varied tracery, dying in 1903, just before they were completed.

One of the eight bells in the tower is 18th century and has lovely scrollwork round its rim, and another boasts that it "rung the downfall of Bonaparte and broke April 1814."

Here lies, as we gather from the register, a bad woman who has found a sure place in our literature. She is Dorothy Matley, buried here in 1660, and she is known because she comes into John Bunyan's Life and Death of Mr Badman, her story being told as an example of sudden judgment:

Take that dreadful story (says John Bunyan) of Dorothy Matley of Ashover, a liar and thief that washed the rubbish that came from the lead mines. Her usual way of asserting things was with imprecations such as, I would I might sink into the earth.

On the 23rd of April she was washing on a hill and was there taxed by a lad for taking twopence out of his pocket. She denied it, wishing the ground might swallow her if she had them. Now a man of good report came by and saw her with her tub and sieve twisting round and sinking into the ground, and a great stone fell upon her head, the earth fell in upon her, and she was afterwards found four yards within the ground, the boy's twopence in her pocket.

Centuries before all this happened (or did not happen) there was buried in the same churchyard an ancient stone coffin with a coped lid, which is now aboveground.

Hand in Hand Down the Centuries

ASTON-ON-TRENT. Clustering happily by the wayside is its little group, the old church, the rectory with a fine yew, the Hall that is now an institution, and the massive oak lychgate, richly carved, with a fine roof of grey stones from the sea.

This lychgate is in memory of a rector who preached his first sermon here in 1869 and was still preaching in the dark hours of the Great War, nearly half a century. There is a window in his memory which shows him as a young man at a christening at this 700-year-old font, and as an old man giving communion to a civilian, a soldier, and a nurse.

His church, one of the loveliest old shrines in Derbyshire, has a tower begun by the last of the Normans and finished in the 15th century, and 13th-century nave and chancel arcades. In charming setting, it is a light and spacious place with fine arches, a 500-year-old clerestory, and splendid windows, most of them 14th and 15th century; the one framing the rector's memorial is especially beautiful with canopied niches in the sides, and at the foot of one niche is a sleeping figure with branches growing from him as in a Jesse tree.

On an alabaster tomb lie a man and his wife of five centuries ago, hand in hand, he in a gown and a round cap, she in a dress fastened with a buckle, a veil falling over her fine headdress. They may belong to the Hunt family, one of whom gave the altar table in the time of Charles Stuart.

There is part of an old coffin stone built into a pillar near the chancel, but the oldest stone here is one wonderfully carved by a Saxon mason, now set in an outside wall near the tower. The village carpenter of the last generation made the beautifully carved stalls in the chancel, and they are not unworthy of the stout oak benches of Elizabethan days. The rainbow light falling in the chancel is one of the things we remember in this attractive interior.

His Name Rang Through Europe

AULT HUCKNALL. He lies in the quiet church on its green hilltop, the poor parson's son whose portrait hangs with those of kings and queens and nobles in the Hall near by; who had among his friends Ben Jonson and Galileo. He was Thomas Hobbes, who died with a name ringing through Europe.

Much of his early manhood was spent at Hardwick Hall as tutor, and in his later years he made his home at Hardwick and Chatsworth. He lived to be nearly 92, his mind vigorous to the last, fond of his dozen pipes of tobacco ready filled in front of him, hating the thought of death for all his philosophy, and afraid to be left in the dark. So much did he dread being left alone that he insisted on coming with the family from Chatsworth to Hardwick even though his end was near, and he had to be carried on his feather bed in a coach.

When he knew he could not recover he said, "I shall be glad, then, to find a hole to creep out of the world at." This he found at Hardwick Hall, dying in 1679 soon after he had expressed his wish that his epitaph should be simply *The Philosopher's Stone*. But the black marble stone which covers his remains tells of his service to learning. It is in the floor of the Hardwick chapel.

In the chapel is a great tomb to Anne Kighley, wife of the first Earl of Devonshire, who died in 1628. On the edge of the tomb stand five draped alabaster figures.

Another memorial has a quaint inscription to a keeper of Hardwick Park who died in 1703:

> *Long had he chased*
> *The Red and Fallow deer*
> *But Death's cold dart*
> *At last has fixed him here.*

It is a fine little church in which they lie, with a charming effect given to the interior by the tower which comes between the nave and chancel. It opens from the nave with a fine Norman archway, ornamented with beak-heads and curious faces. It opens again to the chancel with a smaller arch which some think Saxon, a fine kind of peephole. Other Norman remains are the base of the tower, two round arches of the north arcade, a small west window, and some stones set in the west wall. One of the stones is crudely carved with strange figures: on one side is a tall four-legged animal with a long neck and beaked head; it has clawed feet, and its tail curls between its legs; behind it is a tiny quadruped. On the other side is a half-man half-animal holding a cross. Below this is a second stone, oblong in shape and carved with a man holding a sword and a winged dragon with a protruding tongue. A third stone carved with zigzags is over the little Norman window.

A little 13th-century piscina projects from the chancel wall. The fine three-light west window and the arches of the south arcade are 14th century. The nave roof keeps much 14th-century work with bosses and corbels at the ends of the beams. A massive old font is kept in honour, but it is a modern one that is used.

There is much old glass. In the east window of the chapel are remains of glass erected in 1527 by Sir John Savage. In the upper part of each of the four lights are remains of a figure; they show saints, Christ, and the Madonna. In the lower part are Elizabeth Savage and her daughter kneeling at desks, wearing cloaks embroidered with coats-of-arms; the Hardwick shield of the father of the famous Bess; a man in a blue cloak, and kneeling figures of the two sons of John and Elizabeth, in cloaks of rich blue.

The churchyard has a fine peep of Bolsover Castle; and near one of its many yews is a fine new cross on an ancient stone. Wooded hills and lovely lanes are all about this place, on the edge of Hardwick's fine deer park.

Thomas Hobbes and His Philosophy

THOMAS HOBBES was born at Malmesbury in 1588, son of a vicar who sent him to Oxford and got him appointed tutor in the Cavendish family. He enjoyed the friendship of Ben Jonson, Francis Bacon (who dictated some of his essays to him), Galileo, Descartes, and other illustrious men.

The Spire among the Trees

Norman Arch and medieval Font

The noble west doorway

IN OLD BAKEWELL

Dorothy Vernon with her husband and children

Tomb of Dorothy Vernon's son

Godfrey Foljambe and his wife

OLD MONUMENTS IN BAKEWELL CHURCH

His first literary effort was a poem on the Wonders of the Peak of Derbyshire, followed by a translation of Thucydides, which he thought would be a warning to his countrymen, then in the throes of civil ferment. In 1640 he wrote a defence of the royal prerogative, and fled the country fearing the wrath of Parliament.

During the next ten years he wrote two other works on his theory of government, and in 1651 issued his masterpiece, Leviathan, a work which caused Charles the Second, who had been his pupil, to refuse to see him. The book made him hated by the Royalists because they thought it implied obedience to Cromwell, and by the Church because it made the ruler head of ecclesiastical affairs.

Leviathan is sovereign power, vested in the head of the State by the people. According to Hobbes man is selfish, seeking advantage at the cost of others, and the state of Nature is "contention, enmity, and war," in which notions of right and wrong, justice and injustice, have no place. Fear compels man, according to this theory, to adopt articles of peace, which forbid him to destroy his life or that of his neighbour, and to limit his own liberty by that which he is prepared to allow others against himself.

To enforce these articles of peace it is necessary to invest a ruler with power to punish their infraction. The king is absolute, his power unmodified by Parliament, but his power may be withdrawn by the people if he frustrates the object for which he is ordained, or is unable to secure it.

At 65 Hobbes received a life pension from the Cavendishes, supplemented by £100 a year from the Crown. When over 80 he wrote his autobiography in Latin verse, and translated Homer. He died at Hardwick in 1679, and was brought here to sleep under a marble slab which he had sportively called the Philosopher's Stone.

Here Lies Dorothy Vernon

BAKEWELL. We must all come to this old Peakland town if we would know Derbyshire and feel the thrill of it. It is a piece of rare delight, with green pasture and moorland breeze, a running silver river and the shade of lovely lanes; a group of charming villages about it, exquisite dales, and two of England's far-famed houses, Haddon Hall and Chatsworth.

It lies on the banks of the Wye and has two fine old bridges, one with five arches and huge cut-waters where the river is charming with a mill and a weir; and a little packhorse bridge of 1664, hardly four feet wide with a string of arches on the very edge of the town. By it is an embattled house of 300 years ago.

The wells the Romans and the Saxons knew are of no importance now, but in a wayside garden in the heart of the town is the old ivied bath house the Duke of Rutland built in 1697, where the water still bubbles through the floor.

There are charming gabled buildings and old inns, an ancient market-house refashioned and keeping much of its old charm, the 17th-century Hall with its picturesque ball-topped gables, a delightful row of almshouses as old as Queen Elizabeth, and a stone on the Rutland Arms Hotel carved with these fine lines which we hope are read by all who pass this way:

> *Here's to one who took his chances,*
> *In a busy world of men,*
> *Battled luck and circumstances,*
> *Fought and fell, and fought again.*
>
> *Won sometimes, but did no crowing,*
> *Lost sometimes, but did not wail:*
> *Took his beating but kept going,*
> *Never let his courage fail.*
>
> *He was fallible and human,*
> *Therefore loved and understood*
> *Both his fellow-man and woman,*
> *Whether good or not so good.*
>
> *Kept his spirit undiminished,*
> *Never let down on a friend,*
> *Played the game till it was finished,*
> *Lived a sportsman to the end.*

But among all its ancient sights and its thatched cottages gay with gardens this lovely place has no more beautiful picture than its church in the shape of a cross with its elegant spire among the trees. It is the glory of the town. Its churchyard has lovely views, quaint epitaphs, and one of the finest Saxon crosses in the land. It is about eight feet high and perhaps 8th century; it was found long ago on the moors with its top part nearly worn away. Richly carved with knotwork and elegant scrolls, the Saxon mason sculptured on it a little animal nibbling foliage, five scenes from the life of Christ fading away with the centuries, and a recognisable scene of Christ riding on an ass into Jerusalem.

There are only two churches in Derbyshire in Domesday Book that had two priests, and Bakewell is one of them. Its importance in the old days is shown by what is believed to be the finest collection in England (for number and variety) of ancient coffin stones, carved with all kinds of crosses and other devices—shears, keys, horns, swords, chalices, a bow and arrow, and the curious type showing parts of a figure as if through openings in a coffin lid. About 60 of them, more or less battered, are in the porch, others are at the west end, and some of them are built into the walls as masonry.

The Normans built the noble west doorway with its rich carving of grotesques, beakheads, and animals; over it is their interlaced arcading. A massive oblong pillar at the west end of each nave arcade, the round arches in the west walls of the aisles (built in perhaps to strengthen the masonry), and traces of the old corbel table in the chancel, are all Norman.

The central tower (an octagon on a low square base) and its spire were made new last century in their medieval style. The porch is 14th century, the battlements and clerestory are 15th. There is fine woodwork old and new, the old including the door still swinging on its hinges, a splendid chest made before the Reformation, and a lovely traceried screen nine feet high which has seen over 500 years, but has a modern cornice. The new oak is the chancel screen, the open benches with carved ends, and the 20 miserere stalls all quaintly carved, not unworthy of three old ones that remain. New also is the great reredos reaching nearly to the roof with wood carving of the figures on Calvary, and marble figures of the Twelve Apostles.

The floor of the 13th-century chancel is of fine new mosaic, and the stone pulpit is also modern, a massive structure carved with crosses and knotwork. There are fragments of old glass in the west window. The gem of the medieval relics of this church is the splendid tub font with saints under canopies.

It is a touch of romance, however, that brings so many travellers here, for here is the Vernon chapel (made new last century) in which sleeps the famous Dorothy Vernon who did not elope from Haddon Hall. We may be disappointed that the story is not true, but we are more disappointed with her monument, a ponderous thing with much heraldic display, on which she kneels with her husband Sir John Manners, he in armour with a beard, and she in a long robe, a close-fitting cap, and a little ruff. At the foot of the monument are tiny figures of four children on cushions. They laid the mother here in the reign of Elizabeth, four years before the Armada came, and her husband followed her a few years before Shakespeare died. When Queen Victoria was on the throne their graves were uncovered in the taking down of this chapel, and both these storied people were seen. In Dorothy's hair were *six brass pins*.

Facing them on the chapel wall is another pretentious monument on which kneels their son George. He is at prayer with his wife, and above them are the words nobody believes, The day of man's death is better than his birth. Below them are nine children, each one under an arch with a Bible text. One is in swaddling clothes with the words, Mine age is nothing in respect of thee; another little one, said to have been weak-minded, has for his text, By the grace of God I am what I am.

The oldest of the Vernon monuments is a small table tomb of finely-veined alabaster of John de Vernon of 1477; it has angels at the ends and seated figures at the sides. Dorothy's father, called the King of the Peak, lies with his two wives. His hair is straight, he is in armour with a sword, and he has a double chain round his neck. Both wives have long robes and small caps. But older still is a knight now lying on a modern tomb, Sir Thomas Wendesley, who fell at Shrewsbury in 1403. He is rich indeed with skirt of chain mail, SS collar, and a richly decorated belt. His head is on a cushion supported by angels.

On the wall of one of the aisles is an exquisite little sculpture of Sir Godfrey Foljambe and his wife, both at prayer under a double canopy, he wearing armour and helmet, she in a lovely headdress. It will soon be 600 years since they were buried here.

We noted on the list of vicars the name of Francis Hodgson, who comes into the life of Byron as a friend to whom the poet gave a thousand pounds, which the poet's family afterwards demanded back. We noticed also the grave of a parish clerk with a loud-voiced Amen who is asked to sleep undisturbed "till angels wake thee with such notes as thine." And in Bakewell cemetery we noticed two graves not very old, one of a brother and sister who fell in the greatest aeroplane disaster of our own time, the other the grave of a labourer on the Duke of Rutland's estate on which the aged Duke had put a wreath "To my old and valued friend."

BALLIDON. It has a few cottages and farms sheltering under White Edge, and a lonely chapel away in the fields. Once belonging to the monks of Dunstable, it is now a tiny building with a nave and chancel under one roof; keeping a Norman chancel arch and a Norman doorway, some 15th-century windows, and an old font crudely carved with varied patterns.

The Poet to the Hill

BAMFORD. A Peakland village almost in Yorkshire. It looks out to the great height of Win Hill, which rises 1530 feet above the sea and looks down into five dales. Ebenezer Elliott sang of it in his Corn Law Rhymes:

> *The might of man may triumph or may fail,*
> *But, Eldest Brother of the air and light,*
> *Firm shalt thou stand when demi-gods turn pale:*
> *For thou, ere science dawned on reason's night*
> *Wast, and wilt be when mind shall rule all other might.*

Its people dwell in grey houses with gay gardens, spinning their cotton in the mill by the river, and go to a church they have had for 70 years, with a steeple over a hundred feet high.

A Red Line in Domesday Book

BARLBOROUGH. With a stream between it and Yorkshire, Barlborough is a charming village of old stone houses and cheery red roofs. Within a stone's throw it has the old cross with two sundials, the old Hall, a fine big house and an almshouse, the church, and the parsonage.

The Normans thought it important enough to mark its name with a red line in the Conqueror's Domesday Book, and of their church there still remain four round arches between the nave and aisle, resting on pillars of the 13th century, when rebuilding took place. As old as the pillars is the chancel arch on foliage corbels, and part of the base of the tower with a small window.

On a great stone in the aisle is the battered sculptured figure of a woman wearing a long mantle over a close-fitting gown; she is Lady Joan Furnival, and her monument has come here from the chancel of Worksop Priory where they laid her about 1395. A brass tablet in the aisle tells of Margaret and Mary Pole, two maiden sisters who died within two months in 1755, after restoring part of the church and giving the village its almshouse. The old home of the Poles was

Park Hall, still a substantial house some two miles from the village. A stone on the sanctuary floor is in memory of Sir Richard Pipe, a 17th-century Lord Mayor of London.

A mile from the church is the fine Barlborough Hall, with projecting bays and embattled turrets, built in 1583 by Francis Rodes, who was born a few miles away at Staveley Woodthorpe and was one of the judges who tried Mary Queen of Scots. One of its great possessions is a magnificent stone chimneypiece with the figures of the judge and his two wives. The house, with its glorious approach along an avenue of limes planted at the end of the 17th century, became the home of the judge's son Sir John Rodes, and of many generations of his descendants.

The First of Four Husbands

BARLOW. It looks across a green valley to the slopes of Monk Wood, and has a little aisleless church both old and new. It has been here eight centuries, and we see Norman work in the lofty doorway within the porch, sheltering an old oak door, and in a deeply-splayed window in the north wall of the nave. A very rare possession is the tiny Norman piscina found last century and now built into an east wall. The 14th-century builders made the porch, near which is an outside stairway which once led to a gallery over the little chapel, and two of their windows still remain. The 19th-century chancel is in keeping with the ancient church, and so is the neat oak screen.

A fine 13th-century coffin stone carved with a raised cross, with foliage springing from the stem, is a memorial to Julia, wife of Adam Frauncies. Against a wall is an alabaster stone engraved with portraits of Robert Barley and his wife; he wears 15th-century armour and a helmet, his sword by his side, and is holding the hand of his wife who wears a cloak fastened by a cord.

Another of the family buried here was Robert Barlow, who died in 1532 not long after he married Bess of Hardwick when he was very young and she only 14. He was the first of her four husbands and left her great estates. It is thought that fragments of his stone are buried under the chancel.

The old churchyard cross has been made new in memory of the men who died for peace, the ancient shaft having been lengthened and crowned with a crucifix.

The Pride of the Cross

BARROW-ON-TRENT. Church and great house of this low-land village stand close together, a fine row of yews dividing the churchyard from the garden of lawn and rose-beds. On one side they look across Trent meadows where floods sweep down at times and lap the garden walls. Opposite the church is an old timbered house sheltered by a giant walnut tree.

Within a stone's throw of one another are the fine iron gates of the Hall, a long row of cottages with beflowered walls, and a beautiful cross of which the village is very proud. Made after the fashion of 1000 years ago, from a block of stone weighing 12 tons, it came to this small place after being offered in 1916 to the Derbyshire village which sent the greatest number of men to the war in proportion to its population; at its foot are 36 names.

Nothing is left of the Norman church given to the Knights Hospitallers whose house and chapel are thought to have been at Arleston near by, where ancient stone foundations are in a farmhouse. The earliest work in the beautiful bright church with charming windows, is the 13th-century group of pillars with clustered shafts in the north arcade; most of the rest is 14th century, including the windows. The tower was given its belfry in the 15th. The font is 500 years old. Between the chancel and south aisle is a great peephole, and on the opposite side is a passage which may have served the same purpose. In a recess of the south aisle, which he perhaps rebuilt, lies the battered alabaster figure of a 14th-century priest, his head on a cushion and his feet on a dog. In the chancel is a tomb with inscription to William Sale of 1665; we remember him as one of the figures in the quaint family group in the church at Weston-on-Trent.

A Hero in Shakespeare

BARTON BLOUNT. At the end of a lane which becomes an open road through the park, it lies in delightful country with a tiny church in the grounds of the lovely great house, grown out of the old home of the Blounts who were here from the 14th to the 16th century.

An old manor house at the time of the Civil War, it was partly fortified to watch the movements of the Cavaliers at Tutbury, and perhaps the sorry plight of the old church at the end of the 17th century was due to the war.

Neat and trim and pleasing with its bell turret and lancet windows, it keeps two relics in the massive 14th-century font and the 13th-century figure of a woman holding a heart in her hands. She belonged perhaps to the Bakepuze family who sold the estate to Sir Walter Blount, the famous warrior. The arms of Bakepuze and Blount are in the windows.

Sir Walter Blount lives as the Blunt of Shakespeare's Henry the Fourth. He was standard-bearer for the king at Shrewsbury, and was killed there, it is said, through being mistaken for Henry. The most famous of the Blounts was another Sir Walter who was Lord High Treasurer in 1464 and became the first Lord Mountjoy. Another was made Earl of Devonshire in the year Elizabeth died. He was one of the handsomest men of her court, and was not more than 20 when he fought a duel with Essex, who had been envious of him because the queen gave him a gold brooch for his skill in a tilting match. He was with Sir Philip Sidney at the Battle of Zutphen, and was perhaps close by when Sir Philip gave a bottle of water to a dying soldier. In Armada year he built ships at his own expense and sent them against the Spaniards. He sleeps in the Abbey.

The west window sheds a golden light on the interior, the glass being in memory of the Bradshaws who were here in the 19th century. The east window has a figure of St Chad, the hermit saint.

The Duke and the Four Tall Men

BASLOW. It is delightful, set in a valley of rich meadows where hills and woods and rocks climb up to rolling moors, where the Derwent comes sweeping grandly down on its way to the glory of Chatsworth.

For a magnificent view we climb Baslow Edge to the lonely Eagle Stone and the Wellington Monument, a companion to Nelson's Monument a mile away; and for something altogether charming we go down to the old bridge, with three lofty arches spanning the stream, and still with the little stone shelter built for the toll collector in ancient times.

A young bridge carries most of the burden for the old. Venerable grey houses gather round the bridge they have kept company with so long. A lane leads to the stone-gabled Bubnell Hall, built 300 years ago on the site of a homestead of the Bassets for many generations, a family ever on the side of justice and liberty. One put his name

Ashford-in-the-Water   Sheepwash Bridge

Baslow   Across the Derwent

Bakewell   Across the Wye

THREE OLD DERBYSHIRE BRIDGES

Parwich   Norman Tympanum

Steetley   Norman Doorway

Melbourne   Norman Arches

Bradbourne   Norman Doorway of Tower

Repton   14th Century Nave   **Repton**   The Saxon Crypt

The Majestic Castle from the Valley

The Terrace and the Roofless Walls

BOLSOVER CASTLE

to Magna Carta, another went on the Crusades with Richard Lionheart, a third sat in our first Parliament.

Between the new bridge and the old is the church, in a churchyard a joy to see. Its great elms are reflected in the river, another grand elm is at one of the gates, and here and there are ancient yews. There is an 18th-century sundial on an ancient flight of steps.

The oldest story of the church is told by fragments of stone knotwork thought to be part of a Saxon cross, now in the porch. Built into the porch is a coffin stone perhaps 700 years old, with a carved cross and two keys. Engraved coffin stones are built into the lintels of the clerestory windows. The low tower and its spire are more than 600 years old, and from the 14th century come the nave arcades, and a doorway in which a stout old door still hangs. The chancel is made new.

There is elaborately carved oak of our time in the chancel screen, in the altar, the reredos, and the stalls, and two reading-desks with figures of the Evangelists. Among the windows are three with figures of saints, one of St Luke and St Martin to a doctor who served the village for half a century. A tablet tells us of two vicars, father and son, who were both here for 30 years, and another tells of the third generation, Frederick Barker, who followed for a year before he went to Australia to become Bishop of Sydney. For 28 years he served the Dominion Church with great success, built a noble cathedral, and founded a college. He loved his kingdom overseas, but when he died he was brought to this village he was born in. The story is told of this Barker family that when the Duke of Cambridge came to Baslow church he saw four young men seated near him all over 6 feet 3, and on hearing that they were sons of the vicar said one of them must be a soldier. Within a week a commission in the army was sent to the vicarage, and one of the sons accepted it.

An odd thing we noticed in the vestry is a whip which tells a story, for it was used for driving dogs out of church.

At the Gate of Chatsworth

BEELEY. At the gate of Chatsworth's glorious park and set among the hills, Beeley has wonderful views whichever way we turn. Sheltered by Beeley Moor and Beeley Woods, it looks over the Derwent Valley to fine wooded slopes rising to Stanton Moor, a panorama all the more lovely when the heather is in bloom.

The village has joys of its own, hidden from those who rush by. Its roads go up and down and twist and turn as they take us by houses of old grey stone, by cottage and school and old grey hall (still proud above the wayside though a farmhouse now), by a little green with a lovely lime, to an ancient church with sturdy tower close to the gabled vicarage.

There are splendid limes round the churchyard, with a fine shapely yew to keep them company. It was planted nearly 200 years ago; but another gnarled yew which was once a massive tree is said to be as old as the oldest part of the church, the Norman doorway within the porch it shelters. With three heads carved on its hood, but with new marble pillars in place of the old shafts, this doorway is all that is left of the Norman church except for a corbel in a corner of the aisle and the font so altered that its ancient character is lost. The yew has looked on many changes as its glory has waxed and waned. It saw the coming of the 13th-century builders whose masonry is in the north wall of the chancel. It saw the 14th century add to the tower, and the 15th crown it with battlements and pinnacles.

In the chancel is a Jacobean chair and on the wall is a brass not quite nine inches square in memory of a man who was born while Shakespeare was still at Stratford, and lived to be 95. He was John Calvert who died in 1710, and the interest of his brass is in the engraved figure below the inscription, clad in a shroud but showing face and hands.

A 17th-century sanctus bell once here now hangs over the school. A window has glass in memory of 13 men who did not come back, showing Christ and two soldiers with Beeley church in the background.

There are memorials to the Saviles, and a stone in the baptistry to John Greaves of 1694, the last of the Greaves of Beeley. With these two families the story of the village was linked for five and a half centuries, and their memory clings to a quaint gabled farmhouse nearly a mile away.

Chatsworth is another story, but there belongs to this little village at its gates a peep of the old stone bridge spanning the Derwent with a great round arch, and a view up stream of a glistening cascade.

Treasure Lost and Found

BEIGHTON. Its church has been made new, and in making itself new it found and lost a Norman arch.

The church was in such a sorry plight before the restoration that the chancel walls were taken down, and on the plaster being removed from the pointed arch there was found above it the splendid arch the Normans built 800 years ago. It was a delightful surprise, and there was great joy, but unhappily the arch was so decayed that it could not be saved. Its old proportions have been kept, however, and also the zigzag design.

The tower is 15th century, with earlier work in the capitals of the arch opening to the nave, these being carved with nail-head ornament and curious heads. An ancient stone with a pair of shears by the stem of a cross forms the sill of one of the windows; and the big stone of the chancel floor, engraved with a cross, is to John Tynker who was vicar here when Joan of Arc was hearing her Voices.

The church has lost its Norman arch but has found some of its medieval treasures. The restoration brought to light fragments of 15th-century glass now in the windows of the aisles, and an altar stone with five consecration crosses which is now in use again, set in an oak frame. This was once part of the roof, 500 years old.

The sad story of the ancient font has had a happy ending, for, being old and too much worn for further service owing to its abuse as a water butt, it was buried in the churchyard by the vicar, "like a good and faithful servant."

Here Sleeps Jedediah Strutt

BELPER. The Derwent has made it into a busy little town, for it was its water power that moved Jedediah Strutt to build his cotton mills here. In the shadow of their great walls some of Belper's beauty lies, delightful gardens where the water mirrors the wooded hillside. Just beyond the mills the river is spanned by a fine stone bridge of 1795, replacing the old one washed away by a flood. Here, in a lovely natural setting, the river makes a crescent waterfall on its way to the gorge beyond the bridge. About the time we called there had been found in the river here original timbers from the foundations of the only viaduct constructed by George Stephenson, as good as new after 94 years immersion in the river bed.

It is thought that Edmund Crouchback, who had a seat here and called the village Beau Repaire, built the ancient chapel of St John the Baptist, which has become a sacred place again after being a school. It is a simple nave and chancel with a single roof on five ancient beams. There are two stone seats for priests and a piscina niche, and the church has a rare possession in a stone altar table still in its original position. It has one of the five consecration crosses still visible. Two old things here have had their adventures. One is the 15th-century font, whose bowl was at the vicarage while the base was buried in the churchyard, both now together again. The other is the old cross, whose shaft has been used as a lintel stone for the porch. The top of the cross is modern.

St Peter's Church has completed its first century, a fine building outside with a great tower and pinnacles, though inside it looks as if it has turned nonconformist. It has two fine avenues of limes in its churchyard. Christ Church, a little younger, has a lofty hammer-beam roof and lancet windows with lovely saints. The bowl of its font rests on a finely carved cluster of leaves.

By the side of a busy street is a garden of lawn and lovely trees in memory of 230 men who did not come back, their names on a high column; and just outside the town, at the top of a lovely hillside graveyard with very fine trees, sleeps Jedediah Strutt, high above the valley where the river flows which turned his mill-wheel to fortune.

The Inspired Wheelwright Who Founded the Belpers

FOUNDER of the fortune of the Belper barony, Jedediah Strutt was born at South Normanton, son of a farmer. Distinguishing himself by a faculty for mechanics, revealed by his making water-wheels and improving his father's ploughs, he was apprenticed to a Findern wheelwright. He followed his trade for seven years after his apprenticeship, and then, inheriting a farm from a Blackwell uncle, married Elizabeth Woollatt, with whose family he had lodged at Findern, where her brother William was a hosiery manufacturer.

At the suggestion of Woollatt, Strutt invented a machine with turning-needles which, applied to the stocking-frame, produced, as desired, either ribbed stockings or unribbed stockings. Adapted to other machines it furnished a variety of fabrics such as manufacture had not previously known. We may still see the attic at Blackwell where the invention is said to have been perfected.

With factories at Derby and Nottingham to utilise it, the firm of Strutt and Woollatt, with a third partner, named Need, prospered greatly. When Arkwright appeared at Nottingham and the bankers, doubtful of the feasibility of his cotton-spinning machine, declined to finance him, Strutt came to his aid and is said to have suggested improvements in the machine which was to revolutionise the industrial world. A new firm (Arkwright, Strutt, and Need) was formed, and in 1769 opened in Nottingham the first cotton-spinning factory.

The factory had horses as motive power for the machinery, but after two years a move was made to Cromford, where water-power was available, and there in 1773 the first calico was produced.

Many lesser contrivances stand to the credit of Jedediah Strutt, who, dying in 1797, left sons who inherited his inventive capacity, enabling them to contribute in turn to the wealth of their generation.

The Storied Rocks

BIRCHOVER. Its grey stone houses cling to the hilly road which climbs to Stanton Moor with its stone circle, monoliths, and barrows, and brings us to a glorious panorama of wooded hill and valley. At the foot of the village are the famous Rowtor Rocks, a ridge of millstone grit 80 yards long, rising in places to 150 feet.

This massive pile, one of Nature's fantastic formations, has evidence of the hand of man working on it, and some believe that the hewn stones, the steps, and the caves, were part of a temple of the Druids. To them two small rooms cut in the rock become a priest's room and a room of sacrifice, a tiny hole through the wall becomes a confessional, a hollowed stone at the mouth of the cave becomes a font, and a socket in a stone becomes an altar, while a seat like three arm-chairs at the summit were for the Arch-Druid and his priests.

It is probably not so, though no man knows. It is probable that the rocks were shaped according to the whim of a parson who lived in a Tudor manor house at their foot, since made new. He was Thomas Eyre, one of a famous Derbyshire family, who is said to have built himself a study in the rocks, and to have had the seats hewn out for the entertainment of his friends, so that they might sit and enjoy the glorious prospect of the valley far below giving way to beautiful hills. He built a chapel in the shadow of the rocks near his house, and in this bright little place made new is a tablet to his memory, put up in our own day. He died in 1717.

Near enough to be neighbours are the fine rocks of Cratcliff Tor and Robin Hood's Stride. Cratcliff Tor has a shallow cave at the foot in which somebody has carved a crucifix and hewn out a seat and a niche for a lamp, probably the work of a hermit 700 years ago. The other pile of rocks has been given its queer name because the distance between two upstanding pinnacles (about 22 yards) is supposed to measure the length of Robin Hood's stride.

Close by are the Bradley Rocks, on which is a huge block of stone over 30 feet round, resting on two others and forming a tunnel.

Jedediah Strutt in His Attic

BLACKWELL. A rural oasis in a countryside of collieries is the old part of the village, with fine views from its hilltop, and a cross in its churchyard taking us back a thousand years. It is the lower part of a Saxon cross, five feet above the ground, two sides carved with interlacing knotwork and two with braid work. It was marking time when the Saxons worshipped on this spot, perhaps before the first church was built. The early church was one of the oldest in Derbyshire, but all that is left of its olden days is a round pillar and capital of a lost arcade, built into the new nave wall.

Not far away is a farmhouse which has come into England's story, for its attic, whose little window looks out to the church, saw the working out of an invention which was to revolutionise the hosiery trade. Here came Jedediah Strutt when his uncle died and left him all his stock. It was here that he brought his bride in 1755, and here he turned from his farming to follow his bent for mechanics. Under this old gabled roof he brought his ribbed stocking frame to perfection, and here his first child was born, the oak cradle he made for it being one of the cherished possessions of the Strutts today.

A Father to His Sons

BOLSOVER. It glories in its situation, its old remains, and its story. It had a market 700 years ago. Once it was famed for making spurs and brilliant buckles which had to stand the test of a loaded cart passing over them, and it is still getting stone from the quarries which helped to build the Houses of Parliament.

It is said to have been fortified in ancient days; it came into the Conqueror's Domesday Book as part of the vast possessions of William Peverel. It was he who built a fortress on the rocky spur where Bolsover Castle stands now, a lofty pile, part house, part ruin, crowning the fine ridge 600 feet above the sea, a splendid landmark from the valley round.

Nothing is left today of the Norman structure which was given to

46

John as a wedding present by King Richard, and had fallen into ruin by the time Sir Charles Cavendish came into possession about 1613. True to the tradition of his mother, Bess of Hardwick, he set about rebuilding the Castle as we see it. He preserved the site of the Norman Keep in the square and lofty house with corner turrets and tower, and a domed lantern rising from the roof. He preserved the site of the old bailie in the massive wall enclosing an old-world garden.

Over the main entrance of the house a great figure of Hercules supports a balcony and the Cavendish shield. Some of the 30 rooms are notable for their vaulted ceilings, fine chimney-pieces, their panelling and decorations; the finest and largest room, the Star Chamber, has a ceiling of blue and gold, and portraits of the Caesars. Sir William of the next generation carried on the work, building the splendid range stretching along a natural terrace outside the precincts of the old keep, their great rooms and magnificent gallery now roofless ruins. He also built the picturesque Riding School adjoining the stables.

Three times did Sir William Cavendish receive Charles Stuart here with lavish entertainment. He garrisoned the Castle for the king and was made general of the northern army. He fought bravely, lost at Marston Moor, and fled to the Continent, where he lived (often in great poverty) till the Restoration. He accompanied Charles the Second to London, the poorer, it is said, by a million pounds for his loyalty, with his Castle more or less in ruin.

Sir William (he was Duke of Newcastle in 1665) sleeps in Westminster Abbey, but his father and his son are buried here.

The church is said to have been begun by William Peverel, but nearly all that remained of his day was destroyed by fire in 1897 which left the 13th-century tower and spire, a small part of the chancel arch, the Cavendish chapel of 1618, and a few interesting relics. Fine fragments of coffin lids in the porch are carved with a sickle, shears, and a hatchet as well as a cross. A tympanum over the south door of the chancel, carved with figures of Mary and John by the Cross, is 12th or 13th century. A great battered sculpture on the wall of the north aisle was found face downward in use as a step at the door: it is thought to have been the altarpiece of the Norman church, and is crudely carved with the Wise Men adoring the Child on Mary's lap, two camels in the background.

Made new after the fire, the church is spacious with high roofs and fine arcades. There is fine stone carving in the pulpit, and in the reredos with figures of St Lawrence and St Mary; and two oak screens have lovely modern craftsmanship.

Two elaborate monuments in the Cavendish chapel are to Sir Charles who built the Castle and died in 1617, and to Henry Cavendish (second Duke) of 1691. Sir Charles lies under a canopy, wearing armour; his wife is on the tomb below, on the side of which kneel their three sons. To them the father addresses this quaint poem,

> Let such as have outlived all praise,
> Trust in the tombs their careful friends to raise:
> I made my life my monument, and yours,
> To which there's no material that endures,
> Nor yet inscription like it. Write but that,
> And teach your nephews it to emulate:
> It will be matter loud enough to tell
> Not when I died, but how I lived: Farewell.

The monument to Henry Cavendish has a pediment on four massive columns, and sculptured figures of Fame and History.

There is a memorial to the architect of the castle, Huntingdon Smithson who sleeps in the church. A lovely silver lamp burns in memory of a headmaster, and a tall white cross in the marketplace is in memory of 172 men who did not come back from the war.

Henry Hopkinson of Lincoln's Inn

BONSALL. Once famous for its lead mines, it is tucked away in a deep cleft of the hillside, with the lovely Via Gellia just below and Masson towering above, a hill well worth climbing for its glorious panorama and its view of the Matlocks in the valley of the Derwent.

Charming is the grouping of old stone houses and the 17th-century inn round the picturesque old market-cross, a slender ball-topped pillar on a great flight of 13 steps. And fine is the church above the housetops, with a story centuries old.

The striking tower and spire are 14th century, the tower low and sturdy, with embattled parapet, pinnacles, and gargoyles, and the lovely spire with three encircling bands of quatrefoils, flowers, shields, and fleur-de-lys. Of the same time are the porch and the doorway through which we enter the church, and the pillars and capitals of the north arcade, with a curious animal carved at the foot of one pillar. The oldest remains are 13th century, including the clustered pillars of the south arcade, a tiny piscina, and fragments of coffin stones. The font is 15th century. A small headstone cross with crude carving, now in the church, may be 600 years old.

There is a brass inscription to an honest 17th-century lawyer, Henry Hopkinson of Lincoln's Inn:

> *A barrister, a Bachelor of Art,*
> *A practiser that chose the better part;*
> *That pleaded more for just defence than gain,*
> *That for the poor and common good took pain!*
> *He's buried here, his soul in heaven doth rest*
> *Without all fear, for peacemakers are blest.*

BORROWASH. We may be grateful to it for the colour its beautiful nursery gardens, with their pools and rockeries, lend to a great highway from Nottingham to Derby. On a road leading to the Trent meadows is the little church in a garden of trees, a cosy building of our time with a pulpit and screen of lovely wrought iron over 200 years old, and two finely carved chairs of the 17th century.

BOULTON. It is almost touching Derby, but its old country lane keeps an air of peace as if to be in tune with the little church which, though made almost new, has something left of Norman days.

It stands in a pleasant churchyard, its porch sheltering a Norman doorway with shafts and capitals and zigzag moulding. A holy-water stoup of curious shape, with four outer ribs, has had its adventure after its life of 800 years, for this Norman treasure was found in a farmyard.

Near the pulpit (made from an alabaster gravestone in the sanctuary, and inlaid with marble) are old tiles set in the floor, one with the unusual pattern of two keys on a cross, while on two others are the heads of a king and a queen, perhaps Edward the First and Queen Eleanor. Some of the windows have glass of lovely bright colours.

Cromwell's Men Waiting

BOYLESTONE. Little happens to it now, for it is a quiet place, yet it had its hour of drama long ago. Here came a little company of Cromwell's men in the night, dismounting from their horses and silently surrounding the church that stands so high above the sunken lane. They waited for the peep of dawn to call upon the enemy to surrender. Indoors were 200 Cavaliers sheltering for the night on their way to the relief of Wingfield Manor. They had set no watch outside the church and so were caught in a trap of their own setting. One by one as they came through the priest's doorway they were taken and stripped of their arms, "men, colours, and all, without the loss of one man on either side."

An avenue of stately limes has grown along the way the soldiers must have trod, bringing us to the church whose tower with odd peaked roof is barely a century old. It is snow-white indoors save for the grey walls of the chancel and the nave arcade. Its oldest stones are in the 13th-century buttresses of the chancel, the rest of the church having been made new in the 14th century, perhaps by Walter de Waldeshef who was chief butler to the king, and Governor of the Castle and Honour of the Peak; but the east window is a century later, and some are new, as is the chancel arch. The font is 600 years old.

Here still is the priest's doorway through which the Cavaliers walked out to meet their captors; and there are still oak tie-beams and bosses in the roofs which looked down on that dramatic day.

The Last Supper is finely carved in oak above the altar, with a background of little squares of diaper work, about 120 of them, no two quite alike.

Roofless and Alone

BRACKENFIELD. Tucked in a steep hillside above the highroad to Ashover, looking out on a fine panorama where distance lends enchantment to the patchwork fields, the towers, spires, and chimneys of an industrial countryside, is a little grey ruin, roofless and alone, almost hidden from view by the chestnut trees in front of it, and glorying in the bracken which gives the place its name.

A soft green carpet grows within its walls, and wild flowers have rooted in the crevices, but the windows, the bell turret, and the two stone seats of what was once a porch tell the tale of an ancient chapel made new in the 16th century, and abandoned in the 19th when a new church was built.

The new church is about a mile from the ruin, down in the village of winding lanes, fine trees, and the River Amber bounding Ogston Park. It shelters a few oak benches and the 15th-century screen from the old chapel, the screen now against the west wall of the nave, with tracery in its bays. A low brass screen leads into the chancel, which has linenfold panelling on the walls.

All the Men Came Back

BRADBOURNE. In charming setting on its peaceful hilltop, it feels the blast of the north winds from the moors, but sees the kindly green of Haven Hill on the other side. Down in the dale the Haven Hill Brook flows to the moss-grown wheel of an old mill by the Ashbourne road.

A very happy group is the vicarage, the ancient church, and the fine old Hall which has come through the years with so much grace. A stone house with many gables in an old-world garden, it is said to have something yet of the old place built here for a few monks of Dunstable Priory looking after great flocks of sheep on these rich pastures. It was enlarged and given its fine oak staircase early in the 17th century by the Buckstons, who have memorials in the church. One is to Thomas Buckston, who was 87 when he died a few years after Trafalgar, one of the oldest officers in the army. He was proud that he fought at Culloden.

Bradbourne has a grateful memory of the Great War, for it is one of that group of 30 Thankful Villages we have found in our tour of England, which sent a gallant company to the war and received them home again; 18 men went from Bradbourne and 18 came back.

In all the thousand years of its story the village can have known no prouder day than when all its men were safe and sound at home again. The church in which there would be great thanksgiving has in its keeping the oldest possession of the village, all that is left of a very early Saxon cross carved with foliage and crude figures. Part of it stands about three feet high in the churchyard, and in the church itself are two other pieces which have been used as posts for a stile and a gate.

The fine tower stands almost as the Normans left it, massive like most of their structures, but unusually high. It has a turret stairway, and a Norman corbel table of tiny heads below a 15th-century parapet, but the glory of the tower is its charming south doorway with three orders of moulding, one of beak-heads, the other two of birds and animals. The doorway of the porch and the one through which we enter the church are also Norman.

The nave arcade with clustered pillars is perhaps 600 years old, and the windows are of the three medieval centuries. There is an old stone coffin and two fonts; the fine square one in use is over 600 years old, the round one is older still. The arms of Edensor are among old glass fragments. Four pieces of wood, carved with quaint heads, leaves, and flowers, are about 400 years old, and may have belonged to the pew of the Bradbournes who held the manor from the 13th century till the end of Tudor days. Their old home, Lea Hall, is a farmhouse.

Dr Johnson Meets a Friend

BRADLEY. With its beautiful bowers of trees and winding blue-bell lanes, it knows the stillness of the dreaming countryside. Its wayside church by the open fields, with the great house over the way, is a bright place with chancel and nave under one fine old roof, calling the people to prayer with its bell on the west wall outside.

It was made new in the 14th century, the east window and those in the nave being of this time. Stone faces adorn their hoods outside. Two 14th-century brackets in the chancel have carvings of men with beards and curly hair, and in the south wall of the nave is an ancient stone with crude figures under a tree, perhaps Adam and Eve. The lovely 13th-century font has a round bowl enriched with arcading.

One of two windows with stained glass has in red, gold, and green the figure of Christ with the children and again as the Good Shepherd. Fine carving of our own day is in the oak pulpit, and the altar table with eight spandrels in eight patterns.

The Hall opposite the church was converted out of stables which had been built in advance for another house. It was here that Dr Johnson used to visit Mrs Meynell and her daughters when staying at Ashbourne with his friend Dr Taylor, and here he began his friendship with Miss Hill Boothby. Their friendship was one of the fine things of his life. A gracious woman with many accomplishments, she encouraged Johnson when he needed encouragement most, and his letters show how greatly he valued her friendship. Her death in 1756 robbed him of the precious thing he found here. Long afterwards, when his great Dictionary had made him famous, he looked back with thankfulness to the happy times this village gave him.

Two other men who made their name in the world have known this place: John Bingham the Nonconformist, who lived here for three years after being ejected from the living of Marston-on-Dove in 1662, and Thomas Bancroft, known as the small poet, and remembered for his epigrams.

About three feet of the shaft and the base stone of the old cross remain in the churchyard.

The Glittering Beauty Down Below

BRADWELL. Plain amid much loveliness, encircled by lofty hills and sheltering under the fine height of Bradwell Edge, it is all very old, lying near the Batham Gate, the Roman road which ran from Brough to Buxton.

It was in its busy lead-mining days that it found its proud possession, the Bagshaw Cavern with its famous crystalline formations. A flight of 130 steps leads us down to grottoes of singular beauty.

Reached through a short avenue of limes is the plain little 19th-century church, with good modern oak in the chancel.

At the end of Bradwell Dale, the mile-long gorge with towering cliffs sheer on each side, is Hazlebadge Hall, a farmhouse with the arms of the Vernons on a gable. It was part of the dowry Dorothy Vernon of Haddon Hall brought to her husband John Manners.

Craftsmen of a Thousand Years

BRAILSFORD. Trim and pleasant, midway between Derby and Ashbourne, is this old village which belonged to one of the few Saxon families who kept their lands through the days of Norman England. It has still one thing that Elfin, its Saxon owner, knew, the remains of the churchyard cross. Long buried under its old base, the shaft was found some years ago and set up on a new stone, leaving its old foundation a few feet away. There are fine modern benches in the church, so that we are able here to see the work of craftsmen separated by a thousand years.

The lovely old church stands with great limes and a splendid old yew in the fields between the village and Ednaston, for it was built to serve both places. Of the church the Normans built when the cross was young only three things remain, an arch at the end of the aisle, the great pillar adjoining it (helping to support the tower), and a sturdy column and capital holding up one side of the chancel arch.

The rest of the pillars of the arcade are 14th century, but their arches and the clerestory over them are at least three centuries younger. The chancel with its sedilia and piscina and an arched recess is also 14th century. The fine embattled tower was built about 1500 in the western bay of the nave, leaving the aisle longer than the nave, and shortening two of its own buttresses which end in hideous gargoyles.

The medieval porch, made new in the 17th century, shelters a massive 400-year-old door with heavy ironwork, the great lock and key-plate bordered with chevrons and flowers. An old chest is about six feet long, and on a wall is a piece of panelling from a 17th-century pew on which we read that somebody paid 22s. for this seat to Mr Barnabas Pool, rector. Several sturdy benches are all that is left of the fine seating which filled the church in Elizabeth's day, but the benches of last century are delightful. Their ends are carved with handsome borders, and in the traceried panels are shields with an endless variety of figures and symbols, among them a bird, a harp, a ladder, a pelican with her young, a holy lamb, a king with his crown, and a fox with her cub peeping from its earth.

The font is 15th century, its base carved with the Tudor rose. Built into the outer wall is part of a coffin lid engraved with a cross and a pair of shears, in memory of a 12th-century wool merchant or sheep farmer.

In the hamlet of Ednaston, lovely with trees on the other side of the Brailsford Brook, was born in 1790 Thomas Beighton, one of the bravest missionaries who ever went to the Malay Straits. Soon after his ordination at Derby and his marriage with another earnest evangelist, Abigail Tobitt, he left England in 1818 for ever, giving the rest of his life to mission work in Malaya where he was the best-loved white man. He not only went about preaching and teaching, but set up his own printing press at Penang, so that he could publish books in the Malay language. Every year he issued thousands of copies of books and tracts, the crown of his labours being his own translation of Pilgrim's Progress.

The Oldest Inhabitant in the Tower

BRASSINGTON. This grey village on a green hill has old houses and an ancient church set high above the wayside. Its tower comes from Norman days except for its embattled parapet, the tops of the old buttresses, and a 13th-century window over a much later doorway.

From the Norman also is the entrance arch of the porch, the plain bowl of the font, a fine nave arcade of round arches on massive pillars with bold capitals, and two small bays between the chancel and the chapel. The lofty chancel arch is 14th century, the clerestory and a chancel window 15th.

We may spare a thought for a 17th-century Yorkshire rector who died on a journey and was buried here; he was Michael Adams of Treton, and this is what we read of him:

Pause, Traveller, for a while and drop at least a passing tear for the lamentable death of a certain traveller, whom perchance travelling hence, when a fierce winter was raging without, the more raging heat of an inextinguishable fever seized him within, and carried him without a doubt to the mansions of the Lord in a chariot of fire like unto Elijah.

High up in the wall of the tower, only seen with much difficulty, is a stone 12 inches by 10, carved with the quaint figure of a man with one hand on his heart. Its story is unknown, but it is probably the work of a Saxon sculptor found by the Normans and built into their tower. He is the oldest inhabitant of the village, and the one most rarely seen.

About 800 feet above the sea, Brassington is famous for the scenery around. We can trace a Roman road and find the graves of ancient Britons; near by are the splendid Rainster Rocks and Hipley Hill with its caves, Hoe Grange Quarry where remains of some of the first animals in England have been found, and Harborough Rocks with strange fantastic shapes, where barrows with chambers go back to the Stone Age, and are 1200 feet above the sea.

And less than three miles away rises the mass of Minninglow Hill, crossed by a Roman road. It is well worth climbing to its rocky spur where a ring of beeches surrounds the rock-chambered graves, a sleeping-place for a chief, maybe, carried up here perhaps 20 centuries ago. We are alone on the top of the world, looking out to a mighty panorama of moorland hills, in the solitude of the earth with the wonder of the Past.

The Treasure That Escaped the Fire

BREADSALL. It lies on the hillside above the Derwent, with a treasure it lost and found, and memories of a strange man sleeping in the church.

A charming road under the trees brings us to Breadsall Priory, a stately 17th-century house with tower and turrets (now modernised) on the site of a small priory of 700 years ago. Many families have lived here since the monks were turned out and the estate became the property of Henry Grey, who married a daughter of Mary Tudor. Here the Darwins lived from 1799 to 1858, and here Erasmus Darwin died in 1802. He was a physician, poet, and philosopher, and there is a memorial to him in the old church on the hill.

The massive 13th-century tower with a 14th-century spire is a fine landmark, and its churchyard has lovely views. All that is left of the Norman church is the fine south doorway, in which swings a modern door on beautiful iron hinges, at least 500 years old, some of the curves forming graceful necks and heads of birds.

Towards the end of last century some of the rood stairway and a big peephole were found and it was then that Breadsall found a rare and beautiful thing it had forgotten, an exquisite carving in alabaster of Our Lady of Pity. The artist has depicted a wonderful pathos on her face as she holds her Crucified Son on her knee. The sculpture was found under the floor, having mercifully survived a fire; it is thought to be 500 years old, though the style of the Madonna's dress seems to be 12th century.

The chancel has a 13th-century lancet. From the 14th come the nave arcade, the south walls of nave and chancel, and the porch. The east window and the great embattled font are 15th century. The nave roof has beautiful bosses, and angels support the richly moulded beams. The lovely chancel screen with a vaulted canopy is of our own day.

One of Breadsall's rectors was the scholar John Heiron. He used the Old Hall near the church as a vicarage, a building of stone and timber now a church room, once the manor house. It has still some 14th-century work. The old scholar was one of the ejected Nonconformists at the Restoration. It is quaintly recorded of him that he had many Providential Deliverances when he was but a child. He was tossed by a cow; he fell out of a chamber; he fell into the Trent and yet received no harm. He was carried down the river in a boat alone when the wind was high, and he had in all probability been drowned in a whirlpit if one that saw him had not taken the private boat and stopped him. He survived all these excitements to preach in 66 churches in Derbyshire and in 30 churches in other parts.

Even without his two illustrious grandsons, Erasmus Darwin, whose useful life ended at Breadsall, would be famous.

Darwin the First

AS Scott thought his poet's fame would suffer if he acknowledged the authorship of the Waverley Novels, so Erasmus Darwin feared his standing as a physician would be compromised if he permitted his name to appear on the poems which keep his fame alive.

By his first marriage he was the grandfather of Charles Darwin, and by his second he was grandfather of Sir Francis Galton, a title indeed to renown, but Erasmus stands broad-based and secure in the goodwill of posterity apart from the celebrity of his descendants.

Trained at Edinburgh, he established a lucrative practice and a delightful circle of friends at Lichfield, stronghold of Dr Johnson. Diametrically opposed in all that matters in politics and philosophy, the two men met, admired, and disliked each other.

But Darwin, who was not only the best physician of his age but a man of deep learning and original thought, was king of the Lunatics, as they called themselves, friends who met in turn at each other's houses: Anna Seward, who wished to marry him; Richard Lovell Edgeworth, father of Maria; Thomas Day, author of Sandford and Merton; Josiah Wedgwood, the potter; Samuel Galton; the inventors James Watt and Matthew Boulton; and the discoverer of oxygen, Joseph Priestley. They did not practise plain living, perhaps, but they certainly rejoiced in high thinking.

Erasmus Darwin lives for us today by virtue of one work which in effect was two. He published first the Loves of the Plants, but this was really the second part of his Botanic Garden, which followed. The first poem teems with wit and fancy no less than with extravagant absurdity; the Botanic Garden is rich with foresight and prophecy. In it occur the famous lines:

> *Soon shall thy arm, unconquered steam! afar*
> *Drag the slow barge, or drive the rapid car;*
> *Or on wide waving wings expanded bear*
> *The flying chariot through the field of air.*

His mind ranged over an immense field, and, however dimly, he foreshadowed a host of things which were to come, ideas which incurred the ridicule of his own age in England but now prove him to have been of the true fellowship of the prophets.

The Boy Looking On

BREASTON. Its trim houses and gardens have views of the meadowlands where the Trent and Derwent meet.

Four fine limes lead to its church, most of which was made new 600 years ago, though the tower and the spire are 700 years old, and a blocked-up doorway was used in the time of King John. It is remarkable for the unusual carvings of the arch stones (now very worn), no two of the patterns being alike.

The interior is bright with pointed arches and windows, and has a fine roof. There is a rich oak reredos with four figures under canopies, an unused Jacobean altar table, and three old oak chairs. A graceful alabaster font of 1720 had six coloured bell ropes hanging round it when we called.

For six centuries the wide-open eyes of a chubby-cheeked boy have been looking on the happenings in this place. He came into being during the rebuilding of the church and has held up the end arch of the nave arcade ever since. He saw the raising of the walls and the lowering of the roof when he was a hundred years old, and must have smiled to himself when in 1887 a clock was put in the tower to commemorate only the first century of Mrs Stevens.

A good place for long life Breaston would seem to be, for a weatherworn stone on an outside wall is to Sarah Dyche, who died a centenarian before the Victorian Era had begun.

Our Oldest Cedar of Lebanon?

BRETBY. Four pairs of brothers and five other men are remembered on its green, where two great elms make a fine setting for an oak pump shelter in their memory.

This quiet and charming spot has seen the glory of a castle wax and wane; it has seen the destruction of a wonderful house built by Inigo Jones; and the passing of an ancient church on the eve of our own time. It is said that the stones of the old castle were used for the building of the great house which Inigo Jones designed, a magnificent place, full of treasures of art and set in gardens with lakes and fountains. Its chapel, most richly adorned and lined with cedar wood, was finished in 1696; it was here that John Heiron, the great Nonconformist, used to preach for the Countess of Chesterfield. In the Civil War the house was fortified for the king and plundered by the Roundheads. The wife of the second earl was one of the famous beauties of the court of Charles the Second, and lived here often.

The splendid pile was destroyed in the 18th century, owing, it is said, to a mistaken idea that it was unsafe, and the present hall was built last century, being now a hospital.

In a corner of the gardens, close to the house, is a lofty Cedar of

Lebanon towering like a monarch higher than the roof. It has a magnificent trunk 15 feet round, and fine clean limbs. The death of Uvedale's cedar, planted before 1670 at Enfield, has given Bretby's giant the reputation of being the oldest tree of its kind in England, here since 1676.

The 13th-century church was pulled down when the new one was built on its site; all that remains of it is masonry in the west wall. The reredos Crucifixion was once a picture in the Hall.

It is strange to find in this little church, so hidden from the busy world, an inscription to Lord Beaconsfield. We understand why it is here when we remember that one of the joys of Disraeli's life was to leave his troubles in London to spend a few quiet days as the guest of Lady Chesterfield. The memorial was put here by the countess, one of the two beautiful sisters Disraeli loved, and we read that it is in memory of the foremost man of his age, a record of a much-prized friendship and a lasting regret. Lord Beaconsfield used to say of Bretby that it scattered flowers and fruit over his whole existence.

Derbyshire Delight For Disraeli

IN the years after the death of his wife Disraeli found great consolation in the friendship of Lady Chesterfield and her sister Lady Bradford. He seems to have been very much in love with both.

He made them members of a little group he had playfully formed of his woman friends; he called it the Order of the Bee and he gave his members a brooch with a bee on it. Lady Chesterfield's house was always open to him, and his table was regularly furnished from its gardens, its dairies, its coverts, and its poultry runs. One of his letters to her begins by saying that as he walked into dinner a duchess said to him, "You are going to sit between two of the fattest women in London," and ends by saying that the servant was perpetually coming in and announcing Fruit from Bretby, Flowers from Bretby, Butter from Bretby; Blessed Bretby!

On the eve of a General Election Disraeli came up from Bretby where he had been suffering severely from gout, and, writing to Lady Chesterfield to describe a visit to Balmoral, he spoke playfully of receiving his sovereign in slippers and dressing-gown.

Once he wrote from Bretby to Lady Bradford expressing his great concern at the burden he was imposing on Bretby by remaining there as an invalid. The dear angel, he said, was more than kindness to him as he sat in silence, quite unable to read, musing over the past twelve months, and he added these human words:

I have had at least my dream and if my shattered energies never rally, which is what I must be prepared for, I have at any rate reached the pinnacle of power and gauged the sweetest and deepest affections of the heart.

The Highest Town in England

BUXTON. Set amid great natural glory on the River Wye, it is assumed to be the highest market town in England, 1000 feet above the sea, like a cup in the everlasting hills of the Peak. The rude hamlet of long ago has become a great spa through the fame of a warm spring known down the ages for its healing virtues, unfailing and unchanging in all seasons at a temperature of 82 degrees. It was probably the Aquae of the Romans, who brought roads here from some of their military stations.

In the Middle Ages, in spite of its remoteness and its poor accommodation, pilgrims flocked to the well at the foot of the cliff, and the walls of the old well chapel of St Anne close by were hung with the sticks and crutches they were able to discard. Under Henry the Eighth the relics were removed and the well and the chapel locked up and sealed, but in the time of Elizabeth the waters were again in good repute. Mary Queen of Scots was brought here for the benefit of her health; she stayed at the Old Hall, and the story is told that on her last visit she scratched on a window with her ring the words:

Buxton, whose fame thy milkwarm waters tell,
Whom I perhaps shall see no more, farewell.

The old Hall was rebuilt in 1670, but has some remains of the older house, including the pillared entrance. It is now a hotel and stands at the end of the Crescent.

The town is old and new, Higher and Lower Buxton. Higher Buxton is the older part beyond St Anne's Cliff, where the old village green has become a busy market square, but keeps its old stone cross. Here Buxton's oldest chapel stands in a secluded corner of the busy road. It was built in 1625 after the well chapel had been abandoned. It has a stone roof and a bell gable, and is lighted by small square-headed windows. Fine stout old tie-beams support the roof. The Jacobean font is oblong carved with a shield, a cross, and a Greek letter. There is a 17th-century oak reading-desk handsomely carved. In the little churchyard is the grave of John Kane the 18th-century comedian, restored by J. T. Toole a hundred years later.

Lower Buxton is the new, with fine houses and buildings, lovely gardens and walks. It has the fine Pump Room where the waters are drunk from the flowing source, and the splendid Crescent built by the Duke of Devonshire about 1780. Designed by John Carr of York and said to have cost £120,000, it is built in the Doric style of architecture with three storeys and a fine arcade. The curve is 200 feet long with wings 58 feet, and there are 380 windows. It looks across to the Pump Room and the terraced gardens of The Slopes.

In the gardens looking down on the Crescent and out to the en-circling hills is Buxton's peace memorial, a lovely bronze figure of a winged angel with sword and laurel wreath. Behind the Crescent is the Devonshire Hospital, converted from the old stables and riding school, with a clock tower and a great dome said to be the biggest in the world, covering a round floor 50 yards across.

The classic church of St John has an imposing portico and a cupola for one bell. Bright and spacious within, it is all the work of the early 19th century. It has a massive pulpit of marble and alabaster and a pleasing font. One of the windows has fine glass of rich colour in memory of men who died for Peace, with figures of St Michael and St George. Two windows have lovely Kempe glass, one with St Anne teaching the Madonna to read and St Agnes with a lamb; the other with two martyrs and the emblems of their martyrdom: St Stephen with stones and St Laurence with his grid.

The splendid Duke's Drive, made in 1795, runs from the Bakewell to the Ashbourne road; it rides for a while above the Ashwood Dale and has a fine peep of the Lovers Leap. At its foot the delightful ferny Sherbrook Dell comes to the Dale, with a profusion of wild flowers and plants and a stream flowing to the Wye.

From a new tower crowning the fir-clothed slopes of Grin Low, a mile from the town, is a wonderful view 1450 feet above the sea. The tower has replaced the old Solomon's Temple which once stood near a tumulus here. Under the slopes of Grin Plantation is Poole's Cavern, where a brigand stored his treasure long ago and Nature has stored treasures longer than men have lived. Thomas Hobbes counted it one of his Seven Wonders of the Peak, and Charles Cotton sang the praises of this cave, which we can explore for 700 yards, with masses of rocks of strange shape and formation, and a great wealth of stalagmites and stalactites.

Lovely are the Corbar Woods with winding walks about the great hillside, a transformation from old quarries and shattered rocks to a glory of trees, ferns, and wild flowers. From the top of Corbar Hill is a magnificent view of Buxton close at hand, and away to Kinderscout, Mam Tor, and Axe Edge.

From this fine town we may best enjoy the beauty of much of the Peak: Axe Edge, the Goyt Valley, and glorious moorland rides. Axe Edge is a gritstone ridge of heath and moss and bog, looking out from 1810 feet high to a glorious panorama over three counties, and giving birth to four rivers, the Dane, the Goyt, the Dove, and the Wye. The wildly romantic Goyt Valley, dividing Derbyshire from Cheshire, begins as a wooded ravine with the charming little Goyt's Bridge of one arch spanning the musical meeting of the waters. From the bridge we have a view of Errwood Hall on the hillside, famed for its rhododendrons. A fine moorland walk of five miles from Buxton takes us to the Cat and Fiddle in Cheshire, one of the highest inns in England, 1700 feet above the sea, with views over the great plain of Cheshire, with the Mersey on the horizon, into Staffordshire and Lancashire, and to the Welsh Hills.

For those who love to read Nature's wondrous story of our Past the museum at Buxton is a famous place.

A Home of Man Ten Thousand Years Ago

BUXTON was a home of man 100 centuries ago, when the Ice Age was retreating in the Peak; it is one of the most suitable places in which we can study the things our prehistoric ancestors left behind them in the caves and gravel-beds.

Here also we may compare their legacies to the Peak with things found all over our Motherland, for in the library of this fine museum is the collection of reference books kept by that matchless discoverer of our wondrous past, Sir Boyd Dawkins. We may see his many informing notes on the margins of these books which are kept under a window given by Lady Boyd Dawkins, with a picture of Elaine the fair, Elaine the lovable, holding a shield of her Lancelot as she talks to her brothers.

Hereabouts great discoveries have been made of historic and prehistoric time. Dr Dawkins found an amazing number of bones and teeth of extinct animals, the very oldest collection from caves that had been found at that time. He discovered them at the Victory Quarry, Dovehole. They included bones of the mastodon, sabre-toothed tiger, rhinoceros, and the elephant; here they are in this museum, the marks of the hyena's teeth plainly visible on the bones of these great animals.

Here also have been found flints and pebbles worked by the Stone Age men, jaws and teeth of men and animals, stones and flints from Arbor Low Circle nine miles away, sometimes called the second Stone-henge. With all these we may compare the fine and comprehensive collection of implements from all over the world lent to the museum by Mr F. A. Holmes, a tireless friend and advocate of the Peak as a National Park. With it all is a collection of things from the Roman period, coins, brooches, vases, altars, quern stones; and we noticed a milestone which told the Roman traveller the number of miles to Brough, near Castleton.

The Echo of War

CALDWELL. This quiet place of a few homes, an old great house, and a small church made almost new, was old over 600 years ago when a king and his earls halted here a while. It was Edward the Second in pursuit of Thomas, Earl of Lancaster, who was at Burton five miles away. They met soon afterwards at Borough-bridge, where the earl was taken and beheaded.

One touch of beauty older even than that touch of war has this little place, for here is something from the church the Normans found—three tiny Saxon lights, two in the nave and one in the chancel. They are the chief possession of Caldwell. For its last twenty years this little light of a thousand years in the chancel has had as company a beautiful reredos of translucent alabaster, with traceried panels and handsome carving of vine and grape, crowned by two angels.

Echoes of other wars we found here. Two of three alabaster stones to the Sanders family are to the parents of Colonel Thomas Sanders who fought for Parliament against Charles Stuart in the Civil War. A Kempe window is in memory of a soldier killed at Mafeking in the South African War; another window has the regimental badges of four men who died for us in the Great War.

In the west window are two medallions of old glass from Nuremberg, one showing the Resurrection with the Roman soldiers round the tomb, the other with Joab slaying Abner.

Beauty in a Deep Hollow

CALKE. Its story goes back to a priory soon after the Conquest, whose site was acquired by Henry Harpur in 1621. He made it his home, and the family home it has been since.

Sheltered by the rising ground about it, and hidden from the road, it was made new in the 18th century and given the name of Calke Abbey, keeping some of the old masonry in walls six feet thick. We have a glimpse of an embattled tower across the park, built last century for the church which was being refashioned from the Norman.

We may all know the joy of the glorious ride from Melbourne to this quiet place with a handful of dwellings and the great park in which roam hundreds of deer. Three miles we go up and down among the rolling border hills, with a beauty spot that bids us loiter by the way, for here is a real bit of beauty where a farmhouse and an old mill lie in a deep hollow, with fine woods for a background and a stream flowing under a bridge of stately arches.

Poor Sarah Tissington

CARSINGTON. It nestles in a valley, sheltered by a steep wooded hillside to which its tiny church seems to cling for life.

It is a simple place 50 feet long and 20 feet wide, with something of the 14th century left in the east window and part of another in the vestry, and in the fine font carved with four small heads at the base. Old oak pews now line the walls, and there is a sundial of 1648. Two interesting windows are in memory of the Gells of Hopton close by, one with the names of all their women from 1452 to 1862, the other with the names of all their men from 1404 to 1926. In the glass are figures of St Helena, St Giles, St Margaret, St John, the Good Centurion, and St Philip.

Two odd items we found in the church register here, one of the planting of the yew tree in the churchyard in 1638 and another of Sarah Tissington, who was born here in 1664 without arms but learned to knit with her feet.

One of Carsington's rectors was John Oldfield, who was driven from the church in 1662, and here was born his son Joshua. Both have found their way into our national roll of fame, and we meet them at Alfreton, where the father lies.

Buxton   The Tower on Grin Low

Buxton   The Famous Crescent

The Cat and Fiddle Inn across the Cheshire border near Buxton

The Goyt Valley near Buxton

In the Romantic Valley of Hope

CASTLETON. It nestles snugly in the heart of Peakland, in the gentle loveliness of the Valley of Hope and looking up to wild and romantic scenes. It is an old, old place where rocks are riddled with wonderful caves and the earth with old mines. It knew the ancient Britons, who left their camp on the top of its highest hill. It knew the Romans, who worked its mines. It saw the splendour of the proud Peverels who had these lands from the Conqueror among their vast estates. Time has left us something of these proud folk, in the Castle they built at the top of a precipice, and in their church down in the valley.

Crowning the top of Castle Hill is the Castle of the Peak, like a tireless watcher over the valley, one of the most interesting survivals of a Norman fortress, almost invulnerable except on one side where a winding path climbs to the summit. It frowns above a precipice dropping down to the grim and narrow Cave Dale, and towers above the entrance to the Peak Cavern in the sheer face of the rock.

Something of the castle wall which still remains, with ruins of a gateway, is said to be the work of William Peverel of the Conqueror's day, but the keep, whose roofless shell still stands, is from about 1175; its walls are 8 feet thick and nearly 60 high, enclosing about 400 square feet. Sir Walter Scott has made the castle famous by his Peveril of the Peak, but the book has little foundation in historic fact.

At the foot of the hill is the charming village to which the castle gave a name, stone-built, all twists and turns, proud of a little three-corner green sacred to the men who died for the peace of our fair countryside. At two corners is a monument with the names of all who went out, at the other the names of the eight who did not come back.

Close by is the little church in a lovely churchyard of trim lawn and sycamores, long known as the Church of Peak Castle. Through all its many changes it has kept one thing of the early days when it was built by William Peverel or his son; it is the handsome chancel arch with chevrons. The 15th-century tower has long been associated with the festivities of Garland Day, when the whole village does honour to the old custom now observed on Oak Apple Day, the 29th of May. The merrymaking begins with a procession of dancers and musicians in attendance on a king and queen in fine array. The king wears a massive bell-shaped garland, and at sunset rides to the tower, where the garland is hoisted by a rope to one of the eight pinnacles and left till the flowers wither.

There is an old font, 17th-century box pews with the names of those who once sat in them, a fine modern oak pulpit, and a reredos with a small oil painting of the Adoration of the Magi, by Van Eyck. In the vestry is a library of hundreds of books left by a vicar, among them a Cranmer's Bible of 1539 and a Breeches Bible of 1611.

John Mawe, a mineralogist who was buried in London in 1829, has here a marble tablet according to his wish. It was at Castleton that he acquired his love of geology, and for many years he came here every autumn. He toured England and Scotland in search of mineral specimens for the King of Spain, was in Cadiz when war broke out between the two countries, and was arrested as a spy. He visited the diamond mines of Brazil and wrote many books about rocks and precious stones.

This quaint epitaph, said to have been written by himself, has Micah Hall, an attorney who died on the eve of Trafalgar:

> *What I was you know not:*
> *What I am you know not:*
> *Where I am you know not:*
> *Be gone.*

If we would fathom the secrets of the hills and of the earth there are wonderful caves and mines to explore at Castleton. The magnificent natural entrance arch of the great Peak Cavern, known as the Devil's Hole, rises for 50 feet in the wooded face of the cliff on which the castle stands, opening into the weird and yawning mouth of the cave, 114 feet wide, where ropemakers ply their craft. From here winding passages lead to chamber after chamber, galleries and halls, for a mile into the heart of the hill, while all the time the sound of hidden waters add weirdness to the place. Almost at the mouth of the cavern the Peak Hole Water bursts into life from the rock and hastens down the village street to join the Noe beyond Hope church.

This remarkable cavern was described as one of the Seven Wonders of the Peak in a Latin poem by Thomas Hobbes. At one place the roof shelves down nearly to the floor, though blasting of the rock has given more space here than of old. At one time visitors to the cavern had to lie flat in a punt which the guide pushed along the surface of a stream. Byron came here in those days with Mary Chaworth, and wrote of his strange adventure:

DERBYSHIRE

I had to cross in a boat a stream which flows under a rock so close upon the water as to admit the boat only to be pushed on by the ferryman, a sort of Charon, who wades at the stern, stooping all the time. The Companion of my transit was M.A.C., with whom I had long been in love and never told it, though she had discovered it without. I recollect my sensations but cannot describe them, and it is as well.

The Speedwell Cavern is made partly by Nature and partly by man, reached by a disused mine abandoned after a vain search for lead. A long flight of steps and a voyage down a subterranean canal ends where the sound of waters becomes a roar as they fall with eddy and whirl into the abyss of the Bottomless Pit, and the great cavern rises above to immeasurable height into the heart of the mountain.

The Blue John Mine is famous for a spar coloured like amethyst and topaz, a lovely product of the limestone which is made into ornaments. Here we have a feast of spectacular beauty, where spacious vaulted chambers, reached by labyrinths of passages, reveal magnificent scenes of glistening fairylike formations of stalactites and stalagmites. The Romans probably worked this mine; two vases found at Pompeii are said to have been made from its spar—treasures from the heart of an English mountain buried for 18 centuries under the ashes of an Italian volcano.

One of the glories of Castleton is the magnificent scene from its heights: from its own Castle Hill; from Mam Tor, another of the Seven Wonders of the Peak, 1700 feet above the sea and crowned with an ancient camp; its curious crumbling of shale has given the Tor the name of Shivering Mountain; and the sudden vision of the Vale of Hope as we come from the steep, wild, romantic gorge of the Winnats, whose very name (Wind Gates) is eloquent of the fury of the winds that haunt this winding mile.

At the head of the Winnats is the cavern of Windy Knoll, where have been found the bones of the rhinoceros, the bear, and the wolf to remind us of the days when Castleton was in the heart of a world in which wild life was King.

Two peeps of the living world today we found most interesting here. One was of a little workshop with antiquated foot-driven machines which men have been working a hundred years, making lovely chalices out of Blue John Stone. One of these chalices may take a month or two to shape and they go all over the world. The other interesting peep of life here was of an old craftsman, a man weaving ropes by hand. He was Joseph Marrison and was 82 when we found him carrying on the work his family has done for generations. He has made ten thousand miles of rope an inch thick, miles of it for the Allies in the Great War.

A Shining Deed at Lucknow

CHADDESDEN. It has an unspoiled peep in the quiet ways by the church, which stands with a shapely yew for company and a fine plantation behind, while the shadow of its massive 15th-century tower falls on a charming row of brick and timber almshouses with shuttered windows, six little dwellings 300 years old, with only a narrow cobbled path between them and the church where their old folk lie.

The great house once lending beauty to this scene has gone, but the name of the Wilmots will not soon be forgotten. An old family with a Thane at the court of Edward the Confessor, it has at our end of the line a soldier who won the Victoria Cross. It was Robert Wilmot who founded the almshouses. Sir Edward Wilmot, who was 93 years old when they buried him at Monkton, was physician to two of the Georges; his wife was Sarah Mead, daughter of a famous physician through whom inoculation came to be adopted in England. He spent his last years giving his service to the poor of Derbyshire.

The fine linenfold panelling of the sanctuary and the oak and alabaster reredos are in memory of Sir Henry Wilmot who won the V.C. with two of his men for a shining deed at Lucknow. He and four others found themselves opposed to a great number, and one of the men was shot through both legs. He was lifted up and carried away under fire, while Captain Wilmot covered the retreat of the party by firing with the men's rifles. By what was like a miracle he managed to keep a clear course for his companions and the four men with their wounded comrade were able to get back.

The old chapel was made new in the 14th century, and from that time come the arcades, two old stone altar screens, fine stone seats and piscinas, and a stone lectern. An unusual chalice-shaped font with a very shallow bowl is also 600 years old.

A great treasure of the church is the 15th-century chancel screen, which has a modern vaulting on the western side and beautiful old tracery in the bays. Two massive stall-ends at the entrance are richly carved, their enormous crockets climbing to the tracery in the screen, and having two charming figures as poppyheads.

In the old stone reredos of the south aisle is a beautiful painted panel of the Adoration, in memory of Arthur Wilmot, a rector.

Apostle of the Peak

CHAPEL-EN-LE-FRITH. Industry has come creeping into this little stone town on the slope of a fertile valley, but it keeps its old-world marketplace and its stocks for ne'er-do-wells, and it rings its curfew bell.

All round are Peakland heights: Combs Moss, bleak and threatening; Bolt Edge and Rushup Edge; South Head 1620 feet above the sea; Chinley Churn's bold mass; and the conical hill of Eccles Pike.

Of the chapel founded over 700 years ago by the foresters and keepers of the old Forest of the Peak, little, if anything, is left in the church, which was largely made new in the 18th century. The chancel arch and the nave arcades are 14th century; some of the capitals have nail-head ornament, and one has a very quaint face.

In the oak-lined tower stands the 15th-century font, and across the tower arch are the altar rails carved by a vicar in Cromwell's century. A stone coffin now indoors has been a coping stone in the churchyard wall. A brass candelabra by a Flemish craftsman has been here 200 years.

One of the windows pictures for us the tragedy of Thomas Becket. We see the king appealing to his knights to rid him of this priest, Becket in his cathedral saying he is no traitor but a priest of God, and the murder and the scenes of remorse and penance.

The medieval chapel was consecrated in 1226 by the 41st Bishop of Lichfield, and we read on the back of the pews at the west end of the nave that at its 700th anniversary a sermon was preached by the 93rd Bishop of the same cathedral. Two other things the pews have to tell: the names and dates of the vicars from 1339 to 1927, and the record of three centuries of service as sextons and churchwardens by the Bramwells.

In the chancel sleeps William Bagshawe, a much-loved Nonconformist minister known as the Apostle of the Peak, with his coloured arms on the wall. He was ejected from the living of Glossop in 1662 and spent the rest of his life working in the wildest parts of the Peak. Several chapels were built for him, and, though warrants for his arrest were often issued, they were never enforced.

It was at Ford Hall, an Elizabethan house much changed since his day, that the Apostle of the Peak lived after his ejection from the church. It is one of about a dozen old houses that have stood for centuries near the town. Some survive as houses, some are farms, some have only a wing or a gable left; and many of them have grown out of the old homes of the foresters who lived here and built the medieval chapel. Of the Ridge, the home of the Bagshawes, part of an original gable remains in the modern house; Slack Hall's twin gables can still be seen; Marsh Hall has still a wing known to 18 generations of the Brownes, guardians of the Forest six centuries ago.

On the friendly slopes of Eccles Pike is Bradshaw Hall, now two farmhouses, with an ancient gable of the home of the Bradshaws and the fine 17th-century gateway with their crest and the name of Francis, the last of his line to live at the old house. The house has old beams and panelling, and round a landing are the words:

Love God but not gold. A man without mercy of mercy shall miss; but he shall have mercy that merciful is.

John Bradshaw, President of the Court which sent Charles Stuart to the scaffold, belonged to a branch of this family.

Perhaps the oldest possession of the village is in the churchyard, about three feet of the shaft of a cross with knotwork, said to be Saxon; it was found built into a wall three miles away.

Near Whaley Bridge, not far away, is a strange depression in the hillside known as the Roosdyche, a broad stretch of land between wooded banks three-quarters of a mile long. It was long thought to have been a Roman chariot way, but is more probably a natural feature of the land, a remarkable phenomenon.

The church stands on a site which has become known as Derbyshire's Black Hole. In 1648 the Scots under the Duke of Hamilton marched in to England to help Charles Stuart. They were defeated at Preston, and 1500 of them were brought as prisoners to this little town. With a brutality that amazes us, they were crowded into the small church here, though there was hardly room for half the number. Unable to lie down, pressing one against another in the chancel and nave, with not enough air to breathe, the poor wretches were imprisoned 16 days. It was War's way. Over 40 of them died before the door was opened and the miserable prisoners, more dead than alive, were allowed to stagger out to begin the fearful march northwards.

Ten of them fell down before they reached Cheshire, and with the others they were buried in the churchyard, a pitiful company who sleep far from the land they loved.

The Glory of Chatsworth

CHATSWORTH. It was said long ago of this great house of the Duke of Devonshire that it was the noblest private house in England commanding influence with the Whigs who set Dutch William on the throne; and we can well believe it, for it is perfect still. It has not the ancient memories of many of our great homes, for it comes from Stuart times, but no house has a finer setting than this majestic pile on a rising slope above the River Derwent.

It stands in a deer park ten miles round, with hills and woods, gardens and lawns, far-reaching vistas, cascades and terraces, within its vast enclosure. The beautiful three-arched bridge across the river was built to give the house the best approach and seems a part of the creative scheme; the wild moorland behind the wooded hill is another. The picture is perfect, a worthy house even for our Dukes of Devonshire.

The house was built for the first Duke of Devonshire and was planned by William Talman, the king's architect. It is a vast block of great dignity, with a decorated balustrade and finely spaced windows. The duke gave twenty years of his life to the development of this great house on the site of the old house of his grandmother Bess of Hardwick in which Mary Queen of Scots was imprisoned five times with the Earl of Shrewsbury as her guardian. The Duke of Devonshire called in the greatest artists of the day to decorate it, carvers in wood and stone, craftsmen in iron, the great Verrio to paint the walls and ceilings. In the ironwork we see the master hand of Tijou, and in the wreaths and festoons of flowers, the carvings of fishes and birds, and the delicate profusion of ornament everywhere, the inspiration of Grinling Gibbons, though the work was done by Thomas Young and a Derbyshire carver named Samuel Watson from Heanor. Gabriel Cibber did much of the sculptural ornament, and Sir James Thornhill painted one of the rooms.

Where every room is fit for a king we may take it for granted that all is magnificent, but even amid this splendour some things of interest stand out. Everybody has heard of the fiddle on the back of the door which so many people have tried to take down before discovering that it is a painting; it is in the music room—the room with the lovely ceiling of Phaethon and Apollo. In the sculpture gallery is Canova's marble of Napoleon's mother, and in the painted hall (60 feet long), and hanging elsewhere on the walls, are paintings by Titian, Tintoretto, Holbein, Van Eyck, Teniers, Poussin, Zucchero, and Sir Joshua Reynolds.

The collection of original drawings of old masters is unrivalled, and the library has a precious collection of manuscripts and rare books. There are 15th-century tapestries with hunting scenes, Limoges enamels, and two coronation chairs that have been used in the Abbey. In the chapel the reredos is built up of Derbyshire marble with an altarpiece by Verrio, and statues of Faith and Hope by Cibber. We may imagine how beautiful everything has always been at Chatsworth from the accounts which exist showing the lavish spending on it; there is an item somewhere for over a mile of fringes and lace, and work in silver and gold.

No word will serve for the gardens, which are beyond all our imagining, English gardens, French gardens, Italian gardens, a fountain sending its water 260 feet high (perhaps the highest yet anywhere), and a wonderful cascade falling 60 feet and running down steps for 200 yards before the water sinks into the earth and disappears. The temple of the cascade has sculptured dolphins and symbolic figures, and above the gardens are stone sphinxes on the piers, statues and relief panels, and the Willow Tree Fountain, which has always been a popular attraction. There are lovely iron gates, delightful walks, and stately avenues, and we do not wonder that this princely house in its kingly situation attracts a crowd of visitors numbering nearly a hundred thousand every year.

The Glory of a Thousand Places

CHELLASTON. It has had for centuries a great share in the beauty of the world, for the alabaster quarried in its hillside has added to the glory of a thousand homes and churches.

Chellaston Hill was one of the chief alabaster quarries of the Middle Ages. Its deep deposit of marble covered several square miles, and was much worked. Some of the most gorgeous alabaster tombs in the country came from these quarries, and it was here that the practice began of putting on tombs small angel weepers holding shields. These first appear about 1390, and are characteristic of the

Chellaston workers. The carving of the huge blocks for the tombs was done at the quarry, smaller pieces being taken to convenient towns.

All that is left of the 12th-century church here is the great bowl of a Norman font set on a new base 600 years ago. The chancel arch, the nave arcade, the doorway and windows of the nave and aisles are 14th century. The chancel was made new in the 15th century and enlarged last century. The tower was built in 1842.

It is said that many memorials from the old church were used by a churchwarden to make a stable floor, but two 16th-century mutilated floorstones remain. They are in memory of the Bancroft family, who gave the neighbouring village of Swarkeston its 17th-century poet, Thomas Bancroft.

The Mystery of the Font

CHELMORTON. One of the highest villages in England, it straggles along the steep slope which goes on climbing to the summit of Chelmorton Low, a lofty height crowned with two great burial mounds, looking out to neighbouring lows, and High Edge and Axe Edge loftier still.

Its little church clings to the hillside, and it is its 15th-century stone-roofed porch which tells us the story of its past. Its walls are lined with ancient coffin stones; its floor is laid with them. We noticed a round dozen of them carved with crosses, swords, and shields, two fine ones known to be 12th century, another carved with a pair of scissors and a cross 700 years ago, others from Norman days. Even the two stone seats for the priest in the chancel wall are made from an ancient cross-stone.

A rare possession of the church is its stone chancel screen; it is 14th century, and there are very few of them. It stands between 5 and 6 feet high and has an embattled parapet above traceried panels. The 15th-century font is unusual for having mysterious letters and signs on its eight sides, nobody knowing what they mean.

The base of the tower, the north arcade and the pillars of the south arcade are 13th century. The top of the tower, the spire, and the clerestory are 15th century. The chancel roof has a few old bosses. The old chest is 300 years old. The churchyard has a shapely yew and the broken shaft of its old cross.

Somewhere hereabouts, on a farm between Chelmorton and Brierlow Bar, was a farmer's hut familiar to the village folk of last generation. It was still in a garden when we called. This is its story.

The Marvellous Adventure of the Old Tin Hut

IT is a generation since two brothers of Chelmorton, Jonathan and Barnaby Swan, sold the moorland farm on which they had toiled all their lives. They were growing old and longed for change and travel; but they could not bear to be without a home.

An idea came to them. They built themselves a little house on wheels, made of pitch pine and covered with corrugated iron; and one day, to the astonishment of the neighbourhood, these old bachelors set out in their Tin Hut, harnessed to two strong cart-horses, to wander the country like raggle-taggle gipsies. They spent the first night on the common, where a fair was in full swing, and were lulled to sleep by blasts of music and noisy roundabouts.

This was the beginning of long and happy days of wandering. The children in the lanes would watch for them and bring them posies and pails of water; and many times they were invited to tea in the Tin Hut. Often the old men would take their delighted nephews on holiday tours.

The years rolled by, and the sad day came when Jonathan died. A home had to be found for Barnaby who was helpless alone, and very old, but there was little money left—only ten pounds found hidden in the Toby jug.

So it was that, out of very limited means, Nephew Rowland paid for Uncle Barnaby's board in a Derbyshire cottage. They were all so kind to him that the old man passed the remainder of his days in happiness. As for the Tin Hut, it was sold and resold, used as a pavilion for cricket and football clubs, turned into a children's play-ground shelter, and made a canteen during the war.

It was years afterwards that Rowland Swan one day had a great surprise; he came across the Tin Hut in a sale room, and for the sake of old times he bought it as a tool-shed. While he was carrying in the tools a heavy fork fell and splintered the matchwood of the hut, starting up a plank of the floor. It struck something hard, and there. wrapped in sacking, they found a heavy parcel. *As Rowland Swan seized hold of it out rolled eight hundred gold sovereigns.*

For twenty years the old hut had served many masters; it had been in the hands of navvies, soldiers, athletes, and parties of children; but in the end it yielded up the secret unguessed by any of them, and it delivered its treasure to the right address.

The Town of the Twisted Spire

CHESTERFIELD. It stands among the clustering hills, set in the heart of Derbyshire's coal and iron, but within reach of some of its most famous beauty spots.

For centuries it has been famous for its twisted and leaning spire; for more than a hundred years its wealth has come along the straight lines planned by George Stephenson, to whom the town owes its rise. He came here to supervise the construction of the Midland line, and he lived and died at Tapton House, built on the crest of a wooded hill and almost on the site of a Roman camp, now a fine school. He lies in Holy Trinity Church, where there is a memorial east window to him, and a tablet to his wife. The grave is under the altar, with a plain stone over it marked G. S., 1848. The memorial window is a group of three lancets with his initials nine times, and there are small scenes of the Last Supper, the Ascension, and the Entombment. In the town itself is a memorial hall to keep his name alive, as it should be kept, for he led Chesterfield along the straight way to prosperity.

This busy town is not too busy to be concerned for its appearance; it finds its recreation in attractive parks, and is reclothing itself in some of its busiest haunts in Tudor dress of timber and gables. In the narrow Shambles on the east side of the marketplace are timbered buildings of 400 years ago.

Chesterfield has nothing else so old or fine as its church of All Saints, and near it has been put its finest modern thing, a beautiful stone Calvary on a flight of steps in memory of the men who died for us. It is set on a stone terrace in the old burying ground, its base enriched with shields of our patron saints, and of St Nicholas for sailors and St Michael for soldiers. In the building of the cross there were placed in the masonry a bottle of wheat and a message from the clergy for those who may read it in centuries to come.

Very proud is Chesterfield of its crooked spire, rising 230 feet, as singular a curiosity as any church has. It is eight-sided, built of timber and covered with lead plates set in zigzag fashion, so that in addition to its decided twist the spire has the unusual appearance of being ridged and channelled. The twist which has made it famous is believed to be due to the warping of the wood and the pressure of the lead. It was only the town's affection for the old spire which saved it last century, when experts declared it unsafe and urged that a new one should be built. It was repaired instead.

Like the tower, the spire is 14th century, and it crowns a stately 14th-century church built in the shape of a cross. The central tower rests on four lofty pointed arches on clustered pillars, all resting on the foundation of a Norman church which William Rufus gave. Fragments of moulding in the tower and perhaps the font remain of this place, the round tapering bowl of the font carved with crude foliage and stem-work. There are traces of the 13th century in a half-pillar against the south wall of the south transept and the pilasters of two bays between the north transept and the north chapels. The middle pillar of this arcade is 14th century, having an unusual capital carved with rows of foliage. A corbel table under the cornice of a chapel is 13th century. The clerestory is 15th. The handsome 14th-century porch has a gable cross and a rich recess over the entrance with a modern Madonna; it has a projecting stair turret to the roof ending in a pinnacle like a pyramid.

The church has a lovely interior with fine arches, their grace rather lost among much screenwork. The nave is light and lofty, contrasting strongly with a chancel dimmed by the heavy colour of the east window. The nave arcades of six bays on each side have clustered pillars. There are four chapels at the east end, the chancel opening to two on each side with 14th-century archways, one with a peephole to the altar.

The glass of the west window tells the story of Joshua and his smiting of the country of the hills; we see him under a canopy in a tented field with the soldiers, and the field of battle with the sun and moon standing still. The south aisle has a peace window glowing with blue, red, green, and gold; it has figures of Christ and four saints, and below are three groups of a nurse, a sailor, and a soldier; an old woman, a child, and a widow kneeling before the town's lovely peace memorial, with the church and crooked spire in the background; and the workers at home, a girl munition-maker with a shell, a man with a hammer, and a parson.

The church is rich in old screenwork. In the north transept is part of the 15th-century chancel screen with six angels below the cornice. A slightly later screen runs the length of the south transept, with delicate tracery in its transomed bays and a wide cornice coved on both sides. The screen behind the choir stalls under the tower was originally a screen of the Foljambe chapel, and has been a reredos; it is richly carved. The fine modern screen across the chancel has traceried bays and a coved cornice.

The Jacobean pulpit is of black oak ornately carved, standing on a single pillar. The splendid modern reredos of richly carved oak shows the Madonna, with scenes of the Annunciation and the Holy Child in the Temple. In the Foljambe chapel is an oak chest on which is a mass of ironwork with 16 bands, two locks, and six padlocks: so much ironwork is there that little of the oak can be seen, yet for all its seeming security a leaflet in the register tells of a reward of 40 guineas for information about thieves who robbed it in 1808. On the top of it stands a smaller chest, also heavily banded with iron. A queer relic to find here is the jawbone of a small whale, about seven feet long, relic of the days when our churches were museums for any odd or curious things found round about.

In a handsome canopied recess in the south aisle lies an unknown priest in simple robes, his feet on a lion and his head supported by an angel. He is perhaps from the first half of the 14th century.

The monuments of the Foljambes are huddled together behind a grille in their chapel. On a fine alabaster tomb of 1510 are the brass portraits of Henry Foljambe and his wife, both at prayer, he in armour with sword and dagger, his feet on a dog, she with a girdled cloak and a headdress with lappets. Under richly carved canopies are figures of knights and ladies representing their 14 children. On this tomb is the kneeling figure of a knight in richly chased armour with hands in prayer and a four-roped chain round his neck. His helmet has quaint spy-holes like stars. He does not belong to the tomb, and may be Sir Thomas Foljambe, who died in 1604.

Henry's son Godfrey and his wife have brass portraits on a floorstone, with three sons, five daughters, and four shields. Sir Godfrey is in armour, his head on a helmet and his feet on a stag: his lady has a long mantle and a girdle held at the waist by a clasp of three roses. She has a headdress with lappets and a chain round her neck. His coat and her mantle are decorated with arms. A wall monument shows Sir Godfrey's son James kneeling in armour with a helmet and gauntlets at his feet. Below him kneel his two wives and a dozen grown-up children with a little tot among them. He died in 1558. A gruesome wall monument, perhaps to his brother Godfrey, shows a figure tied up in a bag on a stretcher; above it is a fearful figure of

Death with an arrow and a spade and a foot on a skull, with a fat little boy at one side of Death and at the other an old man hobbling along.

An alabaster monument is in memory of Sir Godfrey Foljambe of 1585 and his wife. He lies in elaborate armour with sword and dagger, his wife in fine Elizabethan dress with a ruff. Their only son Godfrey lies in armour with his wife on plaited matting; his wife has a fine gown with buttoned bodice and slashed sleeves, and a charming ruff. An alabaster floorstone has the engraved portrait of George Foljambe in armour, who died in the year of the Armada.

Here George Stephenson died and here he sleeps—the creator of our railways and one of the founders of the Age of Transport.

George Stephenson's Way to Prosperity

IN the day of his triumph, rich and admired, with his engines thundering over railways that he and his son had laid in Europe as well as at home, he came here for rest and happiness. A Northumbrian, born at Wylam in 1781, he passed from poverty and squalor through a superb triumph of invention to the luxury of Tapton House with its flowers, fruits, and agricultural experiments, the greatest mechanical genius of the age turned country squire.

He grew up in a cottage which had only one room to house the family of six; he earned twopence a day among the turnips, and thought himself made for life with 12 shillings a week, plus extras won from cobbling and the repair of clocks and watches.

On those terms he married the country girl who was to become the mother of Robert, yet he managed to support a mother and father brought to poverty, and to raise £6 to buy himself out of the draft in which he was drawn to go to France and fight against Napoleon.

His work in gassy mines led him to hazardous experiments resulting in the invention of his famous safety lamp, for which, when he was 37, he received £1000. While working in a colliery he mastered the principle of the steam engine by taking one to pieces, repairing and rebuilding it, but as he could not read until manhood (his son Robert then taught him) he wasted time and effort on schemes already in existence. Nevertheless he built a complete engine that began to draw the coal of Killingworth Colliery in 1814, and a year later, with the steam blast added, produced two more of greatly increased power.

The first railway in the open, running from Stockton to Darlington, was laid for horse-drawn vehicles, but Stephenson, with his infectious courage and confidence, induced the owners to try a locomotive, and on September 27, 1825, George drove the first steam train in the world, six wagons with coal and flour, and one coachful of passengers, with a mounted flagman patrolling ahead until the engine developed a speed that put him to flight.

This success did not persuade sceptics or disarm opponents, and the triumph of the 4-ton Rocket with her 30 miles an hour, had become history before Stephenson could establish his right to enrich the country with the greatest improvement in locomotion that had been achieved by man.

It was his fortune to see his work crowned with rich and abundant success, but he remained unspoiled, a born philosopher who loved laughter and played as hard as he worked.

History Lost to Derbyshire

CHURCH BROUGHTON. It has nothing more beautiful than its fine avenue of limes and the old church to which they lead, a gracious place of lovely stone all splashed with streaks of gold, with something left of Norman days and much of 600 years ago when the old church was made new.

The legacy of the Normans is the splendid font (with an unusual pattern of angles and circles), a half-pillar and capital near the chancel, and perhaps the round pillars of the nave. Two oval pillars at the west end are 14th century, their capitals having extraordinary figures which seem to be grimacing at each other. As old as these pillars is the embattled tower with a stair turret and a low spire, the chancel with three stone seats and a piscina niche, a small priest's doorway, an outside recess with a curious little window in the wall, and the capitals of the arcades.

On each side of the beautiful east window (14th century like many others) is an old bracket, one carved with a head. The glass of the window shows the Resurrection and figures of St Michael and St Gabriel, with minstrel angels in the tracery.

Worked into the modern reredos is the tracery of screenwork perhaps 600 years old. The oak roof of the nave with carved spandrels is largely 15th century. The chancel roof is about 1700, the work of the clerestory builders. The oak pulpit is 18th century; though altered since his day, it was the gift of one of the Wolleys of Sapperton a mile away, where the old manor house still stands proudly with its fine old buildings at the foot of a shady lane. William Wolley's manuscript history of Derbyshire, over 200 years old, is in the British Museum. Here it may have been written, but nowhere was it ever published.

In a 17th-century chest with three locks is the old village bassoon, the most curious possession of the church, almost helpless in the throes of the death-watch beetle when we called. An interesting possession of the church is the lovely winged figure of St George and the Dragon in the chancel, carved in Oberammergau in the early years of this century.

A stone in the floor at the west end of the church marks the spot where Francis Fearn used to stand to wind up the old clock in the tower. For 32 years he was parish clerk, and when at last he knew he was winding himself down he chose to be buried near this spot.

Time's Changes

CHURCH GRESLEY. It has miners now instead of monks, but here and there are things to remind us of its vanished glory, and it is proud to remember the great family of the Gresleys, said to be the only Derbyshire family which kept its lands from Domesday Book to the 20th century.

Nothing is left of the castle they built except the grassy mound on which it stood, still known as Castle Knob. Down to our own day the Gresleys lived at Drakelow, a fine old house in a park of 500 acres.

Though today it keeps company with a pit-head instead of its small 12th-century priory, the church has still its links with the past. The chancel and the priory buildings were pulled down in Tudor days, and the church remained more or less a ruin till the time of Waterloo. Sixty years ago a new chancel was built on the site of the old. Many remains of the old priory have been found, fragments of painted glass, medieval tiles, and stone coffins. All that is left of the old church now is the sturdy 15th-century tower and two 14th-century arches leading to the north aisle.

On a great alabaster monument is the figure of Sir Thomas Gresley kneeling under an arch. He has a curly wig, as in the 17th century, and a gown of rich brocade. Round the arch are arms showing the marriages of his ancestors from the time of the Conqueror.

But the pride of the church are ten massive and handsomely carved

The Glory of Chatsworth

Eyam Cross   Norman Carving at Hognaston   Bakewell Cross

Chesterfield Church   Melbourne Church

The curious Chancel Screen of Foremark

miserere stalls brought from Drakelow Hall a few years ago. It is thought they may have belonged to the church in its great days.

It is good to see that in the heart of the village a space of common land has been transformed into a garden, the gift of a village boy who prospered in America and wished to do something in memory of his birthplace, and of his son who died for Peace.

Just before we called, an auctioneer with Drakelow Hall under the hammer said they were seeing a house pass out of a family after 28 generations.

One of the Last of the Domesday Tenants

WHEN the auctioneer's hammer fell that day at Drakelow Hall it snapped one of the last two family links with Domesday. With the Gresleys gone from Drakelow, the Shirleys of Ettington are now the only surviving Domesday tenants, and their house we found empty when we called.

The Shirleys were Saxon, the Gresleys Norman, and both families had their names in the Conqueror's great land register compiled in 1086. For nearly 850 years these two families have lived on the land assigned to them then. Sir Robert Gresley had three sons to inherit Drakelow and its 750 acres of parkland, but the levelling economics of our day have driven them out of their old home.

There are no great outstanding names among the owners of Drakelow Hall. They seem to have kept their heads when heads were falling like ninepins, and their estate when estates were being confiscated and lost like counters in a game. In their absence of great wealth or great ambitions lay the safety of their inheritance. They survived the civil wars of the Roses and the Roundheads, the whims of monarchs and the threat of spendthrift sons; but after 28 generations of quiet victory they have been beaten, a little prosaically and pathetically, by death duties and income tax.

CLOWNE. Many things it has from our ancient past, the old cross crowned by a ball in the middle of the village, and a little church of 800 years ago with a variety of old possessions.

The aisleless church has fragments of Norman England, including the doorway in the porch and the chancel arch (both with carved capitals), the priest's doorway, and the font. On a windowsill is a moulded stone which was the drain of the piscina used by Norman priests. The roof has some of its 14th-century beams, a century older than the embattled tower which has lately received a peal of six bells.

Under the shelter of a spreading yew is a flat gravestone engraved with diamond pattern, thought to be 12th century.

Two extraordinary buttresses support the north wall, projecting ten feet at the base and climbing in steps till they reach the roof. On the chancel floor (now boarded over) is a stone to William Inskip, a parson for 54 years buried here just before the Armada. He must have been here through the troubled period of the church in the reigns of four Tudors.

When the Pond Runs Dry

CODNOR. The ruins at its doorstep, set in billowy fields and woods, make it easy to forget the coal and iron which have made this part of Derbyshire famous.

Once it was a great park of 2000 acres, and the ruins a mighty castle, the feudal home of the Greys. Richard Grey was one of Henry the Third's loyal barons; another Richard was visited here by Edward the Second after fighting the rebels at Burton-on-Trent; another was sent by Henry the Fifth to bring Hotspur's son from Scotland; Henry, the last of them, busied himself in trying to change base metals into gold.

It is thought they built their castle on the site of one which had William Peverel for its lord, making it a great and deeply-moated place with two courts, four massive round towers, and a great gateway. It was when the Zouch family sold it 300 years ago that it began to decay.

Today we see a length of the great boundary wall of the upper court, portions of the dividing wall and of the defending towers, and here and there a doorway, a window, and a fireplace, all standing proudly high and looking over the Erewash Valley into Nottinghamshire.

Farmsteads have been built from the ruins, one the next-door neighbour of the castle since the 17th century. Near it stands the finest relic of all, a splendid round stone dovecot, tall and slightly conical, and crowned by a square wood turret. Here pigeons still find homes in the nest-boxes which honeycomb the walls. Close by is an old pond whose unfailing supply of water gave rise to the saying which every Codnor child knows:

> *When Codnor's pond runs dry*
> *Its lords may say Goodbye.*

The pond is not dry but the lords have said goodbye. The great park has changed, much of it taken up by the ironworks of the Butterley Company, who have laid out some acres as a park on a hill above the ruins. In the midst is a stone tower 70 feet high, built in memory of William Jessop, the founder of the works. It is worth climbing the 150 steps for the fine view of the countryside, with the chimneys and rails and canals of a world of coal and iron merging into lovely hills and valleys.

On the road between Codnor and Loscoe is a church not yet quite a centenarian; a beautiful lychgate opening to a graveyard close by is in memory of the men who died for us.

The Beautiful Mile

CRESSBROOK. The stream of its delightful glen comes down to join the Wye as it flows through a chain of lovely dales.

It has a modern church, pleasant dwellings, and a fine stone Hall built here and there on steep and densely wooded slopes. Its woods are a glory of lilies of the valley in spring, and all its ways are rich in lovely views.

We find it at one end of a most charming mile where the Wye winds like the letter M, deep down in a narrow gorge shut in by rocks and woods, a mile of beauty they call Water-cum-Jolie, which comes suddenly to earth with the cotton mills at each end.

An intrusion of industry into romance were these mills, and it is odd that Cressbrook Mills were owned by one who could make them prosper and be a poet too. He was William Newton, the carpenter poet whom Anna Seward, the Swan of Lichfield, christened the Minstrel of the Peak. Perhaps it was the poet in him that gave his little apprentices more kindly treatment than most boys suffered in cotton mills then.

Tumuli on the hills around tell the story of long ago. In a barrow on Hay Cop close by was found the skeleton of a child.

The Wonderful Story of Pin Hole Cave

CRESWELL. It is a mining village, but it has beauty at its doorstep. It has given its name to Creswell Crags, a lovely ravine of richly wooded limestone rocks rising each side of the road to the Dukeries, where a stream is dammed into a great pool. The stream comes through Creswell as the Wollen, fresh from the meeting at an old mill dam of two streams from the delightful dells of Markland

Grips—deep narrow dells with many trees, by a great plateau where extensive earthworks have been found.

One side of the Crags is in Derbyshire, the other in Notts on the verge of Welbeck Park. At their foot are the famous caves where remarkable treasures made by the earliest men in Britain have been found. These caves have names of their own, Robin Hood's Cave, Church Hole (named from its narrow tapering entrance), Mother Grundy's Parlour, and the Pin Hole.

Nearly 50 years ago Sir William Boyd Dawkins began to dig in these caves, and among many treasures he found the earliest example of pictorial art discovered in our land, a piece of smooth bone three inches long and an inch deep, on which had been scratched the head and shoulders of a horse. The mane of the horse is remarkable, as the hair stands up straight. Drooping manes were seldom shown in drawings by the cave men.

Inch by inch the soil from the first three of these caves was removed and sifted, down to the white sand in which there were no remains. Above the white sand and red sand were bones, and one or two rude implements of quartzite which were also found in a layer of red clay above.

The remarkable thing about these bones is that they belonged to the hippopotamus and the rhinoceros, animals which needed a far warmer climate than ours. Hyenas shared the cave with them, the marks of their teeth being on the larger bones. The hippopotamus is a survivor of the Pliocene into the early Pleistocene age, and the man who made these quartzite implements before the ice ages descended on the land must have had a hot meal from the flesh of these beasts, for signs of fire remain on the bones.

Above the clay we come to the mottled and light-coloured cave earth with implements in a higher stage of manufacture. The hare was the chief food of these men.

On a higher layer still is a red cave earth in which charcoal fragments and blocks of limestone occur with the bones, with implements made of flint brought from a distance. The men who made these were the artists, and used implements of bone as well as of flint. The top layer of all consisted of stalagmite material and other worked flints. These objects are at the British Museum.

A few years ago Mr Leslie Armstrong decided to excavate Pin Hole Cave, which had been left as not worth troubling about. It has proved the richest of all, and from it we have evidence that at least two glacial periods have passed over Creswell Crags, driving men from it. Thousands of years separate the periods of its habitation.

The remains extend over a depth of 15 feet. One of the most thrilling finds was the bone of a mammoth which a cave man split to obtain the marrow and then threw aside, leaving his flint knife embedded in the joint.

Another amazing find was the egg-shell of some kind of goose. At its narrow end was a hole through which the cave man had sucked its contents. Mr Armstrong, with extraordinary cleverness, succeeded in removing this unique shell unbroken.

A rare find was a pendant of mammoth ivory, oval in shape and no thicker than a postcard. A round hole cleverly pierced at one end suggests that it was a charm worn by a lady of the caves. Mr Armstrong was also surprised to come across the skull of a huge bear as big as any at Whipsnade, and the strange thing about it was that all its teeth had been extracted, doubtless to make a necklace for the queen of the cave.

But the gem of Pin Hole was an engraving of a masked man or woman on the bone of a reindeer. The figure is standing erect, apparently engaged in ceremonial dancing of the kind Australian or African natives enjoy today.

Other engravings worked on ivory, and the beautiful flint tools with which they worked and hunted and fished 20,000 years before the birth of Christ, were found in the upper part of this cave which has proved one of the most valuable records we have of the men of the Old Stone Age over a period of nearly a thousand centuries.

Six Proud Words

CRICH. Its story begins with a stream of molten lava, for it is below a volcano which was active when half England was under the sea. Now a great hill 1000 feet high, it is interesting to geologists and notable for the rich lead mines that were about it, and it has an outlook as fair as any in a county of wonderful views.

Today it has something which draws all eyes, a lighthouse tower with a beacon light seen from five counties. It is a noble tribute to 11,400 men of the Sherwood Foresters who did not come back. A new name had been added to the memorial not long before we called, a handsome bronze tablet to the man the regiment delighted to serve,

Sir Horace Smith-Dorrien, their colonel for 25 years. On the bronze his famous message of six words to his men at Le Cateau in 1914 is proudly engraved: *Gentlemen, we will stand and fight*.

Gone are the days of Crich as a little town, but the old market cross still stands, with St Michael slaying his dragon.

Of the old church begun in the time of Stephen there still remain the nave arcades, with square capitals on one side and round ones on the other, and the fine font with heavy cable moulding is also Norman. But most of the church is 14th century—the tower and spire, the chancel with a priest's doorway, three stone seats under trefoiled arches, a piscina drain in the sill of the east window, and a stone lectern. The modern roof of the chancel rests on ten stone heads 600 years old; the nave roof is a century younger.

The oak screen across the chancel arch had an adventure towards the end of its 500 years. Turned out of the church in 1861, it was found in a timber yard and taken to St Peter's in Derby, being returned to Crich about ten years before we called. From the same century is a finely carved oak seat in the vestry with poppyheads of human faces. Very quaint they are, one looking rather astonished, another smiling at us with a good humour 500 years old.

William de Wakebridge lies in a long gown buttoned from neck to waist under an aisle recess. He has long hair and a beard, and his hands are on his breast, his feet on a dog, and a tiny angel is holding a Catherine wheel to his ear. Sir William sat in the Parliaments of Edward the Third, but after the Black Death had bereft him of his wife, his father, his three brothers and two sisters, he gave himself to religion rather than to worldly affairs, and founded two chantries here. In one they laid him in 1369. His old home has gone, but the farmhouse where it stood has relics of it in a 15th-century oak door and an old barn.

In the chancel is the stone of a tomb with the figures of German Pole and his wife, both in Tudor dress and ruffs. His widow married John Claye of Crich, who has a tomb in the chancel showing himself and his first wife, with their five children round them.

Another alabaster tomb has the engraved portrait of Godfrey Beresford in 16th-century armour, and a brass tablet tells of Robert Marshall and his wife, who lived happily in the village for more than fifty years 500 years ago. A tiny brass on the chancel wall has a quaint inscription to the babe whose little shrouded figure is engraved on it, the child of Thomas Shelmerdine, vicar here in Stuart days.

In an arched recess is a stone to Thomas England, vicar 200 years ago. On the other side of the stone is engraved a chalice, and it is perhaps the stone which covered the grave of the first chantry priest, Richard Davy, nearly six centuries ago.

Thirteenth Child of a Working Man

CROMFORD. It is set in a great natural glory, in the midst of some of Derbyshire's most majestic scenery, reached by roads fit to be the roads to heaven.

We come from the Matlocks down by the Derwent, up a delightful stretch of the vale from Whatstandwell, or through Via Gellia's sylvan glades. We come from Wirksworth over the moorland hills, with a feast of splendid views that become a superb panorama if we climb the frowning Black Rocks on our right. Great masses of millstone grit they are, rising 80 feet from the crest of the hill and backed by dark pine woods, piled-up crags like great bastions of varying size and shapes. Into the glorious scene from the top come Wirksworth, Middleton Woods, and the dip of the Via Gellia; the rock-bound Derwent is winding through Matlock Dale, with Masson and the Heights of Abraham looking across to High Tor and Riber's great hill; and down the valley stands Crich's Tower, with the woods of Alderwasley, and the home of Florence Nightingale, Lea Hurst.

Down in the hollow nestles Cromford with its castle, its church, and its mills, the story of them all closely woven with that of the man who turned this secluded hamlet into a busy town, the man who, born 13th child of a working man, was able to give every one of his ten children a Christmas box of £10,000, the man who started life as a barber and lived to build himself a castle.

He was Sir Richard Arkwright, the genius of the cotton world, whose inventions revolutionised the industry by removing what had been its greatest stumbling block, the difficulty of spinning cotton fine and strong enough for warp.

In this lovely corner the first cotton mill in Derbyshire was built in 1771, when Arkwright was in partnership with Jedediah Strutt. Some of the mill remains in the gaunt and lofty works whose grim severity suggests the troublous days when machinery was coming into the world. The Arkwrights spent much of their wealth on the countryside in building, making roads and planting trees. It was the inventor's son Richard who opened a new gateway into Matlock Dale by blasting through the rock.

It was Sir Richard himself who started the Castle at Willersley, but it was burned down before it was finished and Richard died before he could rebuild it. He began his castle and did not see it; he began the church and did not see it: it was left for his son Richard to finish both. Willersley is now a great plain house with a background of fine woods, and lawns down to the Derwent.

The church stands at the foot of the castle grounds, and in it the great Arkwright was laid to rest. There is a memorial tablet to him and to the family, and one by Chantrey to his son's wife and her three children, a marble tablet with a wreath of lilies.

Cromford's beauty spot is at the fine old bridge which spans the river. The tale is told of two artists who painted pictures of the bridge and quarrelled because one showed it with three pointed arches, the other with three round ones. Both were right, for the arches are pointed at one side and round at the other. The pointed side has some of the oldest bridge-work in Derbyshire, being part of the original packhorse and footbridge.

He Founded Our Industrial System

THE creator of the cotton trade on mass production lines was nearly forty and a made man when he arrived here in 1771 to build the first cotton mill in Derbyshire, and to find his last resting-place within sound of his mill 21 years later. Born at Preston, Sir Richard Arkwright was a barber at Bolton and tramping wig-maker with a secret dye before he applied himself to invention.

Hargreaves had just invented a spinning jenny multiplying the number of spindles for each operator, but the product was a yarn too soft for use without other material as strengthening warps. Arkwright one day saw red-hot iron drawn between rollers, and with great difficulty he got a spinning frame constructed on the same principle, the cleaned and carded cotton being drawn between two pairs of rollers, the second pair moving more quickly than the first.

Testing the machine in secret, the inventor was accused of witchcraft, the hum and clack of the mechanism being ascribed to Satan tuning his bagpipes and Arkwright dancing to them. Fearing the Lancashire machine-wreckers, he went to Nottingham, where he erected his first mill in 1769, the mechanism driven by horses. It was the necessity for water power and lower costs that brought him to Cromford.

So fierce was the opposition of Lancashire that he was driven out of spinning until by indomitable will he secured the repeal of an old Act of Parliament that made his oppression possible. Then this illiterate genius invented the most wonderful contrivance textile manufacturers had known, a machine embracing the entire process of carding, drawing, roving, and spinning.

At one stride he was able to multiply output a thousandfold, but a mob smashed the machines he erected at Chorley, and infringements of his patents involved him in costly litigation. But in the end, in spite of the malevolence of ignorance and the rascality of manufacturers, he succeeded in establishing an immense trade which made Lancashire supreme in cotton, yielded him a fortune of half a million, and founded our industrial system. He bought the manor of Cromford, obtained the grant of a market for the town, and died immortal.

The Proud Montgomerys

CUBLEY. It is Great and Little Cubley, some of it high and some low, on the green hillside encircling a valley where streams unite, a quiet spot with memories of the great days of the Montgomerys whose four centuries here ended four centuries ago.

Their old home stood near the church where some of them lie, set in quiet isolation with the rectory and an ancient yew. On the outer walls of the Tudor tower are ten of their shields, while within the church are some of their tombs.

On his alabaster tomb in the chancel lies the battered figure of Sir Nicholas Montgomery of 1435, wearing plate armour with a collar of roses, and a hip belt engraved with flowers; a helmet is under his head, and at his feet a dog with bells on its collar. The brass portraits of Sir Nicholas of 1494 and his wife are gone, and of their tomb itself only the front panel is left (projecting from the chancel wall), with sculptured figures of a man with a book, a knight and his lady, a man in a long robe, and a knight with his shield. The figure of a lady, carved in high relief on a stone in the floor, may be their daughter, Catherine Montgomery.

From Norman days come the round arches and pillars of the nave, the pillars and capitals of the chancel arch, and the great round font. The priest's doorway and five lancets in the chancel are 700 years old, and two of the windows are filled with lovely 14th-century glass. One shows St Catherine with her wheel, the other a kneeling saint. Two other windows have an effective medley of old fragments, and a modern St Andrew.

The east window is lovely for its 14th-century stonework and the glass which fills it, its delicate colouring of blue, red, silver, and gold shedding a soft light on the chancel. It shows the Nativity and the Crucifixion, with the Madonna and three Apostles. It is in memory of a husband and wife of the Victorian era, her grave in the churchyard guarded by a lovely angel holding a cross and a crown.

Montgomery was the great name of this place, but there was a humbler name that will not be forgotten. It was Johnson, and one of them left this place to be a Lichfield bookseller and became the father of Samuel Johnson, the greatest talker in the world, who not only talked but put all our words into our first great dictionary.

The Panorama of the Hills and Dales

CURBAR. A village of rugged charm, it climbs the hillside between the winding river Derwent and the moors above, from a modern church at the foot to a quaint house near the top with a round stepped-roof set cleverly on square walls. An odd little building, it was once a shelter for prisoners on the way to distant gaols, and is now a dwelling.

Has any village in Derbyshire a lovelier outlook? It is lovely where the old moorland road comes down to the church, where valleys meet and a three-arch bridge crosses the stream which swings round the foot of Calver Sough; but from the windswept Edge above, 1000 feet above the sea, the panorama of hills and dales is superb. We look down past the village and the river with Calver in the hollow to a glory of swelling hills rich in pasture and woodland. We get a peep of Chatsworth House and Edensor's graceful spire. We look from Stony Middleton's rocky ravine to Eyam Moor; and up the valley toward Grindleford Bridge, with many a white road threading the hills, and many a shady dale.

In the churchyard is a cross in memory of those who left the charm of this tranquil place for the horror and madness of Flanders, and a stone marking the grave of one whom all fishermen loved. He was George Butcher, known as the Izaak Walton of the Peak, to whom the river and the countryside were as an open book. He was a carpenter and a preacher as well as a fisherman. Just before he died in 1875 the Yorkshire poet John Hall wrote these verses about him:

> *Old Butcher is young; though he's nigh fourscore*
> *He can tramp twelve miles across a moor;*
> *He can fish all day and wade up stream,*
> *And at night as fresh as the morning seem.*
>
> *To those who have wandered in Baslow Vale,*
> *Through Chatsworth's meadows and Darley Dale,*
> *Or skirted the banks of the Silvery Wye,*
> *Where Haddon's grey towers rise steep and high,*
>
> *His form and garb will familiar seem*
> *As the guardian deity of the stream,*
> *With his oval face and his grizzly locks,*
> *And his smile like that of a sly old fox.*

Little Saint Michael

DALBURY. It is Dalbury and Dalbury Lees. Two miles from the Lees on the hilltop is its remote church, content with a cluster of dwellings for company and Radbourne Brook not far away, and proud of a fine treasure 700 years old. It is a beautiful little figure of St Michael, with mitre and bare feet, in 13th-century glass, filling a lancet as old as itself in the nave.

Nothing is left of the church which came into Domesday Book, but of the 13th century there is another lancet in the nave, and a little bell-tower with later battlements, resting inside on an enriched arch which makes a fine frame for the west window.

Bright and very pleasing today, the church tells of the love of a rector of last century who gave it its handsome and unusual wood-work. Two sturdy roof timbers carved on both sides, window adornments like pelmets of wood, borders beautifying the organ pipes, and a very fine panel on a wall with a bracket from which hangs a splendid font cover, were all the work of Charles Evelyn Cotton. He restored the church and gave it an aisle, and built the rectory.

Other treasures are a fine oak chair of 1689, a reredos of five ancient wood carvings of two winged angels on each side of a panel of scroll-work, and a very rare thing in our experience, a beautiful communion chalice of wood, kept in a glass case for all to see.

Village Church—Pocket Edition

DALE ABBEY. It has an ancient cave, a quaint church sharing a roof with a farmhouse, and the majestic arch of a window which was once the glory of a famous abbey, all set in a green valley near the busy world, and all coming into a story 800 years old.

It was between 1130 and 1140 that a Derby baker found his way to Depedale, a wild and marshy place, and made it his home, cutting out of the rock a dwelling and a little oratory where he lived. One day, when Ralph Fitz-Geremund had come from Normandy to hunt in his English woods, he found the hermit, and, touched with pity for his poverty, gave him not only the site of the hermitage but a tithe of his mill at Borrowash. Then the hermit built himself a more pretentious oratory and a cottage in which to end his days. In course of time Depedale passed to Serlo de Grendon, whose aunt built herself a house and chapel here, where her son was priest, she becoming known as the Gome of the Dale. Then monks came from Calke and settled in a priory which flourished till they were removed by the king for hunting in his forest. About 1200 Dale Abbey was founded in memory of the hermit of Depedale.

The hermit's cave is here, hewn out of the rock and measuring six yards by three, with a doorway, two windows, a peephole, and a niche for a light. The division which made it into two compartments for the dwelling-place and the oratory has gone. The hermit's well is in the orchard, now the water supply for the house.

The curious little church which shares a roof with the farmhouse must surely be one of the smallest in the land, yet, while it measures only 26 feet by 25, it is really two churches thrown into one, for it is said that the south aisle is on the site of the hermit's second oratory, and that the nave and chancel are the chapel built by the Gome of the Dale.

About 1250 the aisle we see took the place of the original oratory and new windows were put in the walls. These were altered in the 15th century.

For more than 200 years two gabled buildings stood side by side, till in 1480 the church was given its present form. The roof was given gables north and south, a wooden partition took the place of the stone wall between the chapels, a screen was erected across the nave which, with the wooden partition, was made to support the gallery. This gallery covers all the church except the chancel and is entered by an outside flight of steps.

Such is the story of this pocket edition of a church which might have been built for the goblins of the Dale, thatched until the end of the 18th century, and with an interior in which all things seem askew, held up by props and posts.

The oak pulpit is leaning sideways as if with the weight of its 300 years, perched up in a corner of the chancel and level with a window top. The chancel screen and the partition are those put up in the 15th century, though the old solid panels of the partition have been cut open. There are box pews and open benches, the only seating in the nave being four benches.

There is a great uncomfortable-looking chair, the one massive thing we see in this wee church, known as the Bishop's Throne. It was given in 1824 by an Earl of Stanhope who loved this place and called it in affection his little cathedral. So the chair became the Bishop's Throne, and the whimsical title has crept into the inscription on the tablet to his memory, where he is called Lay Bishop of this church.

By a strange chance this tiniest of churches has one of the biggest things of its kind in the land, a chalice of 1701 measuring 9 inches high and 15 inches round. The 15th-century abbey font is here with worn carvings of the Madonna and Child and the Crucifixion; it was long used as a flower vase in the garden of Stanton Hall. Fragments of 15th-century glass are in two windows.

Traces of wall paintings have been found in the last few years, the finest showing the Visitation—with good line and colour from the 13th century. The figures of Mary and Elizabeth are in black.

The farmhouse with the church has had a varied life. At first the hermit's hut and separate from the church, it was rebuilt in 1480 and attached to it. For some time before 1820 it was an inn, the bar being used as a vestry, with a door into the aisle. It was rebuilt in 1883.

Of the abbey itself, which was finished about 1250 and grew in importance and wealth until its dissolution, there remains the splendid arch of what must have been a glorious east window with fine tracery. The tracery has gone, but the arch stands proudly, 40 feet up to its keystone and 16 feet wide. The sites of part of the nave, the choir, the transepts, two chapels, and the chapter house have been discovered, while some remains of the kitchen, the refectory wall, and a gateway are in buildings round about.

Many relics are preserved in a shed on the site of the chapter house, tiles, fragments of carving, and coffin stones engraved. Here also is a sculpture of a canon in robes of many folds, holding a book.

When his grave was opened there was found a great oak coffin containing a skeleton lying on a bed of leaves, still green though they had been buried about 500 years.

So runs the story of Dale Abbey, and this is how it runs in tuneful ballad by William and Mary Howitt:

> *The Devil one night, as he chanced to sail*
> *In a stormy wind by the Abbey of Dale,*
> *Suddenly stopped and looked wild with surprise*
> *That a structure so fair in the valley should rise.*
> *When last he was there, it was lonely and still,*
> *And the hermitage scooped in the side of the hill;*
> *With the wretched old inmate, his beads a-telling,*
> *Were all could be found of life, dweller, and dwelling.*

Some fine relics of the Abbey have been used in the enriching of other Derbyshire churches. Radbourne has some splendid old woodwork, and Morley church has the old stone framework of the Abbey windows and some rich 15-century glass.

Almost Too Good to be True

DARLEY ABBEY. Almost too good to be true, we thought, when we came to this stone-walled village, for here, with the noise of Derby a mile away and in sight of its towers and spires, was a great estate which seemed like anybody's garden where we might wander at will—along the drive with rhododendrons and great trees, across the park to the winding River Derwent, in and out of glasshouses fragrant with scents and ablaze with colour.

The great house, like the village, is known as Darley Abbey, after the 12th-century abbey which was once the biggest and most important in Derbyshire. Its scant remains are down in the hollow and are used as dwellings. Near them is a great cotton mill on the Derwent, and it is a fine sight to see the mighty rush of water through the sluice gates when the mill is still.

Crowning a hilltop above the village is the 19th-century church; impressive outside, as its walls, adorned with battlements and lofty pinnacles, rise from a lovely churchyard of lawn and great trees. Its fine woodwork is its best possession.

In the churchyard sleeps a man whose voice was often heard within a stone's-throw of Fleet Street, for he was Alfred Ainger, who was born in the first year of the Victorian Era and known all over England as a preacher and lecturer. He was known best of all for the beauty of the sermons he preached in the Temple Church. He was at school with the sons of Charles Dickens, and the novelist taught him to act and recite. He was a friend of Tennyson and of George du Maurier, to whom he suggested many of the subjects for his Punch drawings. He wrote the life of Charles Lamb and some favourite hymns. He loved beauty all his life, and it is all about him now. Here too is a tall stone cross in memory of men of Darley Abbey who died for peace, and the cross has these precious words:

See to it that these died not in vain.

Back into the Mists of Time

DARLEY DALE. Its famous quarries have sent stone to Hyde Park Corner and the Thames Embankment and to a hundred great places, but it is for the stones that remain in Darley Dale that we come to this small wonderland.

It is where Churchtown gathers about an old road off the beaten track that we step into the Past, finding something of Norman and Saxon and perhaps Roman days. Here still lives the famous Darley Yew, almost without a rival in the land if we think of its years and its condition. No man can guess its age, but it is old enough to have seen the coming of the Norman church when the Saxon church came down, and it still stands firm and grand and green with a trunk 32 feet round. Darley Dale's poet John Gisborne wrote of the church and the tree last century:

> *Nor shall thy reverend yew, the sire who holds*
> *His sceptre verdant through the changeful year,*
> *Unnoticed stand. He has beheld, like thee,*
> *Thousands entombed within his shadow.*

Perhaps we find more thrilling still a round stone near the chancel door in the churchyard. It is three inches thick and four feet wide and it was found buried 70 years ago with a twin stone which fell to pieces when they moved it. On top of each stone were charcoal ashes and the earth was burned about them and below. It is thought the stones were used by Romans to cover human ashes buried here.

Out of the far-off past also have come three stone coffins lying in the churchyard, the smallest of them found under a pillar in the nave; it had a little child in it, and its discovery reminds us of the pagan custom of sacrificing a child and laying the body under a foundation stone. No man knows what tragic tale this coffin could tell. About us in the churchyard are many 17th-century tombs, some carved with roses, one with a heart pierced with darts, and one with the handloom and shuttles of a weaver.

From Roman to Saxon and Saxon to Norman, on to our great English building centuries, the stones of Darley Dale come. A piece of a Saxon cross with knotwork much older than King Alfred has been found in the churchyard and is now in a Sheffield museum, but one Saxon relic remains in the walls between the porch and the tower, a dark stone carved with knotwork and showing the heads and legs of two figures whose bodies are worn away. From the Norman days there have survived for us two doorways in the chancel, the bowl of a small font, the capital of a Norman shaft built into the outside chancel wall, a stone outside the tower carved with grotesques, and stones in the porch with the head of a cross and a three-toed animal. From the 13th and 14th centuries come the chancel arch and the arcades, and from the 15th century come the clerestory and the pinnacled tower. By the entrance to the turret staircase inside the tower is a corbel carved into a terrifying fellow with hair on end, sharp teeth, and hands like claws.

These old walls house old monuments. Sir John de Darley, lord of the manor 600 years ago, is in a suit of mail with his legs crossed, his hair curled, and a heart in his hands. Thomas Columbell is here in a fur-trimmed gown such as he wore 400 years ago, his wife in a dress with a girdle. In the chancel kneel John Milward and his wife with their 11 children; they lived at Snitterton Hall, a charming stone-gabled Elizabethan house two miles from the church, and John was a colonel for the King in the Civil War. A fragment of alabaster in the vestry has on it the eight children of Elizabeth Needham, buried here in Tudor days, and a tiny brass in the chancel is engraved with four faces and a death's head in memory of Mary Potts, a rector's wife of 1654.

Finely kept in the north transept are two engraved stones. One of 1513 has the portraits of John Rollesley and his wife, he with eight sons, she with four daughters. John has a chain round his neck, she has an embroidered girdle, their heads are on cushions, and over them are elaborate canopies. On the second stone is the eldest son John, with his wife and tiny figures of their 12 children. John's gown comes just below his knees and his shoes are fastened with straps;

A window of Dale Abbey

The Windmill of Dale

The Via Gellia, near Cromford

Cromford Willersley Castle

South Wingfield The ruined Manor

his wife's dainty dress has a girdle. A remarkable possession is this pair of stones with 28 Rollesleys of two generations.

Only a few years ago did Darley's Elizabethan ship come home, with the discovery of a wall painting of a vessel thought to be one of a series of the banners of the 12 patriarchs once adorning the walls. It is older than the Spanish Armada. The windows have none of their old glass, but one window has fine modern glass, showing the witnesses of the Resurrection with Joseph, Joshua, Caleb, and David above them; and there is a transept window with vivid colours of which Darley Dale is very proud, for its 12 panels, illustrating the Song of Solomon, are the work of Burne-Jones and William Morris.

The roof of the nave is 400 years old, with carvings on its massive beams and faces on the corbels; and ancient stone screenwork has been built round a pew in one of the aisles.

On the other side of the Dale is the hamlet of Two Dales, with an ancient mystery in the grounds of Holt House, where is a long low building 500 years old, now used as a barn. It has an ancient upright stone to keep it company, and it is believed that the barn was once part of a religious house.

Not far away stands a solitary tree which gave Wordsworth a story.

The Brothers Who Did Not Meet Again

FROM the peaceful meadows of South Darley over the river the village of Wensley climbs the steep hillside, with a small church in Norman style but not a century old, and Oaker Hill close by.

On Oaker Hill is a solitary tree which has long been a landmark for miles around, and has found its way into story. It is one of two sycamores planted on the top of the hill by two brothers who parted here to go separate ways into the world to seek their fortune. One of the trees has gone, but the other lives, and round it has been woven the story which Wordsworth made into this sonnet:

> *Tis said that to the brow of yon fair hill*
> *Two brothers clumb, and turning face from face*
> *Nor one more look exchanging, grief to still*
> *Or feed, each planted on that lofty place*
> *A chosen tree: then eager to fulfil*
> *Their course, like two new-born rivers, they*
> *In opposite direction urged their way*
> *Down from the far-seen mount. No blast might kill*

Or blight that fond memorial: the trees grew
And now entwine their arms: but ne'er again
Embraced those brothers upon earth's wide plain:
Nor aught of mutual joy or sorrow knew
Until their spirits mingled in the sea
That to itself takes all—Eternity.

He Changed the World of Machinery

HERE sleeps the man who mechanised half the world, Sir Joseph Whitworth. His motto was Let us Try. Constantly confronted by new problems in mechanics, he grappled with his difficulties and mastered them. In his way he was as true a genius as a poet or an artist; in his life he embodied the principle of self-help.

Born at Stockport in 1803, he finished his schooling at 14 and entered the cotton mill of his uncle, where very soon he was managing the whole business, and then, because the machinery was so inefficient and primitive, he ran away to Manchester and worked for four years to improve his knowledge.

Still dissatisfied, he went to London and entered the service of the great Maudslay, who found in him a kindred spirit and employed him, with one of his best workmen, John Hampson, in his private workshop. Living frugally and saying ever, "Let us try," young Whitworth worked by night at home and there completed his first astounding invention, the true plane, basis of a host of machines that have since covered the cities of the earth.

With quiet pride he showed his invention to Hampson, who, a son of Yorkshire, quietly said, "Tha's done it!" It was the beginning of Whitworth's astonishing succession of creations. Steam-power was being applied to machinery, and there was no exactitude in the making; nothing was true or standard; everything was haphazard.

Whitworth revolutionised it all. Establishing himself in Manchester, he introduced the first series of instruments for refined measurement; standard gauges, taps and dies, true screws precise in thread, power lathes, planing machines, drills, and so on, with machines that would measure to a millionth of an inch.

He made a fortune, gave vast sums to education, bought an estate at Darley, converted a quarry into an unrivalled winter garden, enriched the place with its hospital and institute, and was buried here.

The End of a Saxon Arcade

DENBY. Coal and iron and pottery have made its name, and its old Hall is a farm, keeping company with a pit; yet even now its old ways are unspoiled.

It is in the old part that we find its little church, in a churchyard lovely with trees and a beautiful cross to those who did not come back. It is charming without and within, save for a gallery which it pleased the 19th century to build in place of a Saxon arcade! The round arches and pillars of the south arcade come from the time of Stephen. The chancel with its sedilia, piscina, and aumbry, is 14th century, its lovely old east window with pictures of the Baptism, Crucifixion, Resurrection, and Ascension. Of the 14th century also are the tower and the spire, the porch with its stone roof, and the font, looking like the capital of an eight-sided pillar. The altar table is 17th century.

The richly ornamented bell given by Patrick Lowe in Shakespeare's time still rings in the tower, and in the chancel Patrick and his wife kneel under canopies. He is in armour, she in cap and ruff with a triple chain round her neck. Behind them are a boy and a girl, and two other children with their heads covered by one hood, an odd way of showing that they died before their parents.

Here lies Sir Drury Drury-Lowe, who was buried here in 1908. He fought at Sebastopol, saw the closing scenes of the Indian Mutiny, and in the Egyptian War of 1882 made a daring moonlight cavalry charge which saved Cairo from destruction. Here also was born in 1646 John Flamsteed, a poor boy who became the first Astronomer-Royal, starting his great career among the stars, at a salary of £100 a year, in the new Observatory at Greenwich.

Proud Town of the Age of Transport

DERBY. It is seated at a gateway of the Midlands on the threshold of the North. The Derwent, bringing a tale of hills and dales and rippling shallows, flows here past wall and mill and garden, its swiftness tempered, and something of its romance forgot. So with the town, which, though steeped in memories of Romans who came and went, of Saxons and Danes who fought for its possession, resumed after each irruption its placid course, adapting every change to good advantage and retaining always that sobriety of outlook which is the Midland gift. It is not without significance that here the

Young Pretender turned back from his rash incursion into settled England, and that here the last hopes of the Stuarts foundered.

Its earliest records bear witness to a recognised stability. Saxon kings gave it the privilege of its own mint, where coins of Athelstan and Edgar were struck. The Normans plundered house and mill, but the town found its feet again. King John gave it the right of dyeing cloth, and it kept the trade for centuries. A charter of 1553 speaks of three fulling-mills, and Full Street was the street of the fullers. It has still the remains of the first silk-thread mill in England, and long after that trade had fled it established almost at the door of the town one of the largest firms for the manufacture of artificial silk. The transaction is typical of the town, which, borne forward on the wheels of the Industrial Revolution, has now 145,000 people and a score of industries. It still keeps the china factory William Duesbury established in the 18th century, and prides itself on the fine Crown Derby porcelain, sent all over the world, but it builds the best motorcars and the best locomotives, aeroplane engines, and dynamos; and it is, of course, the head workshop of one of our most enterprising railways, the LMS. As a town it is as ancient as any in England, but it lives in the present. Is there a town in England, we wonder, that would not be proud to turn out such products as the LMS Railway and the Rolls Royce car? It is one of the proud towns of the Transport Age.

It is not unmindful of its past, and a new spirit for its preservation, not wholly confined to the museum, has arisen. Most of its fine old houses are gone, though traces of some of them remain about the marketplace, now turned into shops. It was in a house in the marketplace that Charles Stuart stayed for three days on his march to Shrewsbury, borrowing £300 from the Corporation. Of Exeter House in Full Street, where Prince Charles Edward stayed, nothing remains but the oak panelling of the room where he held his last council of war, and that now lines the walls of the prince's room in the library and museum. There are a few old houses of less renown, a fine Jacobean house in the Wardwick, the old Dolphin Inn in Queen Street, gabled, half-timbered, and dated 1530; and two buildings of less pretensions, but, to our way of thinking, of more account.

The older of them is the fragment of the first silk mill John Lombe built in England on an island in the Derwent in 1717. Nothing is left of his busy factory except the square brick tower surmounted by a canopied roof with ten arches, and now part of another building.

But an old water-wheel in a part of the building still plods humbly along, doing its work in the world of grinding corn as surely as the giants in the town's great power-house. The handsome iron gates, made by Robert Bakewell of Derby, hang no longer in its doorposts, but are against the museum. Another revered building, not so old, is the brick chapel, now a workshop near St Michael's Church, which was the first Methodist preaching-house in Derbyshire. John Wesley preached in it in 1765.

Still one other, more ancient than either, has lately profited by the new care for relics of the past. Near the fine new Exeter Bridge, with its single arch spanning the Derwent, are traces of a bridge rebuilt six centuries ago when already it had an immemorial history of Saxon and Dane and Norman behind it. On it pious men of the 14th century built a tiny house of God. Less pious ages let it fall into disrepair and it became a Presbyterian meeting-house, a carpenter's shop, a storeroom, and might well have been swept away altogether had not the new spirit come to its aid to make it a house of prayer once more. From inside its stone walls we can see the great timbers supporting the roof, or can examine the place on the floor where a way to the river could be found in times of danger. It is good to know that St Mary-on-the-Bridge, this chapel which remains the most interesting relic of the town, is coming to its own again.

From the banks of the Derwent, where the oldest settlement stood, we can read a great deal of the town's history, ancient and modern. The Exeter Bridge, where the stepped embankment follows the curve of the river, has four bronze medallions of the town's four famous sons: John Lombe, of the silk mill; Erasmus Darwin, grandfather of the greater Charles; the historian William Hutton, and Herbert Spencer, the philosopher. Reflected in the waters farther away is the tower of the old silk mill, and beyond it, making one of the more satisfactory pictures of Derby as a whole, the towers of three of its more famous churches, St Alkmund's and All Saints among them.

The embankment on one side of the river has now been completed with charming flower gardens, lawn, and a sunken lily pool lively with goldfish; and at each end of the pool, standing on a pedestal just out of the water, is a giant bronze tortoise. To this garden has come the lovely bronze boy with his pipe who used to stand in the marketplace, and now plays his soundless music by a fountain in a ring of flowers. Still standing in the marketplace is Derby's splendid peace memorial, a bronze statue of a mother with a child in her arms.

Most of the churches gather about the old ways of the town, and are within a few minutes walk of one another. There were six of high renown in the Conqueror's day, and five of them, recorded in Domesday Book, remain, though they have been so much rebuilt that only one, St Peter's, retains any Norman remains in its fabric. All Saints, now the cathedral church, was one of the two collegiate churches in the time of the Confessor. Its great glory, and indeed the architectural glory of the town, is the majestic tower, a legacy of the early 16th century. It rises high above the surrounding buildings, but its stature of 210 feet from base to lofty pinnacle impresses us less than the beauty of the structure, which is one of the finest examples of Gothic architecture in England. The rich buttresses, with their niches and pinnacles, rise above ornamented battlements, and the three stages are divided by bands of ornamental tracery. After Boston Stump it is the highest parish church tower in England, and though too much enclosed to allow a good view from the narrow street, yet, seen from the river or the neighbouring hills, its great size and graceful form are alike impressive. It has lovely traceried windows, and a fine arch.

We may well believe that its church once not unfairly matched it, but it is said that when plans for its reconstruction were being discussed in the days of George the First an impetuous vicar had it hastily demolished, and commissioned James Gibbs, the architect of the Radcliffe Library at Oxford, to build a new one. His effort is wanting both in size and dignity, and the large round windows and column-supported roof are not inspiring.

But the architecture is redeemed by a magnificent iron screen extending on either side of the chancel to the side chapels, its delicate scrolls and foliage as beautiful as anything Robert Bakewell made. It is a monument of fine craftsmanship, but the church has many others of another kind, rescued from the older fabric, and repeating some of the history it preserved. The most striking of them all is the elaborate alabaster tomb in the south chapel, which the autocratic Bess of Hardwick, Countess of Shrewsbury, had designed for herself during her lifetime. She spent a little fortune on it, and often came to admire the huge projecting tomb with pillars reaching now to the roof and supporting a great canopy adorned with stags and shields.

Her stately figure lies on it, apparelled in costly dress. Over her embroidered black gown flows a crimson mantle lined with gold, a small ruff is about her neck, a coronet about the proud brow resting on a cushion. Prideful she was, and seems so here, though her hands are meekly clasped in prayer.

She came to look on her monument for the last time in 1607, and must have observed with satisfaction the long Latin inscription telling of her four husbands, and her great houses. She was the ancestor of the Cavendishes, and to this church more than one followed her, Charles Cavendish who was killed at Gainsborough in 1643, and Henry Cavendish, one of the greatest of the great chemists of the University of Cambridge, where he spent a secluded lifetime in research, and was found dying alone in his room in 1810. He was one of the master builders of the structure of science.

There are other monuments of men and women who left no such name or fame, yet having a place in the annals of the town, and one at least with an interest all its own. This is a rare wooden figure, lifesize, of a canon of the church who has rested thus on his wooden table-tomb with his hands folded in prayer, his vestments about him in graceful folds, for these 400 years. A hound looks up alertly from his feet, and on the front of the tomb is an odd gallery of 13 little monks, some with beads, some with a book or staff, all standing patiently as if they were waiting for the sleeper to wake. Within the tomb lies a corpse.

The oldest monument of all is the figure of John Law, engraved in alabaster, who preached his last sermon here in the 15th century. Also in alabaster we come upon Richard Crowshaw, kneeling in long black robe at a prayer-desk; he was born in Derby, made money in London, and was a benefactor of his town. Near the imposing monument of Bess of Hardwick is the 18th-century white figure of Caroline, Countess of Bessborough, and near to her the bust of her husband William Ponsonby.

Next in order of the churches, and even earlier in time, is St Alkmund's built on the shrine of the saint, Saxon Bishop of Hexham. The old church, pulled down less than a century ago, has been replaced by one famous for a tower with embattled parapet, open trefoils, lovely belfry windows, and graceful flying buttresses springing from the pinnacles to the soaring spire. Inside, the arcades on clustered pillars, the grace of the lofty arches, compel our admiration, and the fine 14th-century font has an added touch of interest because it has come back from the vicarage garden. Some of the church's most precious things are stones which came to light when the ancient church was replaced. One is a huge coffin stone in an outside recess carved by a Norman sculptor, and others are fragments of a cross built into the porch, with carvings of the Madonna holding some unrecognisable instrument, and two other figures in short skirts. It may be part of a crude Annunciation, the handiwork of a Saxon carver. It is at any rate old enough to have belonged to the Saxon shrine. More of these ancient stones are now in the museum.

Under the peace memorial window with its fine stained glass of the Crucifixion and figures of saints and soldiers, chaplain, sailor, and nurse, lies John Bullock on his altar-tomb. John lived at Darley Abbey, and died in 1607, leaving for his monument one of the strangest we have seen in Derbyshire. It is richly panelled, and on it he lies, an immensely elongated alabaster figure in mantle and ruff. Though six feet long the head is so small that we can cover it with one hand.

Facing St Alkmund's is the Roman Catholic church built in 1838 by Augustus Pugin, who was justly proud of it. It is notable for its fine tower, with the Madonna looking down from it on the thousands who pass by. Time was when this church dwarfed St Alkmund's near by, but today the tower and spire of the new St Alkmund's overtop its old rival.

St Werburgh's church has had a very harassed life beside the unruly Markeaton Brook. Domesday Book records it, but the church we see is new, though it keeps an older tower and a chancel which is now a chapel. The 15th-century tower collapsed in a 17th-century gale, weakened by the many floods it had survived, but was rebuilt with some of its old stone on firmer ground. The old chancel comes from a rebuilding of the old body of the church, destroyed by the flood of 1698. St Werburgh's has clung to its old stones, and it has kept some of its old furnishings, notably those of Robert Bakewell's smithwork. One of the most splendid examples is an iron crown used as a font-cover; others are the screen across the entrance to the old chancel, and an iron gateway to a small garden close to the church-yard. The brass pelican, now a lectern in the chapel, was once part of the wrought-iron font-cover.

Filled with light from splendid windows with leaf-like tracery, the new part of the church has arcades with clustered columns, a chancel arch carried on corbels carved with foliage, three lovely sedilia, a lofty oak screen, and a reredos of stone and mosaic. Within the rich framework of stone the mosaic panels have lifesize figures of Christ breaking bread with two disciples, and at the sides are figures of Moses, David, Isaiah, and Daniel. The east window, glowing with colour, shows a Crucifixion with Mary and John; and there are ten prophets and saints, and St Werburgha in a blue robe, holding a model of her church. Small windows near the south doorway, in reds, blues, and gold, picture Lydia and two angel children, St Boniface, St Christopher, and St George, all delightful miniatures.

The peace memorial is a beautiful bronze figure of Christ with outstretched hands, and in the old chancel is a sculpture by Chantrey of a woman weeping by an urn, a memorial to the wife of Edward Whinyates who saw much fighting in the Peninsular War. Here also is remembered Thomas Parker, who preached for 64 years, seeing the passing of Henry the Eighth, the short years of Edward the Sixth and the terrible years of Mary Tudor, the glorious reign of Elizabeth, and its unhappy decline to the Stuart dynasty.

But St Werburgh's pleasantest memory is of one summer's day in 1735, when Samuel Johnson brought his beloved Mrs Porter to the altar of the old chancel. A strange pair they must have looked, she twenty years older than her ungainly husband, dressed fantastically and affected in her manners. Here they were married after driving over from Birmingham, and from Derby Johnson went to be a failure as a schoolmaster at Edial near Lichfield, and an immortal in London.

St Michael's church, near All Saints, was entirely rebuilt in 1858, after much of the old structure had collapsed during a church service, and is the fifth of the churches mentioned in Domesday Book.

St Peter's (with a 19th-century tower) is the sixth, and the only one with any Norman remains in the fabric. These are only slight, chiefly in the capitals of the nave arcades and on each side of the chancel arch. Other survivals are a 13th-century coffin stone built into the inner south aisle wall, with an unusual design of a cross-head in a circle, two stars, and foliage; and other fragments built into a churchyard wall. Among the woodwork is a pillar almsbox by a Flemish craftsman, with a panel showing a woman and her child giving alms outside a castle gate; and, finer still, a big 14th-century chest, the masterpiece of some other Fleming, with elaborate tracery and grotesque animals among a wealth of exquisite carving.

In St Peter's churchyard is an old stone building with a greater fame than the church, for in it Derby School was established when, after four centuries, it was removed from its first foundation. Its second foundation was in 1554, and it is of curious interest that after another three centuries Derby School should have returned to its original site, for it is now at St Helen's House, which stands on the spot where Darley Abbey, to which the school belonged, had an establishment. The old school house, in its centuries of teaching, received many men of worth, and at least two of light and leading, John Flamsteed, the first Astronomer-Royal, and Edward Venables Vernon, who became Archbishop of York.

If in the past the town has seemed to neglect its antiquities, it has always held in high esteem its great men and women. Hutton, the historian, was born in Full Street in 1723 and worked in a silk mill before he was tall enough to reach the machine without standing on tiptoe. He was a book-binder in a small way; he afterwards became rich through the paper trade in Birmingham, and then retired to spend the rest of his life in writing about the places he knew or had visited. Having the writer's knack and the scholar's industry, his book about Derby is still valuable. His fame was a local one. That of Herbert Spencer, who began life in 1820 in one of a row of plain old brick houses near the bridge, belongs not to Derby alone, nor even to England, for he set his mark in the 19th century on the thought and philosophy of the civilised world.

There are others, Joseph Wright, the painter whom all knew in the 18th century as Wright of Derby, and who refused to become an academician, though he was both fashionable and famous. His real worth as an artist has lately won a new recognition; but in his lifetime he was noted most for his subject pictures and for his skill in painting candlelight and firelight. The subjects lent themselves to reproduction in mezzotint, and two at least are extremely well-known, the Air Pump and the Orrery, the originals of which are in the Art Gallery of the Museum. There, sharing the galleries with Roman remains from Little Chester, the name of the Roman camp at Derby, palaeolithic remains from the Creswell caves, and the fine carved Saxon stones from St Alkmund's church, is a magnificent collection of the Derby porcelain which brought new fame to the town; and this brings us to another of the town's worthies, William Duesbury.

After beginning his first china works in Derby about 1750, he bought the Chelsea china factory and the plant at Bow, and reproduced their figures from the old moulds as Chelsea Derby, giving their patterns a second life, and a more successful one, in his own town. For three generations the works remained in his family, and in producing the famous Royal Crown Derby they flourish still. They are one of the sights of the town, which all may see inside and out.

Duesbury's porcelain is his incomparable monument, but the museum keeps alive the fame of other men of Derby. There are bronze busts of Herbert Spencer and Florence Nightingale, and others in stone or marble of Erasmus Darwin, William Strutt, Charles Sylvester the engineer, and John Keys, historian. Michael Thomas Bass gave the museum buildings, and here he stands presiding over his gift.

One name has this town dear to the hearts of all, Florence Nightingale, who belongs to the county. On a stone pedestal near the Royal Infirmary, which many who know Derby always think its most familiar building, her lovely white marble statue looks down on the busy traffic for ever passing by. A shawl is thrown loosely about her shoulders over the nurse's dress she wore in the Crimea; she has a frilled cap on her head, and in her hand a lighted torch such as she carried through the wards of Scutari. At night her gracious figure is floodlit.

Among the bricks and mortar of a town which always seems to be multiplying them is a green oasis with banks of lawn and lovely trees, and formal flower-beds patterned to picture the recumbent stag of the town's arms. It is the Arboretum, and over its entrance gates is a lifesize figure of Joseph Strutt who gave it to the town in 1840. There is another statue by the side of a fish pool, where stands a little bearded bronze man with his hands in his pockets looking thoughtfully down at the flowers growing about his feet. He was Henry Royce, who made the engine of the first aeroplane to cross the Atlantic direct, and the engine which made the first flight to Australia. He was a working boy, one of a family of nine and he sold papers in the streets and delivered telegrams at a halfpenny a time. By his own character he won for himself the applause of the world, for all unaided by influence he forced himself upon the attention of the motor industry. He began with neither capital nor influence, with nothing but a faith in his own powers and in the future, and he it was who fashioned the Rolls Royce car, and, in partnership with Charles Rolls who died too young, raised its reputation to the height at which it stands throughout the world. The boy who sold papers in the streets of London grew up as a man to make the finest engines that had ever been seen running through the streets.

Here sleeps one of our scientific immortals, Henry Cavendish, the strange rich Derbyshire man who weighed the earth.

He Weighed the Earth

THE Father of Chemistry was born at Nice in 1731, a grandson of the second Duke of Devonshire. He left Cambridge without a degree. He inherited a fortune of over a million, yet he made his great rambling house at Clapham a laboratory and a hermitage.

A shy and nervous man, with a stammering speech, he could not tolerate the presence of women and would leave written instructions as to his meals, which always meant leg of mutton for dinner, two legs if he had guests. He would converse only with scientists whom he could not avoid.

With his laboratory in the drawing-room and a forge next door, with his observatory aloft, he first weighed carbon-dioxide, experimented with hydrogen, which he found the lightest of gases, and mixed oxygen and hydrogen in a large glass vessel, exhausted of air. By means of an electric spark he fired this mixture and found that only fluid remained, so startling the world by his revelation that water consists of these two elements.

Cavendish first revealed the fact that carbon-dioxide prevents combustion and is incapable of sustaining life. One of his ancestors was among the first to sail round the earth; Cavendish, by a simple home-made apparatus, was the first to weigh it, and made an estimate wonderfully near the truth, finding it to be 6000 million million million tons.

His work was fundamental, and on his foundations chemistry has erected a structure that has transformed human knowledge and activities. Most of his researches were unknown to his contemporaries, for no man ever spoke fewer words to his fellows. He died at his London home in 1810, left over a million of money to a nephew, a remarkable page of new learning to all who wanted it, and the memory of one of the most extraordinary characters of his age. They brought him here that he might rest in his native county.

The most distinguished son of Derby, the great educator and philosopher, Herbert Spencer, was born here in April 1820.

The Forgotten Philosopher

HE was a schoolmaster's son. Sent to his uncle's school near Bath at 13, he walked home, 115 miles in three days, a first proof of his resolute character. His own schooling formed the basis of his book on Education, a veritable masterpiece which made him the chief educational reformer of his age.

At 17 he began eight years of service on a railway, where he invented an apparatus for testing the speed of engines; following this, when he was famous, with an attempt at a flying machine, a successful invalid bed, and—a mousetrap!

In early manhood he wrote a series of papers on the rights of the individual, maintaining that the function of the State should be limited to the maintenance of justice at home and the repelling of aggression abroad, while every man should be free "to do that which he wills, provided he infringes not the equal freedom of any other man."

Elaborating many essays, he formulated his great system of Synthetic Philosophy, a work of many volumes into which he put 30 years of labour, ruining his health. The founder of evolutionary philosophy, he traced the progress of laws, customs, men, matter, and the universe itself to evolution. It was he who gave currency to the word Evolution in its modern sense; he who, when Darwin's great work appeared, suggested the substitution of Survival of the Fittest for Natural Selection.

He had to spend all he had to secure publication of his work, which long kept him poor; but triumph came eventually, in money and in worldwide fame, but although he lived 83 years he was an invalid and much given to eccentricities, of which amusing examples are recorded in the queer story told of him by "Two," the ladies with whom he shared a home in London.

He would stop his carriage in traffic, they said, in order to test his pulse. When travelling by train he had a hammock slung in a saloon. He put on ear-stops if conversation wearied him. As a housekeeper he ordered so much meat that the bulk of it had to be buried in the garden.

His closing years were spent at Brighton, where he was disheartened by the thought of failure and the sense of having achieved so little with so great a labour. One day in those years of melancholy there came to him an hour of happiness and the feeling that after all, perhaps, he was not forgotten. It was one day when an editor in Fleet Street printed an appreciation of his work in a famous weekly paper, and it is recorded that its appearance much comforted this great man whose life was drawing sadly to its close. He who wrote that appreciation writes this, believing still that Herbert Spencer should be remembered far more widely than he is.

A Village Waiting to be Drowned

DERWENT WOODLANDS. Tucked away in hills that climb to wild and sweeping moors, we come to it in company with the hurrying Derwent, two miles of loveliness from Ashopton. Here, within a stone's-throw, things old and new make up an entrancing picture: a stone Hall of many gables, a modern church with tower and spire, and a charming packhorse bridge.

If it were all the village had we should come to it for this narrow bridge which spans the river with two arches, its projecting piers rising to the top of the parapet and forming recesses on the footway. On one side of the parapet are traces of a Crucifixion.

The church is about the site of one of four medieval chapels built hereabouts by the monks of Welbeck, and the only one remaining after the Reformation. Small, and only a lifetime old, it has a charming arcade on short, slender pillars, and a fine pulpit made from one block of stone and carved with a lily, a passion flower, a dove, and a rose.

A lovely chalice is beautifully chased with figures representing the Elements. The 17th-century font was given by Henry Balguy, who built the great house in 1672. He had a bank and kept his stores of gold in one of the rooms. He was one of an old family with great possessions and many homesteads in the Peak.

The great house became the home of the Duke of Norfolk, who filled its finely panelled rooms with wonderful furniture from all parts of the world, some as old as the 12th and 13th centuries.

But today the house has lost its glory. It was a holiday house when we called, for we found this village, perhaps the saddest in Derbyshire, lying under the shadow of death. Sheffield, Nottingham, Leicester, and Derby were planning its destruction, preparing to drown it in their reservoirs. Two had been built, and when the third is made poor Derwent Woodlands will be no more. Already the work has begun which will take years to complete, and will drown part of Ashopton as well. The last service has been held in the little church. Though it is sad to think so much loveliness must go, the new lake will have a beauty of its own. The Howden and Derwent Dams are a fine sight to see, great lakes with stone walls and embattled towers which will with time merge into their glorious setting of hillsides planted with a myriad trees.

The Home of a Famous Plotter

DETHICK. High above the Derwent, with a fine panorama of the lovely valley, is this secluded village with a story of one of England's conspirators.

In one of the two farmhouses nestling close to the tiny church are the remains of the manor where was born Anthony Babington, who was to bring dire tragedy on the splendour of his house.

Thomas Babington had married the heiress of the Dethicks, and was at Agincourt. His son John was killed at Bosworth Field. His brother William was a famous Lord Chief Justice. Anthony was sixth in descent from Thomas; he spent his boyhood in this village, and he must have known the grand old kitchen which is still here with its old turnspit, its oak beams, and its stone arches.

His father died when he was ten and he was brought up in a strong atmosphere of the Roman Catholic faith. At 16 he was page to the captive Queen of Scots, and it was his pity for her plight which was to bring him to the scaffold. In a few years he was plotting for the death of Elizabeth and the release of Mary, his own share to be the actual deliverance of the queen, who was then imprisoned at Wingfield Manor, four miles away. It is believed that he frequently visited her there in disguise. Well he knew this old church, whose splendid tower was built in 1532 by one whose name he bore; it has a band of 15 shields of arms of his family and their alliances, and a great shield of Sir Anthony and his wife Catherine Ferrers.

The church had its beginnings in the 13th century. Among the remains of those days is the lower masonry of the side walls, two tiny lancets, the south doorway, and the piscina. The clerestory is 16th century.

It would be the bell in Dethick's fine tower which tinkled out a welcome to Florence Nightingale when she arrived home from the

Crimea, alone and unguessed at, while all England was talking of her. She had stolen her way to London, hid herself there for a night, and, refusing triumphal bands and presentations of addresses, had come quietly home to Lea Hurst a mile away, after the two years which had made her the most famous lady in the land.

The Terrible Secret of Anthony Babington

ANTHONY BABINGTON, head of a house which was then still secretly clinging to Roman Catholicism, inherited great estates at Dethick and beyond the Derbyshire border. During the imprisonment of Mary Queen of Scots at Sheffield Castle, he acted as one of her pages, and, fascinated by her charm, formed a passionate attachment for her, although she was 19 years older than he.

Married at 18, he won immediate recognition at the Court of Elizabeth, his wealth, wit, and good looks making him a conspicuous favourite. His Roman Catholic sympathies, however, soon led to his becoming the centre of conspiracies which gradually crystallised into a plot for the furnishing of money and troops by Philip of Spain, the sack of London, the murder of Elizabeth's chief advisers, and the crowning of Mary as Queen of England and Scotland.

All this depended, of course, upon the assassination of Elizabeth, and that fearful mission Babington himself blithely undertook. Plot and counterplot ran their course, and happily the secret was revealed by the discovery of Babington's letter to Mary detailing the plot. Babington fled in disguise, his hair cut off, his face and body stained with walnut juice. He hid first in the wilds of St John's Wood and then in the house of a sympathiser at Harrow, but he was arrested with 12 other conspirators, and condemned to death.

Anxious to save his life, he betrayed the cipher in which Mary had conducted this terrible correspondence, and the day before his execution he wrote this letter to Elizabeth:

Most gratious Souvraigne, if either bitter teares, or pensive contrite harte, or any dutiful sighte of the wretched synner might work any pitty in your royal brest, I would wringe out of my drayned eyes as much bloode as in bemoaninge my drery tragedye should lamentably bewayle my faulte, and somewhat (no doughte) move you to compassion.

But since there is no proportione betwixte the qualitye of my crimes and any human commiseration, Showe, sweet Queene, some mirakle on a wretch that lyeth prostrate in your prison, most grivously bewaylinge his offence, and imploringe such comforte at your anoynted hands as my poor wife's misfortunes doth begge, my child's innocence doth

In the Riverside Gardens

The Peace Memorial

From St Mary's Bridge

DERBY, THE COUNTY'S CAPITAL

Hathersage   The hillside Houses

Edensor   The graceful Spire

crave, my gyltless familye doth wishe, and my heynous trecherye leste deserve.

It was in vain that he pleaded. The terrible sentence of hanging and quartering was carried out in the manner of those days.

DOVE HOLES. It has something like the shadow of an ancient past, for little is left of what once was the great Stone Circle 260 yards round, one of the three most important prehistoric circles in Derbyshire. Known as the Bull Ring, its stones were broken up and used for building 200 years ago, and what is left for us to see is the ditch, with two entrances which were old before the Romans came, and its isolated mound, or pointer, close by. Its companion is a modern church.

The Fearless Michael Sadler

DOVERIDGE. On the border in a charming setting, it spreads down from the highway towards the winding Dove. A pretty lane leads to the church in a green retreat, the vicarage on one hand and a drive to the great house at the other, a narrow lane dropping down from the church to a light suspension bridge.

It was on another bridge, which takes the road into Staffordshire, that a schoolboy was told he would be thrown into the river if he did not curse the Methodists. He did not curse them and he was not thrown in; he showed his tormentors the courage which made him famous as the great Michael Sadler, remembered for his great work for the poor in the 19th century, and especially as a fearless agitator against child slavery in the factories.

In the peaceful garden of the lovely old church is one of Derbyshire's magnificent living treasures, an old yew whose fine upstanding trunk is 22 feet round. Its spreading branches are supported on a ring of posts, and shelter a patch of ground more than 200 feet round, making with the help of another yew a green tunnel from the gate.

Near it is an elegant cross where something old and something new have made a lovely thing, for the broken 13th-century shaft has been lengthened and crowned with panels of the Crucifixion and the Madonna in memory of the men of Doveridge who did not come home again.

The old cross and the embattled tower with its beautiful windows would be young together, for the tower is also 13th century, with a 15th-century spire. The priest's doorway and the graceful lancets of the chancel are some of the finest 13th-century work in Derbyshire. The piscina is 700 years old and the font is also of this time, in spite of its youthful appearance. The nave arcades are 14th century. The 15th-century oak roofs have fragments as old as the walls. A 17th-century chest with a gabled top and three locks is nearly three feet high.

An alabaster stone in the chancel has engraved portraits of a knight and lady fading away after 450 years, Radulphus Okovere and his wife; and another stone has a priest in robes, his head on a pillow held by angels. He was perhaps Robert Kniveton, who founded a chantry in 1392.

A monument with two angels holding back curtains is to Thomas Milward and his wife, who entertained Charles Stuart; and another shows the kneeling figures of their daughter Mary and her husband. He has the dress of a Cavalier, with rosettes to his high boots, and she wears a full-skirted gown. Below kneel three daughters, dressed like their mother and with lace-trimmed collars; and with them is a wideawake baby in a cradle with pretty draperies. We do not forget these happy little faces.

There are a few fragments of old glass in an aisle, and two lancets in the chancel are filled with beautiful blues, greens, and reds showing St Christopher with the Child and St Nicholas with a tiny ship.

In the Valley of the Drone

DRONFIELD. In the valley of the River Drone, it grew into a town and had a market till time gave it easy access to Chesterfield and Sheffield, between which it comes midway. Then its market cross was replaced by a stone shelter in memory of Sir Robert Peel. In the heart of the town is a soldier standing in a small rockery garden in memory of the men who did not come back.

Collieries and iron foundries have given it a workaday dress, but some fine old houses remain, and with all its stir of spades and shovels, tools for the workshop and sickles for the field, it has not forgotten how to treasure the fine old church on the hill.

A beautiful building without and within, it has been the glory of Dronfield for 600 years. In its lovely churchyard is the shaft of the old preaching cross. The fine tower and spire, 138 feet high, is 14th century, though the spire has been much restored after a storm. The nave arcades, 600 years old, were crowned with a clerestory a century after.

The joy of the church is the lovely 14th-century chancel, one of the finest in the county, long and lofty and light with beautiful traceried windows, and a carved band of wavy moulding below the parapet.

In the chancel windows is ancient glass through which the light has been falling 600 years. There are coats-of-arms, and three roundels with quaint figures playing musical instruments. A man is sitting with an ancient guitar, a monk has a clavichord, and another man is playing a primitive kind of fiddle. In a border round a medley of fragments is St Cecilia with an organ and other strange little figures.

Splendid woodwork old and new adds to the charm of the church. Worked into the fine choir stalls are lovely bench-ends and poppy-heads 500 years old. There is a fine Jacobean pulpit handsomely carved, and a splendid old chest with seven locks. The handsome carving of the altar table, and the reredos with Christ and the Four Evangelists in canopied niches, are among the finest work of a modern Derbyshire craftsman (Advent Hunston of Tideswell). Across the tower arch is an oak screen.

The old font was found in the vicarage garden a few years ago. Among the beautiful silver is a paten said to be about 1491. There is a little sanctus bell, and among other survivals is a chained book.

On an alabaster tomb adorned with angels lies Sir Richard Barley in armour, his hands in prayer but his dagger by his side; he lived at Dronfield Woodhouse 500 years ago.

Set in a stone against the chancel wall are brasses of John Fanshawe with his wife and four children, and another of a woman and a child. They lived at Fanshawe Gate three or four miles away; a barn and a dovecot remain of their old home, and they are remembered in Dronfield as the founders of the grammar school in the time of Elizabeth. On the chancel floor are fine brass portraits of two 14th-century priests who were brothers, Thomas and Richard Gomfrey, said to be the only example known of a brass engraved in memory of two brothers.

The old lady chapel, plundered by Henry the Eighth, has been restored in memory of one who fell in the war, and it has still its old piscina and the old altar table. The three windows have in them the Crucifixion, the Labourers in the Vineyard, and the Wise Men and the Shepherds at the manger.

A Message from Anthony Bradshaw

DUFFIELD. It lies in a lovely hollow where the Derwent flows through a fine old bridge after gathering the waters of the Ecclesbourne. It has two tiny almshouses of the 17th century, a fine Hall now a school, and another big house in an enchanting hillside garden with lawns and flowers, pools and quiet walks. Its church is in delightful river setting, with great limes and a splendid yew 21 feet round in the churchyard; and the site of one of the greatest castles in England belongs to this village.

From the road above the river is a glorious view of the valley, with Bunker's Hill where a Norman kiln was found, and Castle Hill where Henry de Ferrers built his Norman stronghold. The foundations of its keep were accidentally laid bare about 50 years ago, and it was found that it must have been bigger than any other Norman keep in England except the Tower of London. It was nearly 100 feet square with walls 16 feet thick. It has a well 80 feet deep, and a moat of which we can see remains to this day.

The church of many gables has a 14th- and 15th-century tower and spire and a fine peal of ten bells. Nothing is left of the Saxon church except its dedication to St Alkmund, who sleeps in the county town, but there are fragments of Norman work in two small shafts and capitals of the 14th-century chancel arch, and a corbel table with 12 grotesque heads on an outer wall of the chancel, now enclosed by a chapel. Norman coffin stones are built into the tower about the belfry windows, and an arched recess in the chancel may mark the burial-place of the founder of the Norman church. The stone with a cross lying under it now is new.

From the 14th century come most of the nave arcades, the south porch, the doorway letting us in, and a fine corbel of a bearded head under the north aisle roof.

There are windows of three medieval centuries, those in the chancel filled with lovely glass showing the Last Days in Jerusalem. Beautiful modern craftsmanship is in the chancel screen with its six slender pillars all differently carved, the screen-work in the arches of the chapel with fine ironwork above it, and the linenfold panelling of the sanctuary and of the bench-ends. Pulpit, altar, reredos, and rails complete the lovely scheme.

On a fine alabaster tomb in the chapel lie splendid figures of Sir

Roger Mynors and his wife who were buried here 400 years ago. He is in armour with his sword and gauntlets at his side; she has a girdled gown with many folds and a mantle with wide sleeves, and lovely pointed headdress showing her hair held by a ribbon. Everything is very rich; both have rings on their fingers, she four on each hand; a big jewel hangs from his collar, and her collar has a double chain with a cross; his feet are on a lion, and two tiny dogs are holding the hem of her robe. There are angels and two priests on the tomb. Sir Roger was a sergeant in the household of Henry the Seventh and his son, and knew Sir Thomas More.

Very quaint is the wall monument with a marvellous company of Anthony Bradshaw, his two wives and 20 children. He set it up in the year 1600, or the children would have been three more. We may wonder if anywhere else in England three children came too late to have their pictures on their father's monument. The figures of Anthony, his wives and the 20 children, all with their initials, are engraved across the middle of the monument between long inscriptions. Worked into the inscription is a rhyming acrostic on Anthony's name, ending in these four lines:

> *A different tyme I wish thee,*
> *Quoth he which here doth lye,*
> *But put thy house in order*
> *For surely thou shalt dye.*

A queer fellow was this Anthony Bradshaw, great-uncle of the John Bradshaw who sat in judgment on the king. He was a barrister, and Deputy-Steward of the then important Duffield Frith, a stretch of forest land between Duffield and Wirksworth where wolves abounded in the 13th century and Edward the First hunted the fallow deer. He wrote an extraordinary poem of 54 stanzas about Duffield and Duffield Frith, and lived in the village for a time. He founded an almshouse here, which was pulled down last century, and left instructions in his will that the old folk who lived there should sit at the back of his pew and keep his monument clean.

A simpler tribute to a simpler man we find on a wall, a pathetic tablet to Reginald Wright. He was one of the very first Scoutmasters. He was on duty with his scouts in 1911 when he met with an accident and died the next day, 21 years old.

Some of the family of Anthony Bradshaw lived at the old hall (now a farm) at Makeney, a stone-built hamlet at the end of a lovely climb from Duffield along the road where coaches used to travel. An old stone near the inn has the words Derby Coach Road 1739.

A Saxon Treasure in the Hills

EARL STERNDALE. It sleeps in the bosom of a wonderful array of hills, which fill the horizon with the wild scenery of the limestone country of the Peak, and abound in lonely graves of forgotten folk. Hitter Hill and Aldery Cliff and High Wheeldon keep watch above, and not far off is Brier Low, while Axe Edge rises 1700 feet three miles away.

An old inn and a centenarian church stand by the green, the church on the site of an ancient chapel. It shelters a crudely-shaped font, perhaps ten times as old as the church itself, for it is said to be Saxon.

From this quiet place went out 15 men for England who did not come back; they have a cross near the ancient one in the churchyard.

Two Views Through a Peephole

ECKINGTON. It has a charming corner about the church, where the little coal town throws off its workaday garb. Here, on a little green, stands a fine cross to those who did not come back.

Its glory is its church, with the work of the Normans in two splendid nave arcades with massive pillars. The Normans also built the west doorway of the tower. The rest of the fine tower is 13th century, with lancet windows below the parapet of quatrefoil and ball-flower ornament. The sturdy spire is 14th century. The 13th-century arches of the tower and chancel rest on capitals carved with foliage.

The chancel is rich in old oak chairs, for it has seven of them as well as a seat. The fine oak screen and choir stalls are modern. There is a very unusual peephole at the end of an aisle, designed so that it gave a view of two altars.

The reredos is a beautiful painting of the Madonna with her dead Son, a copy made about 1600 of a work by Ludovic Carrachi in Bologna. In the east window are shields and medallions of ancient glass.

One of the queerest things we have seen in a church hereabouts is an extraordinary monument showing the kneeling figures of Sir George Sitwell and his wife in comically theatrical attitudes. After losing heavily by his loyalty to Charles Stuart, Sir George recovered his fortunes by founding the Renishaw ironworks, and here he lies.

Renishaw Hall, his old home, has a fine setting near Eckington, a 16th-century house famous for its 17th-century Brussels tapestries, some of which show the Triumph of Solomon.

A marble monument with his portrait marks 50 years of service here as rector by Edmund Hiley Bucknall Estcourt. Many people when we called remembered this rare old man, who was still shepherding his flock on his 90th birthday. Sir George Sitwell, the lord of the manor when we called, was well on the way to equal his record, for he had been lord of the manor for three score years and ten.

The Wonderful Walk

EDALE. It is in the broad and smiling Vale which bears its name, through which the little Noe goes gathering countless mountain streams. Mighty hills surround the valley, from the glory of the Kinder Range with Grindslow Knoll and Ringing Roger, to Brown Knoll, Rushup Edge, Mam Tor, and Lose Hill's 1500 feet.

A secluded little place, it has pretty houses and lovely gardens, an inn 300 years old, honeysuckle hedges, and a delightful wayside dell where a one-arch bridge crosses Grinds Brook on its way to the Noe. The church is the third in three centuries; in the churchyard is a cross in memory of those who died for Peace, an unlucky thirteen.

One of Derbyshire's wonderful walks begins here, crossing the Kinder Range by way of Upper Booth, Jacob's Ladder, and Oaken Clough to the famous Snake Inn where a Roman road crosses the fine road from Glossop to Sheffield. On the way we pass the ancient Edale Cross, a rudely shaped and perhaps medieval stone near the old packhorse track taking us on to Hayfield.

From the road which climbs Mam Tor is a superb view of this quiet village and exquisite vale, and of the splendour of the southern mass of Kinderscout bounding its farther side.

At the Gate of Chatsworth

EDENSOR. Its charming houses gather by a green and wayside edged with lawn, built of every style and shape with irregular roofs and chimneys, with gable or turret or battlement; all at different angles, all in gardens, all looking up to the handsome church.

Everywhere about it is the loveliness of the English countryside, for it stands on the threshold of Chatsworth. We may come to the village from Beeley's fine old bridge across the park, with a view of the

Palace of the Peak, an approach enchanting when the woods are turning to gold and the bracken to bronze. We may come from Baslow by another stretch of the park; from Bakewell through Pilsley for the joy of views and fir plantations; or by the steep way which climbs Ballcross, passing an ancient road stone in a corner of a field. Well worth while is this rough road for the glorious panorama of Bakewell encircled by hills, and the fine views over Chatsworth as we drop down into Edensor.

The lovely spire has reared its great height since 1867 when the old church was made new in 14th-century style, a spacious place of fine arches, beautiful windows, and splendid fittings. There are canopied sedilia and exquisitely carved corbels on the pillars supporting the roof beams and the chancel arch. The clerestory windows are quaint and deeply recessed. The fine pulpit and the font are made from Chatsworth marble, but the church has also an old font like a chalice, the eight sides of its shallow bowl carved with traceried arcading. It is not the only old possession of this new church, for there are Norman pillars in the nave arcades, and a Norman capital with a face and foliage carved on it. The north aisle has a Norman window, and the south porch a Norman doorway.

The embattled porch, with a stone roof, is mainly 14th century. On one side is a gargoyle with an ugly human face, and on the other an angel holding arms; and in the walls are fragments of ancient coffin stones. So we read the story of the old and the new in the stones of the church, and within its walls we glean something of people who have made history in a greater world than Edensor.

We think here of the tragedy of Mary Queen of Scots, for there is a brass in the chancel in memory of her faithful servant John Beton. He helped her to escape and was imprisoned with her at Chatsworth, dying there. The plate, three feet long, has a Latin inscription below which is a tiny figure in armour lying on a tomb. The brass was set here by his two brothers at the wish of the Queen, his most kind mistress, and the epitaph says:

> *The fates, O Beton, envious of thy worth,*
> *Have snatched thee prematurely from the earth:*
> *With thee have gone bright genius, judgment sound,*
> *And we, thy friends, are left in grief profound.*

A costly monument in the Cavendish Chapel is in memory of two sons of the famous Bess of Hardwick and her husband Sir William

Cavendish. At each side is a mythological figure, and at the top a display of arms. Fame with a trumpet is holding Latin inscriptions to Henry Cavendish, and to William, first Earl of Devonshire, a friend of James the First who is said to have helped to colonise the Bermudas and has an island named after him. Beneath the open tomb lie two figures, one a skeleton and one in a winding sheet with its head uncovered. In the upper part of the monument are Henry's suit of armour with helmet and gauntlets, and the earl's robes and coronet; they are lifesize, and as if the brothers had just stepped out of them at the call of death. In the ostentatious style of the time, this monument was the reredos of the old church.

The lovely glass of the east window of the chapel, and the fine alabaster tablet below it, recall a dire tragedy of half a century ago, for they are in memory of Lord Frederick Cavendish, who was murdered within 12 hours of his landing in Phoenix Park, Dublin, in 1882; murdered by those, as Mr Gladstone said, "to whom he had gone full of love to their country, full of hope for the future, full of capacity to do her service." This quiet village had its share in the shadow which fell on lovely Chatsworth when they brought him home, for in the peaceful churchyard he was laid to rest, borne from the chapel of the stately house, across the park where thousands came to do him honour, with Mr Gladstone in the long procession. A plain granite cross marks his grave.

A plain inscription pays tribute to Sir Joseph Paxton, who left the world more beautiful than he found it when he died in 1865. For more than a generation the lovely gardens at Chatsworth became more lovely under his care. He made glorious plantations and designed the colossal conservatory which covered nearly an acre of ground and was one of the wonders of Chatsworth till it was demolished in 1920. It was from this inspiration that he designed the Crystal Palace.

While at Chatsworth Paxton became a devoted friend of the sixth duke, who helped him with his plans. Known as the Good Duke, it was he who rebuilt the village of Edensor and the north wing of Chatsworth. He is said to have spent £50,000 on his mission to Russia for the coronation of the Emperor Nicholas. His collection of books and pictures were among the finest in England. He has lain in the churchyard since 1858 under a nameless tomb carved with a cross, according to his wish:

Accordant with his humble wish
In this grave's narrow room,
Lies an illustrious Cavendish
Beneath a nameless tomb.

Here also lie the seventh earl and the eighth duke. William Cavendish, the earl, was M.P. for Derbyshire when the Reform Act was passed, but devoted his energies to science and industry. He contributed £200,000 towards the Irish railways, and did much to advance the iron and steel works of the north. He was one of the founders of the Royal Agricultural Society, and his name is preserved for all time in his gift to the Cambridge University of the Cavendish Laboratory. The eighth Duke loved nothing better than entertaining royalty in this magnificent house. Better known as Lord Hartington, he was the chief supporter of Mr Gladstone until the split on Home Rule, when he formed the Liberal Unionist party. His statue is in Whitehall.

A fine brass shining in the dim light of the tower has a kneeling figure of John Gregory Cottingham, steward to the seventh duke. The window above it is to his memory, showing scenes in a steward's life. A medallion shows Christ as a master giving a staff of office to a steward who is seen serving the household with food, and there are labourers in the vineyard, felling trees, preparing the ground for seed, building, paying wages, gathering crops, and giving to the poor in winter.

An inscription to Joseph Hall tells us that he died in 1907 after 52 years here as vicar: there is a tablet to John Philips, 60 years in the service of Chatsworth; and in a charming alabaster recess is a Book of Remembrance of the men of the Chatsworth Rifles.

John Kirkland's Hope

EDLASTON. It stands on a hilltop with a lowly church by a lovely lane, looking away to the pyramid height of Thorpe Cloud, rising from a dip between the Derbyshire hills and the Weaver Hills of Staffordshire.

Much of the church is 14th century, including the chancel arch, but most of the windows are a century younger. The bowl of a very old font is still here, though a 19th-century one is now used. A corner of the 17th-century altar table serves as a shelf in the chancel. The pulpit is in memory of those who did not come back.

Perhaps the pride of the village is its ancient yew, exceptionally fine with widespreading branches and a trunk 16 feet round. It keeps company with the old churchyard cross, crowned by a ball. Cut on a stone tomb near the porch is this tribute to John Kirkland, a young man who died when Queen Anne was still on the throne:

> *Who hath a good child to his parents bin,*
> *Hoping the Lord is as good to him.*

The pretty hamlet of Wyaston lies about a green hollow near by.

Dr Johnson Rides Past, Thinking

EGGINTON. It lies in rich meadows, near a Roman road and a common where the Royalists were routed. The River Dove divides it from Staffordshire, here near the end of its journey and crossed by three bridges. A new bridge with a single span has kept for company the old Monks Bridge a few yards away, a monument of the leisured days. Over this narrow graceful bridge, built perhaps by the monks of Tutbury Priory, Dr Johnson must have come with his darling Tetty, the widow nearly twice his age, on their way to be married at Derby, making up his mind as he rode never to let her get the upper hand of him. A stone's throw from Monks Bridge the river is crossed again, this time by a canal raised on sturdy arches, the building of which was one of the triumphs of James Brindley in the 18th century.

The fine church is in lovely setting at the end of an avenue of majestic limes. On one side is the wavy buttressed wall of the rectory, on the other the parkland of the great house, while between them flows a brook under a grove of trees.

Much of it is from the end of the 13th century, when the Norman church was rebuilt, and of this time is the north arcade, with two tiny 14th-century clerestory windows (a very early date for these in Midland churches), the chancel with a priest's doorway, a stone seat and a piscina, and the fine east window with remains of 14th and 15th-century glass. In it are small figures of the Madonna and St John, with a Crucifixion scene.

To many of us perhaps the joy of this bright place will be the south aisle of about 1320, its fine arcade with clustered pillars, and its long wall a mass of recesses and niches and odd windows of later time. In one recess lies the stone figure of a woman with a heart in her hands, perhaps Elizabeth Stafford, a 14th-century heiress.

The Unparalleled Country Yokel

ELMTON. It has lost the glory of its elms, said to have been among the finest in England; and today Elmton has nothing for us to see but a plain church of the 18th century and a churchyard in which sleeps an Elmton man who has curiously written his name into books all over the world, though here he sleeps without a stone to mark the place. Here he was born in 1707; here they laid him in 1772, Jedediah Buxton, son of the village schoolmaster.

There were many odd circumstances in his phenomenal career, but almost equalling his astonishing faculty for figures was the strangeness of the fact that Jedediah, although grandson of the vicar and son of the schoolmaster, never could learn to read or write. He passed his life as a labourer in the fields, dreaming in arithmetic.

The theory of the men who studied him was that, having a genius for mathematics, he unconsciously developed it to the entire exclusion of other mental attributes. Working away in the open, performing his task with unflagging zeal, he was constantly creating and solving problems with which normal mathematicians found it difficult to grapple.

However limited his knowledge, his power of concentration on his favourite subject was baffling. He chatted briskly while working out such a problem as this: In a body whose three sides measure 23,145,789 yards, 5,642,732 yards, and 54,965 yards, how many cubic eighths-of-an-inch are there?

As he walked over a field he could estimate its area to an inch with the accuracy of a surveyor. One of his rapid feats was his calculation of the product of a farthing doubled 139 times. When mathematicians had proved his answer correct, Jedediah calmly multiplied his answer by itself. He could break off a calculation at any point and resume it in a week.

After a short season of triumph in London, where he was disappointed not to see the royal family but was delighted to appear before the Royal Society, Buxton returned home and died here at 65. His widespread reputation was not forgotten in his death, and a learned hand placed a Latin inscription on his coffin. Could poor Jedediah have seen it it would have been no more puzzling to him than the complexities of that native tongue which he was never able to read or write.

The Treasure Thrown Away

ELTON. Hills and moors and rocky ravines are round about this village, which has a modern church and ancient memories. It was perhaps through delving for lead that the foundations of the ancient chapel were weakened in the 18th century, causing the old steeple to fall in Trafalgar year. Some of the old stones are still in the rectory garden, with one that may have been the base stone of the village cross.

The new church has a font with a story. Of most unusual design, it has on one side a small stoup fashioned out of the same block of stone, seeming to be held in the mouth of a dragon carved on the bowl. But, alas for Elton, this font is only a copy of a rare treasure it had but did not value, now the pride of Youlgreave, a Norman font perhaps unique in England, for it has a bracket beneath which the head of a dragon peeps out.

It is curious to learn that, when the new church was built after the fall of the steeple, the old font was cast out. Twenty years later it found itself in the vicarage grounds at Youlgreave, and there wise people took it back to church. The day came when Elton asked for it back again, but nothing would persuade Youlgreave to let it go, and Elton must needs be content with its copy of the priceless thing it threw away.

One of its bells was here before the Reformation; exceptionally fine and ornate, it is inscribed, Jesus be our Spede.

By the Golden Gates

ELVASTON. It is five miles from Derby, completing a happy group with the hamlets of Ambaston and Thulston on a level stretch of meadows near the winding Derwent. Away from the road, facing a fine avenue, are the blue and gold gates of Elvaston Castle (called by the people here the Golden Gates) from a royal palace in Madrid. Famous these grounds have been for their avenues and groves of trees, their gardens with lake and rockeries, and a lovely yew garden where one of a maze of yew hedges, fashioned into many arbors, encircles a lawn.

The stately castle, made new over a century ago, has been a home of the Stanhopes for nearly 400 years. The first Stanhope of Elvaston was Sir Michael, who lost his head in 1552 for being faithful to Protector Somerset; the story of some who followed him is told in the beautiful church by their home. Before the Stanhopes the Blounts were here for generations, and traces of the home they knew are said to survive in the castle. The first here was Sir Thomas, Treasurer of Calais during the wars of Henry the Sixth; and here is said to have been born his son Walter Blount who was Lord Treasurer to Edward the Fourth and became the first Lord Mountjoy.

A fine embattled tower, with eight pinnacles above the high tree-tops, crowns the church which came into Domesday Book but has now nothing older than the 13th-century lancet in the aisle. The chancel arch, the nave arcade, the porch, and the beautiful font are 14th century; most of the windows and most of the fine nave roof (with carved and gilded bosses) are 15th.

The handsome medieval chancel screen is carved both east and west; two richly carved stall-ends once attached to it are in the chancel, with poppyheads of an antelope seated and a lion chained. Another lovely 15th-century screen encloses the Stanhope pew, where is also some 17th-century carving.

In the chancel, on a monument with a wonderful canopy and a shield which is almost a monument in itself, lie the marble figures of Sir John Stanhope and his second wife, he with golden hair and gilded armour, she in a black hood, resting on a tasselled cushion of red, green, and gold. He was knighted when James the First came to England. One of his sons was the Philip who became Lord Chesterfield in 1628. Another son John sat in Charles Stuart's first Parliament, and his striking monument of white marble shows him wide awake, resting on his arm. He died in 1638, and this costly monument is said to have been damaged by Sir John Gell (his bitter enemy) when the Roundheads plundered the castle. We read how Sir John Gell wooed the widow and married her, only "to destroy the glory of her husband and his house."

The great-grandson of this Sir John Stanhope became first Earl of Harrington. The fifth earl lies in the Stanhope pew, a fine marble figure, and in the chancel we see his eldest son Algernon, who died at nine years old; it is a lovely sculpture of a sleeping boy, by Westmacott. On the chancel wall is the fine brass portrait of the sixth Earl Harrington, who died before he was 21, showing him in a scholar's dress.

The place of the east window has been taken by a great stone reredos, coloured and gilded, with scenes of Bethlehem and Calvary.

Sir Aston Cokayne, the poet of his family, was born here early in the 17th century. Made a baronet by Charles Stuart, he suffered heavily by his loyalty, and after an extravagant life, joined with his son in selling Ashbourne Hall and other estates. He died a poor man.

Three Tudor Gentlemen

ETWALL. Like a bit of the old world among the little hills, it has a church high by the wayside with a shapely yew, and a delightful group of almshouses with a central archway adorned with painted heraldic panels, and two sundials on the chimney stacks. Nestling in the trees below, and approached by fine gates made by Robert Bakewell, is the stately 17th-century Hall, built from the ruins of Tutbury Castle and keeping some part of an older house. It was once the home of the Ports, of whom three generations, three gentlemen of Tudor times, have memorials in the church where they sleep, two having found a place in our national roll of fame.

The first is Henry Port, a merchant of Chester who died in 1512. His brass has gone, but those of his wife in her widow's mantle, and groups of their 17 children, are here. His son Sir John Port has a rich tomb with a small battered figure of himself in his judge's robes, and his two wives. He was a benefactor to Brasenose College, Oxford.

Under the lovely canopy of his tomb are the charming brass portraits of the next Sir John, his two wives and five children, all kneeling in prayer. He gave Etwall its almshouses, which were made new in the last years of the Stuarts, and he founded Repton School, whose badge (a pigeon with a cross) is seen on his armour and in the heraldry of his monument. His heiress married Sir Thomas Gerard, a Roman Catholic suspected of plotting to get Mary Queen of Scots out of prison. Sir Thomas tried to evade Elizabeth's spies by attending service in the church, but trouble came one day when he compelled his younger brother to accompany him, for he began chanting psalms like a good Roman Catholic as soon as the minister began the reformed service in English, and the scene ended in his being seized and carried out of church.

Much of the old work left in the church is 15th and 16th century, including the low embattled tower. Part of the chancel walls and its buttresses are 13th century, and two round arches and pillars remain of the Norman arcade. The massive font is 500 years old, there is an ancient stone lectern on the chancel wall, and in the Port Chapel are beautiful carved seats and a prayer desk 300 years old.

The Village of the Heroic Spirit

EYAM. In a land of moorland heights, ravines, and pretty dells lies this charming Queen of the Peak, whose old stone houses line the long, wide, oldworld street on a terrace of the hills. It looks up to Eyam Edge towering 400 feet above the village, and reaches down to the grand gorge of Middleton Dale with its own delightful Cucklet Delf and Eyam Dale shut in by rocky heights and a fine plantation. Its hills are riddled with caverns and the earth with old lead mines; its moor, crowned by Sir William Hill 1418 feet above the sea, is rich in barrows and stone circles, among them the Wet Withens.

It has a fine house, an old church, and in the churchyard one of the finest ancient crosses in the land: it has associations with a group of lettered folk through whom it came to be called the Athens of the Peak. It has its humble cottages, its simple graves, its church not made with hands, its memories of simple folk, and it is with these that its story lives, imperishable.

It was in September 1665 that a box of tailor's cloth and some old clothes came from London to the cottage by the church, and with it bitter tragedy for Eyam, tragedy which turned the peaceful village into a place of death, for it brought the plague that had raged in London many months. The first of its victims was the journeyman who opened the fateful box; he died within four days. By the end of the month five more had died, in October a score and more. For more than a year the pestilence pursued its savage way, abating with the winter months only to burst out with greater violence in the spring. In March 56 are said to have perished.

All the time this village of grief and despair was a place of quiet heroism, the heroism of a little band who stayed to serve, of a panic-stricken people who in the very face of death resigned themselves to follow the path they were asked to tread.

Names that will live while man has memory are those of William Mompesson the rector, his wife Catherine, and Thomas Stanley who had been ejected from the church for nonconformity but had remained among his people. They set themselves to isolate the village for the sake of the outer world, asking no more of the others than they were willing to do themselves. They arranged for food to be

Eyam   The 17th Century Hall

Hartington   The Jacobean Hall

Glossop
Modern Marble Font

Derby
Florence Nightingale

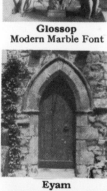

Eyam

Chesterfield

Tideswell

Wirksworth

Wonderful Saxon Carving

brought from outside and left at certain places on the boundaries they fixed, the money left for payment being carefully washed before it was taken away. One of the appointed places, since known as Mompesson's well, is covered with a block of stone, half a mile north of the village.

The horror of it all increased as the months went on, and deaths were so frequent that the passing bell ceased to toll, and the graveyard ceased to take the dead. Graves were dug in gardens and fields, and often those yet spared had to bury their own loved ones. At Riley Side a woman watched her family die within eight days, husband and six children. The Riley Graves of the Hancock family can still be seen, a pathetic circle of six headstones and a tomb. The tomb of John Hancock, the father, is in its original place, the stones having been brought together from about the field.

Time came when the church door was closed, and the rector took the remnant of his flock to Cucklet Delf, a haunt of peace and loveliness among the trees which June had filled with the song of birds and the joy of flowers. The pitiful procession was to grow pitifully less as the days went by, wending its way down grassy slope and slowly up again to where Mompesson found his pulpit on a picturesque rock with natural arches, and carried on his ministry to the stricken people. Every year when Feast Day comes, on the last Sunday in August, a great procession treads the selfsame way to the simple Cucklet Church in memory of the heroes of nearly three centuries ago.

In August Catherine Mompesson died and was buried in the churchyard, a yew tree now sheltering her tomb. By October the last toll had been paid, and out of 350 village folk 259 had died, as well as 58 children. Among those who were left were the two ministers William Mompesson and Thomas Stanley. They saw this bitter tragedy through to its appalling end. Mompesson left the village soon afterwards for the living of Eakring in Nottinghamshire, and became a Prebend of York and Southwell. Very different was the reward of Thomas Stanley, who remained at Eyam till he died in 1670, for after all his labours, there were those who would have turned him from the village for his nonconformity had not the Earl of Devonshire rebuked them.

There is a stone in the churchyard by the chancel wall in memory of Thomas Stanley with these words:

He stood between the living and the dead,
and the plague was stayed.

In the church is a brass tablet in memory of Stanley and the two Mompessons. The solid oak pulpit was here in their day; in it both these brave men must have preached. The old oak chair carved with *Mom. 1665. Eyam* is said to have been rescued from a dealer's shop in Liverpool. In the vestry is a little oak cupboard said to have been originally in one of the Plague Cottages, as those by the church are called.

Much of the old work of the church has been lost in rebuilding and restoration, but from the Norman church there is still the plain round font, and another ancient font with round arcading is preserved. From the 14th century come the archway to the tower and from the 15th the clerestory windows. There is an old oak chest, ancient tiebeams and bosses in the nave roof, and remains of an urn found in a barrow on Eyam Moor. Some windows have pleasing glass, one showing St Helena, and a lancet in the chancel in memory of a rector who helped with his own hands to restore the church last century; it shows John Green with his trowel, the architect with his plans, and the workmen with scaffolding.

In the chancel is a memorial to Ralph Rigby, a curate here. Three Yorkshire clergymen who had been to his funeral in 1740 were lost in the snow while returning; one was found next morning and survived, but the other two perished.

The churchyard with its fine trees is rich indeed in story. There is an elaborate sundial of 1775 on the wall of the church showing "the parallel of the sun's declination for the months of the year, the scale of the sun's meridian altitude, points of the compass, and a number of meridians." Many of the epitaphs were written by two poets who knew this place. One was Richard Furness, a village boy born in 1791 and buried here, a preacher and soldier before he was 20 and afterwards schoolmaster of Dore, where he designed a new schoolhouse and was doctor for all. He wrote a queer poem called the Rag Bag. The other was Peter Cunningham, who was curate here for 18 years and wrote poems that no one reads. While he was curate the rector was Thomas Seward, who thought himself a playwright, poet, and author, and published an edition of Beaumont and Fletcher. He was buried in Lichfield Cathedral where he was a Prebend, and after his death Coleridge said of him, "Mr Seward, Mr Seward, You may be an angel now, but you were an ass."

It was his daughter Anna who made his name familiar. Born at Eyam rectory in 1747, she could repeat a poem of Milton's before she was three and she became known as the Swan of Lichfield. Her poetry was very affected and has been forgotten, but while she lived at Lichfield, where the Sewards were often visited by Dr Johnson, she became the friend of many men of letters of her day.

The most precious thing the village has is in the churchyard, a wonderful cross which has come through a thousand years and more in almost all its glory, complete with head and arms, only two feet of the top of the shaft missing. It stands eight feet high and is carved all over with fine design. On the head and arms are angels with crosses and trumpets, while the shaft has knotwork and lovely scrolls with foliage, and figures of a man with bugle horn, and the Madonna and Child.

Very proud is the village of its charming great house, at the roadside facing the stone pillars of the ancient stocks. Grey-stoned and many-gabled, set in terraces and lawns, it has been the home of the Wrights since it was built in 1676. It is said to be a copy of the old Bradshaw Hall of Eyam whose stones were used in it. A wing of Bradshaw Hall remains on a farm.

The Strange Motto

FAIRFIELD. It is almost on Buxton's doorstep, but it keeps a character of its own, for all at once the busy road opens out to a breezy common where men play golf 1200 feet above the sea, one of the highest courses in England.

Just beyond the common is Water Swallows Green, its name coming from the curious behaviour of a stream near the wayside, which disappears into the earth with swirling eddies and runs underground about three miles till it bursts out in Chee Dale.

The modern church has an old font which may have been in the chapel here 700 years ago, when the Dakins were living in the village. One of two 19th-century memorials to them has on it the strange motto: "Strike, Dakin, the Devil's in the hemp."

In memory of 72 men who died for Peace the east window has figures of our four national saints and groups of soldiers and sailors with a nurse and a priest.

Sixteen Sons for the Wars

FENNY BENTLEY. It is watered by the little Bentley Brook which found its way into Izaak Walton's Compleat Angler, thanks to its trout and grayling.

The old Hall is a farmhouse, but picturesque with gables and a square tower making it look like half a house and half a church. The tower is part of the old manor of John Beresford who fought at Agincourt with a soldier son now lying in the church across the way.

This great soldier, who is said to have marshalled his 16 sons for the wars of Henry the Sixth, has one of the most extraordinary monuments in Derbyshire, an alabaster tomb on which he lies with his wife Agnes, both in shrouds tied up above the head, at the ankles, and below the feet, so that no part of them can be seen. Round the edge of the tomb are helmets, shields, breast-plates, swords, banners, and drums, the things these Beresfords loved, while on one side and at one end are engraved the tiny shrouded figures of 21 children, five of them girls, who must have thrilled to see their 16 brothers riding to battle. In a window of the chapel, with a great heraldic display, are Thomas and Agnes with their son James, who became Canon of Lichfield.

Another window showing the death of St Edmund is in memory of Captain Hans Busk, the gift of a daughter who married a Beresford. Born in Waterloo year, Hans Busk was the founder of England's volunteer army, author of many books about rifles and shooting, and one of the earliest advocates of lifeboats.

The east window shines with blue, green, silver, and gold, and has the four Marys and a picture of Jesus with the children.

The fine little church has nothing older than the 14th century except the red bowl of the font and a doorway perhaps Norman. From the 19th century comes the fine hammerbeam roof of the nave and chancel, with 26 angels looking down. Some are singing, some playing instruments, others praying.

There is a splendid chest with ironwork perhaps 600 years old, and a bench with 14th-century carving; but the precious possession of the church is its ancient screens. The chancel screen, the older of the two, still keeps its roodloft, though the fine vaulting and exquisite cornice has been made new. In the spandrels we noticed a fox with a goose in its mouth. The other screen, now between the aisle and north chapel, once enclosed a chantry founded by James Beresford.

The Flower from the Holy Land

FINDERN. A quiet old place gathered round a shady green on a little hilltop, it has a lovely tale, belonging to the Crusades and the Findernes, who were here 200 years. Sir Geoffrey fought in Holy Land, and when he came home he brought a narcissus to plant in his garden.

The flower took root and flourished. It saw the great days of the Findernes and said Goodbye to the last of the line when Jane Finderne married Judge Harpur and went to Swarkeston. When the last traces of the old home had gone the narcissus went on blooming, growing wild as the garden became a field, until it seemed, as the villagers believed, that it would never die. It found its way into the gardens of the cottages and vicarage, and we think it saw the passing of the little Norman church 70 years ago before a careless hand up-rooted it from the soil.

When Sir Bernard Burke came here to look for a memorial of the Findernes he looked in vain. No stone was left of their old home; there were no monuments to be seen in the church. Sir Bernard asked an old inhabitant what remained of the Findernes. "Nothing," said the old man, "nothing except the little flower in the vicarage garden." Walls and tombs had gone, but the little flower brought to England by a Crusader was growing and blooming still. Now there is only its memory, but in the church an alabaster monument has come to light, bearing traces of shields in memory of Isabella Finderne of 500 years ago.

All that is left of the Norman church is a tympanum crudely carved with a cross, a pattern of squares, and little figures like Dutch dolls. One of its great treasures is an exquisitely engraved chalice of beaten silver. It is 1564, among the oldest in Derbyshire.

We are told that the church-register records the burial of John and Sarah Woollet, who lived together for more than 60 years and were buried in one grave on the 14th of January 1747, he being 91 and his wife 92.

It was here that Jedediah Strutt, the inventor of the ribbed-stocking frame, served a seven-years' apprenticeship with a wheelwright, and no doubt learned much about hoisery from the family with whom he lodged. It was in this family of hosiery makers that he found his wife.

The Rich Man of Good Courage

FOREMARK. It is all charming here, high above the Trent, and lovely are the ways bringing us to it from Repton or from Ingleby. Fine gates lead to the handsome stone Hall with a huge portico and corner bows with domed roofs, built by the Burdetts in the 18th century. It stands at the head of a lake in grounds with groves of trees, noble yew hedges, and a brook for ever babbling over the pebbles.

One who loved this quiet place and made it his home was Sir Francis Burdett, a vigorous opponent of injustice and a 19th-century champion of liberty. He had denounced flogging in the Army and advocated its abolition for fifty years when Queen Victoria was still advocating its continuance as the only means of keeping order in the Navy. He was imprisoned more than once for his advanced views, and suffered through his protest against the Peterloo massacre. It was his courageous efforts which brought about some of the early prison reforms; and as far back as Trafalgar he was urging reforms which were not accepted for another generation. He died in 1844, a man widely loved, generous to the poor and a supporter of every good cause. His youngest daughter was Baroness Burdett-Coutts, and he left her the richest lady in the land.

The little church with the low tower was built in the 17th century, when the old chapel and the neighbouring chapel of Ingleby fell into decay, the stone and wood from Ingleby being used to rebuild it. There are three sundials on three buttresses, and above the chancel window are the Burdett arms and figures of Faith and Hope.

Much old woodwork has been saved. The flat roof has massive beams, the nave walls are lined with oak panelling, and the box pews are so high that we do not wonder the parson climbs up into a three-decker pulpit, a fine Jacobean piece. An extraordinary oak screen between the chancel and the nave is crowned with a pediment of painted glass showing angels and a dove. The font is 13th century; the altar table of grey marble was here on Consecration Day in 1662.

Where the road crosses a belt of wood, a sharp dip between two groves of trees brings us to the river and to what is called Anchor Church, a hermit's rude shrine cut in the rocks centuries ago.

Mugginton
Nicholas Kniveton
and wife, 1475

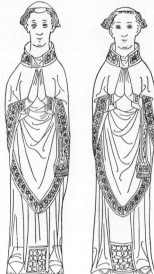

Dronfield
Thomas and Richard Gomfrey, 14 c.

Ashbourne
Francis Cockayne
and wife, 1505

Chesterfield
Sir Godfrey Foljambe
and wife, 1529

Kedleston
Richard Curzon and
wife, 1496

Etwall
Sir John Port (founder of Repton School) with his family, 1557

Its Historian Sleeps in the Abbey

FOSTON. A patch of beauty on a green highway, it has a few picturesque houses, a Hall in a park, a pretty corner where the roots of an ancient elm have escaped from a garden, and a brook winding to Scropton, where the hamlet people go to church.

It has given England a distinguished antiquary. Its great house took the place of the old Hall burned down last century, the home of the Agards, who had lived here from the 14th century till the time of Charles the Second. Here was born in 1540 Arthur Agard, who spent most of his time in London, a patient searcher among old documents in the chapter house at Westminster. He made a wonderful collection of writings, some of them still used by students. A friend of Camden, Stow, and Cotton, he loved nothing better than ancient manuscripts on law and heraldry. He died in 1615 and was buried in the cloisters of Westminster Abbey, close to the marvellous old chapter house in which he had spent the happiest hours of his life, doing things that would have been tedious to most men. He was one of the first members of the Society of Antiquaries.

The Winding Road to a Wonderful Scene

FROGGATT. It lies on a gentle slope above the Derwent, mantled in trees and with gay gardens that are a joy to see, a village so girt with beauty that only those who have time should seek it.

There is a charming viewpoint from the 17th-century bridge which spans the river with two arches odd in size and odd in shape. It is a scene of a wide stream making a marvellous curve, of the softness of lovely meadows and the grace of fine wooded slopes, of the rugged strength of Froggatt Edge stretching like a rampart behind the village.

The glory of the village is this gritstone Edge under which it nestles, magnificent in length and in its precipitous height, with great boulders jutting from its sides and all of it softened by the green of heath and fern and tree.

A winding road climbs to a scene of almost surpassing beauty at the top. With moorland all about us and across the valley, we look deep down below to where the Derwent stretches like an endless snake of trees, winding to Grindleford Bridge and Padley Woods, on towards Hathersage, and beyond to the glorious background of Bamford Edge and Win Hill.

The land which rises across the river to the heights of Eyam is eloquent with a tragic story. On the slopes are the Riley graves where seven of one family in plague-stricken Eyam were buried in eight days. Between them and the river are the deep woods sheltering Stoke Hall, the 17th-century home of William Cavendish, the famous Royalist who smoked a pipe at Marston Moor and spent nearly a million pounds in the cause of Charles Stuart, losing his estates in the end.

Northern Gateway to the Peak

GLOSSOP. It is Derbyshire's little cotton town, busy with printing calicoes and making paper, but finding romance in its glorious situation as the northern gateway of the Peak.

We remember it as the beginning of a magnificent 12-mile stretch of road unrivalled in this lovely county, beside the wild grandeur of Kinderscout, a world of mountain and gorge, moorland and trackless waste and many a waterfall, and the beauty of green valleys as Ashopton draws near. Four miles from Glossop, after climbing nearly 1700 feet above the sea, the road is joined for a spell by the Doctor's Gate, which leaves it again near the inn which is the only sign of life on the road.

The Doctor's Gate is part of the old Roman road from Brough to Melandra Castle, where, on a slope between the meeting of the Etheroe and a brook, can still be seen a few stones and a corner of the wall of the fortress. At Dinting an impressive railway viaduct 120 feet high, with 16 arches each 125 feet wide, strides across road and valley, and north of the town the Etheroe is dammed up into five miles of lakes to supply Manchester with water. South of the town, on the old Monks Road, is the Abbot's Chair, perhaps the base stone of an ancient cross; and a mile from the Chair are Robin Hood's Picking Rods, twin monoliths set in a massive stone.

The charm of the town itself is in its older haunts, where gabled houses climb the road by the church and the tall market-cross stands in the square.

The fine church has little old work left, the nave and chancel having been made new and a lady chapel added in our time. The tower and spire were built last century by the Duke of Norfolk, whose arms are on the spandrels of its doorway. There is an elaborate reredos coloured and gilded, with a lovely rose window above it;

a fine oak pulpit has three angels in niches and three fine groups of figures on the panels; there are three old oak chairs, and the choir stalls and the reredos in the lady chapel are of fine modern craftsmanship. The unusual font of pure white marble has a bowl in the shape of a shell held up by two children, and behind the font are sculptured figures of an angel and a child in front of a cross. William Bagshawe, the Apostle of the Peak, was vicar here till his ejection in 1662.

Not far from the church is a Roman Catholic chapel, with a lovely view of dipping hills. A century old, it has a beautiful altar, fine paintings of the Twelve Apostles, and an old copy of a famous Dutch Crucifixion.

Opposite the chapel is Glossop Hall, a fine 19th-century house now a school, its lovely grounds of 60 acres a public park of rare delight, with a wealth of trees, stream and waterfalls and lake, and playgrounds for all. At the top of the park is an old stone wishing well in the shade of two magnificent beeches, where we have a glimpse of the great house.

The Heroic Doctor

GREAT LONGSTONE. It lies under Longstone Edge, a ridge five miles long rising 1300 feet at Bleak Low, where human skeletons have been found in a barrow. A splendid row of 14 great elms by the roadside adds to its charm, and on the small green is the old cross on its steps, and a monument to 13 men who died for Peace.

Facing the manor house and the Crispin Inn (with its sign of the Cobbler's Saint) is the 18th-century red-brick Hall, reached by an avenue of fine elms and lawn, keeping still a ball-crowned gable of the older home of the Wrights who lived here most of the time from the 14th century till our own day.

The church, in company with two fine old yews and a splendid cross with a new head, comes from the medieval centuries. The lower part of the tower and the south doorway are 13th century; the priest's doorway and the nave arcades are a century younger.

Its glory is in its splendid 15th-century roofs with fine moulded beams, embattled cornices, and bosses of flowers and foliage and arms, one showing a man holding the cover of a tub from which a weird figure has just come out. An old oak screen with a deep cornice shuts off the end of an aisle which was once the family pew of the Eyres. On the wall is an engraved copper plate of 1624 with the portraits of Rowland Eyre and his wife, kneeling as if in a chapel with a window at each side; he in a long robe with lace ruffs at the wrists, she with a ruff and a flowing veil. Both have a rosary.

The eight panels of the fine old font were splendidly carved early this century by a Tideswell sculptor, and its fine new cover has eight figures of kneeling angels. A cross built into an outside wall may once have adorned a gable.

There is a tribute here to a well remembered hero of Great Longstone, Dr Edward Buxton, who early last century, as an old man of 73, sacrificed himself to tend the villagers during an outbreak of typhus. Though the fever visited every house but one, no one died.

Traveller's Surprise

GRINDLEFORD. Time brings changes even here, but nothing can rob it of its glorious setting in a wild and lovely land. It lies under Froggatt Edge, where the Derwent comes down through a glory of woods and meadows to its three-arch bridge, only lately joined by the Burbage Brook which left a moorland home for the joy of a sylvan glen.

The village keeps its charm of other days on the hillside where the road comes down from the great Sir William Hill to the creepered inn; where old grey cottages gather round a green with an old sundial, the only touch of our own day being a pathetic thing it is proud to have, the finely carved cross to the men who died for us.

The village lies at a point of a triangle of roads enriched with scenes it would be hard to surpass, ten miles of river and rock, of lovely woods, of hill and moor. We climb from Grindleford Bridge through Padley Woods to the heather moors, past the stately Long-shaw Lodge to the Fox House Inn. The lodge is an old shooting box on whose pastures famous sheep trials are held (the pastures now with the National Trust); the inn, standing where the roads divide, is a spot endeared to lovers of Charlotte Brontë as the Whitcross where Jane Eyre was set down from the coach during her flight.

And then the road rides by the moors from east to west. We see Burbage Brook near the beginning of its journey, passing under the road where the Toad's Mouth Rock rears its realistic shape. On the moor beyond the rock we see Carl Wark, where Nature and man combined to make a remarkable fortress, mysterious yet in its name and age; near it rises Higgar Tor 1420 feet above the sea, its great mass of rocks heaped in fantastic fashion and weathered to curious shapes.

At Millstone Edge an entrancing panorama comes upon us with such startling suddenness that it is known as the Surprise. A great surprise it is. From this top of a moorland world which is wonderful whatever its mood, kind when the heather is all aglow and magnificent under snow, we look far down to the Derwent in its wooded vale, joined by the Highlow Brook at the end of its lovely journey between two moors with ancient graves; we look beyond Hathersage nestling round its charming church to Bamford Edge, and on to Crook Hill rising between the Ashop Vale and the reaches of the Upper Derwent; we look from Win Hill, Lose Hill, and Mam Tor to a dim horizon of Peakland heights beyond the broad and lovely Vale of Hope.

From Hathersage back to Grindleford the road runs in the valley, through deep plantations under the slopes rising to Eyam Moor, crowned by Sir William Hill.

The Beautiful Home of Dorothy Vernon

HADDON HALL. Set on its gentle hill with the Wye flowing at its feet, it is not a vast structure like Chatsworth, but a lovely English home that has taken nothing but beauty from the centuries it has seen. It stands as a mirror of 600 years in the history of the dukes of Rutland, whose roots were planted by our Norman conquerors. It is one of the finest medieval houses and one of the best pieces of domestic architecture now existing, and is magnificently preserved. There are Saxon and Norman stones within its walls. Its oldest gateway gives entrance to the lower courtyard, a gem of architecture with stone steps, turret and tower, and traceried windows. Here is the oldest part of Haddon, the chapel, still keeping its Norman font and one round Norman column of its arcade. There is a remarkable peep-hole high up in the chancel wall, through which an attendant on the rood-loft could watch the altar and know the right moment for ringing the sanctus bell. There is medieval glass in the windows and wall paintings of the early days of Our Lord.

We cross the courtyard to the banqueting hall which rises to the full height of the building. It has a minstrel gallery fronted by a splendid screen, and at the opposite end is the raised dais, its high table lit by a traceried window. We pass what is now called the dining-room, one end of which is filled by a window of eight lights brilliant with heraldic glass, the other end having an exquisite oriel window. Over the fireplace are the royal arms and the motto, Drede God and honor the kyng; and on two of the panels are the heads of Henry the Seventh and Queen Elizabeth. From this room we climb stone stairs to the state apartments and find ourselves in the drawing-room, which has a fireplace with a surprising splendour of metal work. The Long Gallery, 110 feet from end to end, is reached by six semi-circular steps of solid oak cut from the root of one tree, and it is said (though truly it seems incredible), that the whole floor of this room came from the timbers of this oak. The wainscoting here is probably unequalled anywhere. Big and little arches are divided by pilasters with flowering capitals, and running along the top is a frieze and a battlemented cornice. The design, with its flutings, its geometric patterns, its shields, its wealth of carving, is exceedingly intricate, and the general effect is overwhelming. One end of the room is filled with a window of 24 lights, and from near the other end a rich doorway leads into a room with a strongly barred door opening on a flight of steps leading down to the terrace.

It is this doorway that is known to lovers all over the world as Dorothy Vernon's Door, but she did not go through it to meet John Manners and fly with him over the hills and far away. The legend so dear to all who visit Haddon is spoilt only by being untrue. The state bedroom has in it one of the finest medieval beds still in existence, in which at least one king has slept. A doorway in it behind the Gobelin tapestry leads to the archer's room, with a wooden frame for stringing cross bows, and beyond is the eagle tower, with its 70 steps commanding a view which seems to embrace half a county, with the River Wye winding in the meadows below and the hills of the Peak far away. It is a noble landscape, yet nothing in it can surpass in charm the beauty near at hand.

Bess of Hardwick's House

HARDWICK HALL. It does not impress us as some Elizabethan houses do, for a cold splendour dwells about its great magnificence; but, chilling as the tremendous front of 290 feet may seem, Hardwick Hall, one of the great houses of the Duke of Devonshire, is redeemed indoors by its richness of decoration, its balanced proportions, and its unequalled tapestries.

It has six lofty towers and a mass of closely-packed windows seeming to occupy almost the whole of its great front, so that there has grown up a derisive old Derbyshire rhyme, Hardwick Hall—more glass than wall. Again and again we find on the walls the initials of Elizabeth Shrewsbury with a coronet over them. They stand for Bess of Hardwick, Countess of Shrewsbury, a commanding woman even in the days of Elizabeth, who built this overpowering pile to supersede the old Hall which was crumbling before her eyes. Its ruins stand still in sight of it.

One room of Hardwick Hall, much smaller than the rest, has a story which sets it above all the great rooms with their sumptuous decoration. It is known as the Mary Queen of Scots Room, because her arms are over the door. For fifteen years she was a captive with the Shrewsburys as her guardians, and it is thought she might have made visits here and that this room may have been dedicated to her as a pitying memorial by a woman who was very jealous of her while she lived. The black velvet bed-hangings in the room are beautiful with silk flowers embroidered by the captive Queen. All day she wrought with her needle, and what hopes and fears and memories are woven with these gay colours none of us can know.

In the state bedroom is a bed nine feet square, and in the room we found also a huge travelling trunk made in 1727.

From room to room we pass at Hardwick in an ascending scale of grandeur. The lofty entrance hall has tapestries so wonderful that they must be counted as national treasures, and from this hall we come to a severely beautiful chamber deeply panelled with eight grand pieces of tapestry designed by Jacob Jordaens.

The Hall is imposing, the Presence Chamber is magnificent, the Long Gallery is overwhelming. In the Presence Chamber a great plaster frieze of forest glades, branching trees, browsing deer, and galloping hunters goes round the room, the work of an English craftsman, Abraham Smith. Under the frieze hang tapestries coloured with old dyes and shimmering with gold and silver. The Long Gallery, 160 feet from end to end, with deep window recesses, is a royal spectacle, the architectural masterpiece of the house. It has a painted frieze, and a vast range of tapestries illustrating the story of Gideon. It has portraits famous all over the world, portraits of Elizabeth and Mary Stuart and the beautiful Duchess of Devonshire, and among them reigns one of the countess herself when she was growing old, her beauty gone, though still she looks out as one having authority.

Perhaps the most interesting historic fact concerning Hardwick is that Thomas Hobbes, the philosopher, died in this great house, having been a tutor to the Cavendish family and a frequent visitor here.

Izaak Walton and His Friend

HARTINGTON. Fine hills are round this little upland country town of old stone houses, where an ancient church and a fine old Hall look across to each other from opposite slopes, and an inn reminds us, with its name and its relics, that this is a place our most famous angler loved.

Here a lovely reach of the Dove divides two counties and, within a mile of the town, flows through Beresford Dale, an exquisite haunt of precipitous rocks, luxuriant trees, and green banks mirrored in a crystal stream. Here is Pike Pool in still and green seclusion, with a great lichen-covered rock rising like a slender spire from its depths; and we have a glimpse between the trees on the Staffordshire side of the one-roomed Fishing House built by Charles Cotton in 1674, where he and Izaak Walton talked of everything to do with rod and line. Here, too, is the cave where Cotton hid from his creditors, and the ruins of a tower in the grounds of the old Beresford Hall.

The picturesque and gabled Hartington Hall was built in Shakespeare's day by one of the Batemans and restored 300 years later by another. Robert Bateman was born at Hartington in 1561 and became a merchant in London, one son being knighted by Charles the Second, and one becoming Lord Mayor of London.

The church in the shape of a cross is chiefly 14th century, including the fine west tower with unusual carvings on its west window, the nave arcades, the chancel with its priest's doorway and fine east window, and the two-storeyed porch with a niche for a saint. The sundial on the porch says, So marches the God of day.

Fragments of ancient stones are built into the walls, some engraved with crosses being in the porch. Oldest of them all is a small Saxon stone in the wall of the north transept; carved with interlaced knotwork, it is the oldest thing Hartington has. We found a rose among old glass fragments, four piscinas, and an old font with shields and tracery. In a transept recess is a long tapering coffin stone showing in openings at each end the sculptured head and shoulders of a woman holding a heart, and her feet. Found under the floor of the nave, it is thought she may be Margaret de Ferrers, lady of the manor.

The Disappointed Man

HARTSHORNE. It gave England a great preacher, and has in its church an unfortunate historian.

The preacher was George Stanhope, born in the village after Cromwell's day, a few years before his father became rector. He grew up to be a famous preacher, a bold critic, and a daring writer of Queen Anne's reign.

The historian was Stebbing Shaw, Hartshorne's most pathetic rector, who followed his father in 1799, and was buried here in 1802. With Sir Egerton Brydges he travelled much in Staffordshire, Leicestershire, and Derbyshire, and together they edited the Topographer. In 1788 he published a diary of his travels in Scotland but no one read it. His only popular book was about Cornwall, but he was always trying to write something that everybody would read, and his failures made him bitter. It was during his three years here that he wrote what was to have been a monumental history of Staffordshire, though only the first volume was published. A disappointed man, sometimes insane with grief, he walked about the rectory garden with his eyes to the ground; and often he would be found playing his fiddle trying to wile away his melancholy.

His church has been much changed, but it keeps a 15th-century tower with a row of carved stones in an outer wall, one with arms, and two with figures of dogs; the nave arcade may be as old. There is an ancient font, and a splendid old chest has nine iron clamps; two bells are older than the Reformation, and a silver paten may be about 1480.

On a fine altar tomb lie the alabaster figures of Sir Humphrey Dethick of 1599 and his wife, both with ruffs; Sir Humphrey in armour has a pointed beard, his wife has a pretty French cap and lies on a cushion with a beautiful border. On the front of the tomb are three sons and three daughters. It was one of the Dethicks who went to Cleves to find a fourth wife for Henry the Eighth, and his son Sir William laid a pall of rich velvet on the coffin of Mary Queen of Scots.

From the yew in the churchyard we see a fine old house of brick and timber by the roadside, and two great beeches in the rectory garden.

The Bridge across the winding Wye

The Terrace and the Battlemented Walls
LOVELY HADDON HALL

Barlborough Hall

Hardwick Hall

Lord of Twenty Manors

HASSOP. It shelters under Longstone Edge, charming with its cluster of pretty houses, its great house, and a little church.

For centuries the home of the Eyres, it has seen the waxing and waning of the splendour of this family, once with 20 manors in the country and 20,000 acres in Derbyshire. They built the Hall in Jacobean days, set in a noble park with a fine lake. A mighty chestnut and a giant beech are among the splendid trees guarding the gates to the drive enclosed by an ivied wall and a high yew hedge.

They garrisoned their house for Charles Stuart, fighting the Roundheads at its gates. One of them won distinction at the siege of Newark, and later had to pay £21,000 to redeem his estates. One married Lady Mary Radcliffe, whose father and his brother (the Earl of Derwentwater) were also friends of the Stuarts, both being captured at Preston in 1715 when the earl was beheaded. Charles Radcliffe escaped from Newgate, only to be taken off the Dogger Bank in 1745 when he too was beheaded, a piece of the red baize from his scaffold being treasured at Hassop Hall till a few years ago. It was through Mary Radcliffe that the Eyres were for 40 years Earls of Newburgh, one of whom built the Roman Catholic church, like a little temple, just after Waterloo. Five of its windows have continental glass of vivid colour, and over the altar is a fine painting of the Crucifixion by Luigi Caracci.

Here was Charlotte Brontë

HATHERSAGE. It comes into our literature; it is said to have the grave of Little John; and it has a lovely treasure-house.

For long it knew the Eyres, and some of their old homes are near. Highlow Hall and Offerton Hall stand high across the valley, and beyond the church and towards the moors are Moorseats and North Lees Hall. A 16th-century house in a lovely setting is North Lees Hall, mantled in trees. From here the Eyres fled when James the Second ran away, and close by are ruins of their tiny chapel.

Charlotte Brontë knew Hathersage and brought it everlasting fame in Jane Eyre, giving her heroine a name which breathed association with this place and using the glorious country round about for her moorland scenery. North Lees Hall is in the story, Moorseats is the Moor House where the Rivers sisters lived. The house has been much altered but the little window through which

Jane peeped is here, now inside the hall. The cross-roads three miles off are the Whitcross where Jane left the coach to find her way to Morton, which is Hathersage. Charlotte stayed at the vicarage, helping her friend Ellen Nussey to get the house ready for her vicar brother and his bride.

Close to the vicarage is the handsome church, coming mainly from the 14th and 15th centuries. Lighted by splendid windows, its battlemented walls have pinnacles and gargoyles, among which are quaint faces, a tiger's head, and a muzzled bear. The fine 14th-century tower has a lofty spire as old as itself, and an arch with beautiful capitals; its west window is a century younger. The nave arcades with fine capitals, the lovely priest's doorway, the graceful canopied sedilia, and a lovely piscina, are also 14th century. Of the 12th-century church all that is left is the base of a pillar in the north aisle. In the porch is a broken coffin stone 600 years old.

The arms of the Eyres are over the porch, and their fine array of brass portraits are indoors, all in armour. The splendid 15th-century font has their arms, too, and a beautiful little sanctus bell asks for a prayer for Robert and Joan, whose brass portraits have been for nearly 500 years on an altar tomb under an elaborate canopy in the chancel. Robert has his sword and dagger, his wife has a fur-trimmed gown, and their 14 children are all in a row.

On the wall above this tomb kneel their eldest surviving son Robert with his wife, four boys kneeling behind; two little kneeling figures on the other side of the chancel may be missing daughters.

The brass portraits of Joan's son Ralph and his wife are against the chancel wall, and brass figures of a knight and his lady two generations later, kneel at desks on which there are books; they are Sir Arthur Eyre and his wife.

There is a finely carved bronze plaque in memory of the men of Hathersage who died for Peace.

The churchyard is lovely with trees and has splendid views; it has also four feet of the old cross, and a grave that everyone comes to see. It is by an old yew, and we read that here lies buried Little John, the friend and lieutenant of Robin Hood. We are not sure he ever lived but we know he will never die.

Robin Hood's Little John

IT was Little John who disguised himself as a servant in the house of the Sheriff of Nottingham and carried off the silver plate. He loved his master and came back here with a broken heart after laying Robin Hood to rest at Kirklees. It was he who gave the dying Robin his bow and arrow, and sent him from the world with the praise of his last feeble shot ringing in his ears; he it was who heard his master's last request and obeyed it:

> *Lay me a green sod under my head,*
> *And another at my feet:*
> *And lay my bent bow by my side,*
> *Which was my music sweet:*
> *And make my grave of gravel and green*
> *Which is most right and meet.*
>
> *Let me have length and breadth enough*
> *With a green sod at my head,*
> *That they may say when I am dead,*
> Here lies bold Robin Hood.

The wise will be content with the story, content to hear how his little cap and his bent bow used to hang in this church, and how there was found in his grave a thigh-bone of a man of tremendous stature, 32 inches long.

Every year a band of pilgrims lays a tribute on his grave, a wreath of laurel, or of cotton grass from the moor above Hathersage where he is said to have roamed with his friends. They come in Lincoln green and Sherwood red, from the Ancient Order of Foresters which has taken upon itself the care of this grave which is for ever Robin Hood's England.

The Village Blacksmith and His Sons

HATTON. This little place must have had a great share in Tutbury's pageantry, for such near neighbours are they that we stand on the five-arch 19th-century bridge spanning the Dove with one foot in Tutbury and one in Hatton, looking up to the ruins of the castle crowning the wooded hillside. Hatton saw the rising of the noble castle walls in Norman days and their dismantling in the Civil War; saddest of all its memories was the passing this way of Mary Queen of Scots to be a prisoner there.

It has known the days when a treasure chest was thrown into the Dove while Thomas Earl of Lancaster was fleeing from the castle with the king's men after him; and it has known the excitement of the finding of some of the treasure a century ago, when a hundred thousand silver coins were picked up in the gravel of the river bed near this bridge. We have seen some of them in the British Museum.

A story we heard of this village was of the craftsmen who are appearing in our countryside, for we came upon the Wright family, who began in Tissington where Robert Wright made fine blacksmiths of his four sons and sent them out to establish forges for themselves. In due time about 30 descendants were carrying on the tradition all over Derbyshire. Edward had six sons, four of whom carried the family craft to Brisbane in Australia and Winnipeg in Canada.

The younger generation have added all the modern scientific knowledge to their skill of hand and eye, and are found in all parts of the world. They hold important posts as oxy-acetylene and engineering experts, and one was with the Cunard Company as an expert on oil engines. Far and wide the descendants of sturdy Robert Wright have carried his ringing anvil, his cheerful fire, and the good name of honest workmanship.

Old associations cling to Hoon Hall, a farmhouse now with pointed gables half a mile from Hatton. Here came to live Sir John Pye, a valiant Cavalier, after his king was dead. Made a baronet by Charles the Second, he was brother of Sir Robert Pye the Roundhead, who led an attack on his own father's house when it was garrisoned for the king.

This Way for Kinderscout

HAYFIELD. It is on the threshold of the mighty range of Kinderscout, the great tableland wild and savage in rock and ravine, menacing with trackless wastes of moss and heath and bog, charming with mountain streams and delightful waterfalls, and kindly when the sun lights up the moorland hues of purple, gold, and green. It is a region of solitude that was here when Time began, with a lofty grandeur culminating in the height of Kinder Low, where unknown men are sleeping in a mound 2088 feet above the sea.

We can cross this mountain mass from Hayfield over Leygate Moor, by way of Nab's Brow and William Clough to Mill Hill, with fine views of the Downfall Cliffs and Kinder River. It was round these haunts that Mrs Humphry Ward laid the early scenes of her David Grieve. A few miles across the moorland bring us to the Snake Inn on the famous road from Glossop.

Standing 600 feet above the sea, on the banks of the vigorous little River Sett, Hayfield is busy making paper and printing calico. Like the rest of the village, the church suffered from floods before it was rebuilt last century, for a lusty stream actually flows beneath it. The new church was built on the old foundations, and the level has been raised, the pillars of the old arcades being shortened to serve as props for the new floor.

In the church is a fine marble bust of Joseph Hague, sculptured by John Bacon. Born at Hayfield, he began life as a pedlar, carrying his wares till he was able to afford a donkey, and in 1717 he went to London and made a fortune, which he gave away. It is said that when his own 12 children died, all before they were 21, he adopted another family. He ended his days at Park Hall near here, and was buried in Glossop church where this bust was originally set up. At the rebuilding of the chancel there the bust was placed for safety in the lock-up, where all was well with it till one night it had a drunken man for company, and he, enraged with the silence of his white companion, set about it savagely. It was then rescued from its indignity and set up here in memory of a village boy.

Halfway between Hayfield and Glossop, by the Monk's Road, is the Abbot's Chair, perhaps the base of a wayside cross. A mile or so from it are Robin Hood's Picking Rods, two pillars a foot apart in one massive stone, said to come from Saxon days.

The Story of the Nineteen Arches

HAZELWOOD. It lies on an airy upland between the valleys of the Derwent and the Ecclesbourne, glorying in its fine views; it has a pleasant group with the gabled vicarage, the gabled schools, and a peace memorial hall gathered round the churchyard, from where we see Crich Tower.

The fine little 19th-century church was restored after a fire this century. Some of its lancets have lovely glass, one in memory of one of the Strutts who helped to make Belper famous, another to the Alleynes, one of whom made for the church its finely carved lectern. There is more splendid woodwork in the modern altar table and in the reredos.

It is a lovely ride to Windley down the slope of the Ecclesbourne valley, giving us at the foot of the hill a peep of a house with the delightful name of Flower Lilies.

The tale is told in this village of one of the most astounding examples ever known of human stubbornness. Here just before we called had been blown up a monument to the cunning of a farmer long ago. In the days when the railway came the Midland Railway sought power to cross the land of the tenant of Shottle Farm, and permission was refused unless they would build a bridge for the farmer's cattle from one field to another. The company offered the farmer a level crossing but he would have a bridge, and, there being no way out, a bridge of 19 arches was built, a quarter of a mile long. Then the farmer's cunning was revealed; he prepared to use the 19 arches as his sheds! The Midland Railway, not to be outwitted, dug trenches across the arches and set up fences and made the arches useless to the farmer, and for half a century the bridge remained an astonishing monument of folly. Now it has gone, and the railway from Duffield to Wirksworth runs freely and unhindered.

The Hilltop with a Story

HEANOR. This little hilltop market town, busy with hosiery, coal and iron, and pottery, has more to remember than to see. It has known an interesting group of people.

It knew William Howitt who, with his wife Mary, was writing books for nearly 60 years when there were not so many books to read. William and his brother Richard were born in a house called the Dene, which was being demolished when we called. Close by their old home is the little chapel the family knew, built for the Quakers in 1834. The house, the chapel, and an array of seven stones in its graveyard with the names of Howitt and Tantum (the family name of William's mother) were the only memories we found in Heanor of its most distinguished son. But we remember the delightful bronze busts of William and Mary at the entrance of Nottingham Castle, together intent on an open book.

Heanor has known Samuel Watson, who has been sleeping in its church since 1715. He was a marvellous craftsman, and he did much of the exquisite carving at Chatsworth, where his work is of such striking beauty that when Horace Walpole called he imagined it to be by Grinling Gibbons. His epitaph in the church speaks of his wondrous works in Chatsworth Hall, and declares that his skilful art represented nature "to the very life."

It is possible that Samuel Watson may have been present in his teens at the funeral of a brave rector who sleeps somewhere in the churchyard, John Heiron of Breadsall. He was one of the Nonconformists turned out of their pulpits at the Restoration, a man known in a hundred churches and chapels all over the country, believing in God and fearing nobody. He seems to have escaped from death many times when face to face with it, for he was tossed by a cow, he fell from a window, he was caught in a whirlpool, and fell into a river. But in the end he died a quiet death, and they laid him here in 1682.

By the church, in a house rebuilt on the old foundations, lived one of Cromwell's commanders, General Roper, and at Langley lived a man who gave evidence at the trial of Charles Stuart that he had seen the king unfurl his standard at Nottingham Castle.

On a window sill of the church is a fragment of stone with an inscription of Roman carving, and we recall that 1700 years ago a Roman buried a vase at Heanor with 800 Roman coins in it. Here they lay forgotten until the railway came.

Only the lofty 15th-century tower is left of the old church made new in 1868. There is a small crucifix made from an old oak beam of the belfry, but all else is modern. The oak pulpit has good tracery and a cornice of vine and grape; the oak font-cover was given by the parents of one child who was baptised along with 250 others in 1908; and a window whose interest is in its story has a group of martyrs in memory of a brave sufferer, Jane Burns, showing St Lawrence with his grid, St Catherine with her wheel, St Elizabeth with roses, St Andrew, and St Martin.

The glory of the churchyard is a beautiful Celtic cross carved with scrollwork and knotwork, looking proudly across to the market place. It is a memorial to the men who died for peace.

William and Mary Howitt sleep not far from Keats outside the walls of Rome. This is the story of these two writers.

William and Mary Howitt

SONS of a wealthy Quaker surveyor here, William Howitt, born in 1792, and his brother Richard, seven years his junior, inherited a love of learning and a gift for languages. After schooldays they practised together as chemists in Nottingham but at 29 William married Mary Botham, a Quaker of martyr stock, whose name became inseparable from his own in a long literary career.

Leaving the shop for the study, they wrote jointly a number of books such as the Rural Life of England, and volumes resulting from their wide travels to places of fame and interest, old halls, battlefields, and homes and haunts of our poets.

Mary, like her husband, was a poet and novelist, and was widely esteemed for her books for children. Quiet as was their lives, there was a spice of adventure in their blood, and they settled for some years in Germany, doing excellent translation work there, with works on German life and manners, and the first complete examination in English of the chief Scandinavian and Icelandic writers.

After their return to England William, accompanied by his two sons, joined the gold rush to Australia, worked in the goldfields, and returned three years later, at 63, to publish work which stirred Young England to follow where he had led, and travel about the world. One whom he so inspired was his own son, Alfred, who made a memorable Australian journey to find and carry to Melbourne the bodies of the two heroic explorers Burke and Wills.

It was a Heanor boy, Henry Garnett, born in the middle of the 16th century, who grew up to be a central figure in the Gunpowder Plot.

The Tragedy of a British Scholar

THE son of a Protestant schoolmaster, Henry Garnett left Winchester for London and the Law, but, turning Roman Catholic as a young man, went to Italy. He proved such a brilliant scholar there that it was with great reluctance that the Papal authorities permitted his return on a mission in which his friends pictured him as a lamb going to slaughter. He was to take part in the plots against the Throne, stirring up rebellion first against Elizabeth and then James. It was the Gunpowder Plot which brought to light documents by which he was incriminated.

Garnett fled to Hindlip Hall, near Worcester, where he lay with a companion hidden for four days in a secret chamber, nourished by broth and other warm drinks conveyed by a reed through a hole in a chimney. He was driven out at last by foul air, and more than twenty times he appeared before his judges, but threats of torture and tricks of eavesdroppers failed to betray him into more than one admission. He acknowledged himself "highly guilty, and to have offended God" in not revealing it. He pleaded that he was struck with horror at the proposal, and saw that, as he could not disclose the secret, he used every endeavour to prevail on the conspirators to abandon their undertaking. Sentence of death was passed on him, and he was drawn on a hurdle from the Tower to St Paul's Churchyard and executed.

The Forsaken Treasure House

HEATH. It has left the hollow for the fine view from the hill. In a churchyard bordered with limes is the little 19th-century church with embattled tower and spire and high roofs, looking down over the fields to all that remains of the old church left for the new.

All but the porch was pulled down, but on to that a little chapel was built from the old material which served for a while at funerals. Lonely and forsaken now, it is a modest shelter for a treasure of the past.

The chapel is lighted by a 15th-century window. Old beams and rafters with bosses and shields support the roof. Above the window is a piece of wood which was perhaps once part of the chancel screen, showing carvings of two angels, a rose, a winged lion, and a winged beast with a human face. The masonry of the porch is mainly 15th century, but the entrance arch with two worn heads is 14th. The small stone crucifix over this doorway is perhaps part of the Norman church; the stones with chevrons on the inner doorway were part of a Norman arch, of which the figure of Christ, boldly carved on a stone set in the wall, was perhaps the keystone.

But the great treasure of this deserted chapel is a 12th-century coffin stone in the west wall, its upper part with the head of its cross missing. Each arm of the cross is a star in a circle, and below another circle with a star is a crude human figure with a crowned head, holding a staff ending in a cross. On the other side of the stem are two smaller figures, one holding a bag to the other whose head is like a bird's, and between them is a great cross with another circle on the top.

HIGHAM. It lines the trim road by which the Romans tramped to Chesterfield from Little Chester, its houses (stone-walled and set in gardens), a happy frame for a charming wayside cross.

Higham was a little market town, and the round pillar on the fine flight of seven steps reminds us that butter and eggs were brought here for sale. The cross looks afar to a lovely countryside, or nearer to the busy road at the end of the village, pitying, we may think, the people who hurry on not heeding that Higham is near.

We have beautiful views whichever way we come to it, and especially fine is the panorama from the road from Stretton, looking over the Amber Vale to the Ashover hills.

Here Passed a Queen

HILTON. It has little to show, but it remembers the tragedy of a queen, for the unhappy Mary Queen of Scots would come this way on her journey to Tutbury Castle, one of the many prisons she was to know before she reached Fotheringay. It is said that she called or stayed at the timbered house by the roadside, which was Hilton's glory in other days, built perhaps five centuries ago and known as Wakelyn, from the old family whose home it was. Even now, in its decay, its gables and timbering recall its charm of other days.

HOGNASTON. It is in a pretty lane climbing from a sparkling brook to the Ashbourne road, which rides nearly 1000 feet high along the top of Hognaston Winn.

Its ancient church has fine views of sweeping hills and valley, the trimmed limes making a frame for the sturdy tower. The tower walls, five feet thick, come from the 13th century, the belfry with its pinnacles and gargoyles is 15th. It opens into the nave with a fine pointed arch.

The glory of the church is sheltered by the porch, a handsome doorway of the Normans. The sides have beak-head moulding, the arch has chevrons, while the fine old tympanum is engraved with crude carvings of quaint figures. One is a man wearing a tunic and bearing a staff; he stands between a holy lamb and a group of wild beasts as if to convey the idea of a pastor protecting his flock from attacks. In this doorway still swings an ancient oak door.

The round bowl of the font is Norman, with sunken arches; the chancel arch and the east window are 14th century.

The Flag at Waterloo

HOLBROOK. It is on the hilltop where Derby's invalids find their health again, with houses great and small, and a charming outlook on a pastoral countryside.

The church, lovely with rambler roses, looks out to Horsley's ancient steeple in a wealth of trees on the facing hill. In the churchyard is a row of four Spanish chestnuts centuries old, one fine trunk measuring 14 feet round. They are among the noblest giants we have seen.

The church grew last century from the private chapel built for the Hall which stands above it. Spacious and bright and unusual, it has much splendid woodwork, and a memorial to Samuel Bradshaw who built the original chapel and died in 1768. A round west window has glass in memory of William Leeke who was vicar here. He lies in the churchyard, his gravestone telling us that he carried the colours of his regiment at Waterloo.

Florence Nightingale Comes Home

HOLLOWAY. Sheltering under the crest of a wooded hill, it seems to be at the top of the world as we climb up to it from Whatstandwell. It looks out magnificently over valley and mountain, rocks and trees, which seem to have no end. It has a fine little church built in our 20th century, with a tower forming part of the chancel, nave walls lined with oak, a fine oak pulpit, an alabaster font, and a dazzling east window in memory of those whose names live for evermore and are cut in the stone round the walls. But it is not for this that we come. We come drawn by its memory.

One summer's day in 1856 a lady left a convent on the banks of the Thames, took a train to the nearest station to Holloway, and walked from the station to her home. She was unattended and hardly expected when she opened the door of Lea Hurst to reveal herself to her astonished household. She was Florence Nightingale home again.

We wonder if there has been anything much more dramatic in any village. She was the most talked-of woman in Europe. She had astonished the Government by her courage and frightened every old woman in the Army by her daring. She had torn the red tape of the army to shreds and had scattered her enemies right and left. She had made memorable the great crime of the Crimean War with the opening of another chapter of humanity; she had soothed the last hours of soldiers wounded by war and murdered by neglect. In all our history there was no woman like her, and when it was all over, and she came home, all England waited to acclaim her. The Navy offered her a warship and would have brought her home in state, but she would not have it and came home privately. When it was known that she would go to her Derbyshire home there was talk of triumphal arches, addresses from mayors and corporations, all the panoply and pageantry of regimental bands, and such crowds in the streets as could gather in those days.

But Florence Nightingale would have it not. She arrived unknown in London, lay there lost for a night, and early the next morning knocked at the door of the home of the Bermondsey nuns and spent a few hours with them. Then she went to the station and caught a train at an unusual hour. She arrived unseen at Holloway, walking home alone. A little tinkle of a church bell on the hills a mile away, a little prayer of thanksgiving at the little chapel the next day, was all the greeting she received and all she wished.

She was home again, back in this stone house with many gables in the charming garden above the Derwent. Her father had built it in 1825. Florence, who was born in Florence, came here when she was five. Here she loved to be, to visit the old folk in their cottages, to help with village entertainments; she could be well content, she said, to do this all her life.

Her balcony was a great joy to her, commanding a view of the garden with its stone terraces massed with flowers, and of a meadow beyond, losing itself among the trees running down to the river. Often the sound of the Derwent was in her ears, and she had recalled it one night in hospital at Scutari. There was a great storm, and suddenly Florence Nightingale said: "How I like to hear that ceaseless roar; it puts me in mind of the Derwent. How often I have listened to it from the nursery window!" If ever she lived to see England again, she wrote from the Crimea, the western breezes of her hilltop home would be her first longing.

It was so. It was to Lea Hurst that she came home again, to this house that we may see, to these gardens we may walk round at any time, for here still live the Nightingales, in the spirit of charity for which she gave her life.

One of the precious things she had with her that day was a little tuft of grass. She had brought it all the way, pulled up where our men had fought and died, stained with English blood at Inkerman.

Murray Gilchrist the Storyteller

HOLMESFIELD. Perched at a height of 900 feet, on a ridge of the Pennines which separates the headwaters of the River Sheaf from the headwaters of the Rother, it looks far over Derbyshire to Hardwick Hall, the ruins of Bolsover Castle, and the crooked spire of Chesterfield, while north are the hills round Sheffield.

Where the road along the ridge begins to drop from Holmesfield into the Cordwell valley is a low weather-beaten house with many gables, some panelled rooms, mysterious recesses, fine carvings, and beautifully moulded ceilings. This is Cartledge Hall, home of the Wolstenholmes. One of their sons (Sir John) was a most energetic merchant adventurer, a founder of the Virginia Company. He helped to fit out the ill-fated expedition of Henry Hudson, and his name is preserved by Baffin in his map of the inhospitable region of Wolstenholme Island.

In this ancient hall lived, wrote, and died in 1917 Robert Murray Gilchrist, the Derbyshire novelist, and with him companioned in a David-and-Jonathan friendship, was George Garfitt, who was as devoted to the study of prehistoric man as Gilchrist was to the observation of the present-day people of the Derbyshire hill-country.

Gilchrist was born in Sheffield in 1868. From boyhood he was a writer, and he wrote a dozen or more novels illustrating either modern types of character or 18th-century romance and fashion. Almost invariably his work had a Derbyshire setting. Whether his stories were long or short his literary workmanship was fastidious, and he had the power of making his characters intensely real in the simplest way. He never wrote a best-seller, but many thoughtful judges of literary art have held that his stories have qualities that will always call for notice in any wide survey of fiction.

Gilchrist had a natural gift for friendship, and not a few writers of his day visited him at the old hall on the hilltop, and with him traversed the dales and moors of the Pennine's Derbyshire fringe.

He was a huge man, full of tricksy humour, who could rattle off anything on a piano and surprise the stranger with the sweetness of a tenor voice coming from his massive frame. He died suddenly in his prime, and had a great funeral, including a contingent of Belgian refugees who had found their way to this remote upland village, and to whom he had been kind. He lies in Holmesfield churchyard, on the edge of the hill country he peopled with his fancy. There is a memorial to him in the 19th-century church built on the site of an ancient chapel.

Holmesfield was held by the Deincourts from the Conquest till the 15th century. The old Hall near the church is now a farmhouse, still adorned with a great shield of some of its owners.

A mile below Holmesfield, in the Cordwell valley, is the hamlet of Millthorpe, where Edward Carpenter, the Socialist poet, lived the simple life and evolved his philosophic theories.

The Old Folks at Home

HOPE. We find it in the rich green Vale which bears its name, changing with modern days but with an ancient story. Hereabouts the Peakdale Water meets the little River Noe as it flows from the Vale of Edale between Win Hill and Lose Hill, two fine landmarks towering above the village for another 1000 feet.

Only a mile away is Brough, which the Romans called Anavio, where many relics have been found; some are in Buxton's Museum, with an ancient milestone. There is little to see at Brough today, for the excavations have been filled in, but they revealed an enclosure with walls six feet thick, measuring 340 feet long by 280 feet wide. There was a gateway on every side, and a western tower. Traces of the Praetorium were found, and a sunken chamber dating the fort as 2nd century. For 600 years Brough has had a mill by the bridge, given in early days to the Strelleys for the service of attending the king on horseback whenever he should come into Derbyshire. The mill we see has been made new.

Hope had a Saxon church which may have stood where the church now stands amid fine sycamores. It is thought the round bowl of the font may have been in it; certainly it is very early. In the churchyard is a fine fragment of a cross which was perhaps here before there was a church at all. Seven feet of the shaft remain, carved with knotwork and foliage, and with two figures holding a cross. It is said to be over 1000 years old, and was found in pieces in the walls of the old school. By the porch is a flight of ancient steps on which stood another lost cross.

From the 14th century, when the old church was made new, come the nave arcades of lofty bays, three priest's seats and a piscina, the south doorway, the tower with its short spire, and the lofty tower arch like a lancet window, which gives a charming effect to the interior, framing the west window showing Christ with the fishermen. The clerestory and the fine windows of the aisles are 15th century; two of the windows have lovely glass after the Annunciation of Leonardo in the Uffizi Gallery, Florence.

The chancel has pleasing Kempe glass in the windows, the east showing the Crucifixion in eight panels. Lining the side walls is fine old panelling, some of it the remains of the 16th-century family pews in which sat two great families, the Balguys and the Eyres.

They lived at Aston Hall now a farmhouse, Hope Hall now a hotel, and Derwent Hall now waiting to be drowned. On the chancel wall is a tiny brass with a quaint engraving of old Henry Balguy who died in 1685; it shows him in breeches, doublet, and pointed hat, pen in one hand and a book in the other, and it has this epitaph:

> *Wained from the world, upon it yet I peepe,*
> *Disdaine it, weepe for sinne, and sweetly sleepe.*

There are fragments of old heraldic glass in the windows, ancient tiebeams with quaint corbel heads in the nave roof, a curious old hymn board with a picture of David playing the harp, four big 18th-century pictures of Moses and Aaron, Time and Death, a fine carved oak pulpit from 1652, and two 17th-century chairs in the sanctuary. One of them is said to have been the schoolmaster's chair, and has on it the words, "A Mercury cannot be made out of bent wood."

Two coffin stones at the west end of the church are perhaps 13th century, and are engraved with crosses and bugles, one having also an arrow and a sword. The 15th-century porch has a turret with steps which once reached to the roof of the aisles.

We remember, in this old place, the story of a wonderful group of old folk living when we called. If it is true that where there is life there is hope it is certainly true that where Hope is there is life, long life. Joseph Holme, aged 93, could be seen most days at work in the village forge. Down the street would come Miss Annie Middleton aged 92, shopping basket in hand, for she lived by herself and did all her own work. Every Sunday she was in the church where her ancestors worshipped 700 years ago. Miss Middleton would stop for a chat with Mrs How in her little shop, Mrs How being 90. Another 90-year-old was regularly attending the local lodge of Oddfellows, to keep an eye on the many members of 70 or 80; and Mrs Presser died at the Old Hall three years short of 90.

Round Nimble Jack to Via Gellia

HOPTON. In this delightful green hamlet, with its handful of cottages, is a great house which has long been the home of the Gells, and keeps some traces still of the old home of Sir John Gell, the Parliamentary General of the Civil War. Here was born this extraordinary man who, with a rough and rather brutal spirit, led the forces of the fairest army ever raised in England, and, in Mrs Hutchinson's words, found a place in story which he never merited. His doublet, colours, and other relics are still preserved at Hopton Hall.

Very different was Sir William Gell, famous classical scholar and traveller, born here in 1777. Gentle and kind-hearted, he spent most of his life in Italy, where he wrote books on Rome and Pompeii. His greatest joy was to entertain distinguished people in his lovely home at Naples, where he was often found with his books, drawings, and maps, his guitar, and two or three dogs. There he died in 1836, and he sleeps on a hill above the famous bay. Sir Philip Gell, the last baronet, founded the almshouses in the village.

Their name will long be remembered in Derbyshire, for the Via Gellia, a lovely road through a romantic woodland valley, was named after one of them who made it. One of Hopton's joys is a lovely lane which climbs through a glorious hillside plantation, the way we take to find the Via Gellia two miles away, round the foot of Nimble Jack.

Poets and authors loved and honoured the scholarly son of Hopton, Sir William Gell.

Sir Walter Scott and the Wandering Scholar

THERE were Gells who stayed in and about their ancestral Hopton to strike shrewd blows for the Commonwealth against the Stuarts, but in happier days the family produced in Sir William Gell an even more conspicuous figure in the life of peace. An MA at Cambridge and a Royal Academy student, he went to Greece, exploring and sketching what he believed to be the site and environs of the old Troy, and tracing, as he believed, the footsteps of Ulysses in his little island kingdom.

He settled down in Italy, with homes in Naples and Rome, where he was a centre of an artistic and learned society. Byron, Moore, and Scott were among his friends. Surrounded by noble books, writing, drawing, and publishing, he was a prince of hosts and one of the best known men in Europe.

Apart from these considerations, however, he is endeared to us by one of the most pathetic chapters in Lockhart's Life of Scott. Gell and Scott had met in England and immediately became friends. They did not come together again until 1832, when, although neither knew it, both were dying. Scott had only four months to live, Gell three years. Yet they met with the delight of schoolboys.

At Naples Gell arranged Scott's plans, being warned by him that those who had tried to get classical antiquities into his head had always "found his skull too thick." The two friends went to Pompeii. Scott could not walk, so Gell surrendered his chair to him, and himself obtained another which was tied together with cords and handkerchiefs. So they rode side by side, the old poet surveying the scene in romantic rapture.

It was at Naples that Scott received a letter from his publishers announcing the success of his last two novels, leading him to believe that his calamitous debts had now been paid. "I could never have slept straight in my coffin till I had satisfied every claim against me" he said to Gell. "And now," he added, turning to Gell's dog, "my poor boy, I shall have my house, and my estate round it, free, and I may keep my dogs as big and as many as I choose, without fear of reproach."

Feeling himself free from debt, he confided to Gell that, being no longer forced to write for money, he longed to turn to poetry again, whereupon Gell asked him why he had relinquished it. "Because Byron beat me," he said.

In Rome the old friends laboured at sightseeing, with Gell as guide so solicitous as to remember to tie a glove round the end of Scott's walking-stick lest he should slip on the floor of the Vatican. Scott begged Gell to return home and visit him, and Gell replied that if his health and means permitted he might do so. "If the money is the difficulty," said the poet, "don't let that hinder you; I've £300 at your service, and I have a perfect right to give it to you, and nobody can complain of me, for I made it myself."

Four months later Scott was in his grave, and Gell came no more home to England, for he died at Naples, where he sleeps.

The Gargoyle

HORSLEY. Far back this hilltop had a house which knew the mightiest people in the land. Known as Horeston Castle, with Montforts, Shirleys, and Dukes of Lancaster and Norfolk among its owners, it stood a mile from the village, but not a stone of it remains.

It is the glory of another building which brings us here, an ancient church in a beautiful setting, with carpets of narcissi and daffodils in spring, roses in summer, and always kindly trees. It is seen from afar, and reached by a tree-lined road.

The church is charming to look at, with a strongly buttressed

M

tower and spire, a pretty porch with a medieval crucifix, and a lovely array of windows, with the fine 15th-century clerestory under a handsome parapet of battlements and pinnacles. The church of the Conqueror's day was made new 600 years ago, and from that time comes the tower and the fine spire with two tiers of lights rising to 130 feet. To the 15th century belong the chancel with its sedilia, the fine font with roses and foliage, and perhaps a remarkable gargoyle projecting about two feet from the wall.

Seen in profile, the head of this gargoyle is like some forbidding catlike creature, while a full view of the face shows debased human features. It is remarkable for the carving underneath, which can only be seen standing right below it, seeing the figure clothed in vestments with draped sleeves, an open book in its hands. Below the book, near the wall, is a face. Another great gargoyle with a grotesque head projecting even farther from the wall on the other side of the porch, is not so old.

The south arcade was rebuilt last century, much of the old stone being used again. The reredos is a splendid oak carving of the Last Supper; the fine chancel screen with tracery and a cornice of vine and grapes is in memory of 12 men who died for Peace.

Kept in a glass case is a fragment of an old chancel screen, and in a window are scraps of ancient glass.

Seeing Forty Miles Away

HULLAND. At the end of a fine ridge of high land, it has a magnificent outlook over the hills and moors. From the top of the sturdy embattled tower of the church we can sometimes see the Wrekin in Shropshire, 40 miles away.

The church (hardly a centenarian when we called) has an enormous font, one of the biggest we have seen, its eight sides carved with the symbols of the Four Evangelists. Its bowl is over ten feet round and stands over four feet high.

On a pretty stretch of the Ashbourne-to-Belper road, shaded by lovely trees, stand the old Hall and the new, the old one now a farmhouse, said to have been built with stones from a moated house in the valley which was destroyed in the Civil War.

IDRIDGEHAY. On a busy highway in the lovely valley of the Ecclesbourne, it is part of a golden land in spring, when hills and vale are thick with buttercups. Charming ways bring us to it, but especially pleasing is the long mile from Alton Manor, a fine 19th-century house in Elizabethan style, built of stone from its own estate.

The church and a cross to six men who died for Peace are at the divide of the ways; the church was built in 1855 with tower and spire, and has a porch of stone and timber carved with open quatrefoils.

The Six Famous Windows

ILKESTON. It has fine wide views from the hillside above the valley of the Erewash which here bounds the county, and its church-crowned hilltop is a landmark from afar. A mining and industrial market town, it has nothing finer than its church, whose story is one of many changes since its building late in the 12th century.

The church has grown with the town, and is today a spacious place with lovely windows and arcades like a graceful avenue. Of the three eastern bays of each arcade, dividing the old part of the nave from the aisles, those on the north are about 1300; those on the south are of special interest, for, coming from the close of the 12th century when the Norman style was changing to English, they show the two styles in the chevron moulding on the slightly pointed arches. Their capitals are square, resting on the original round pillars, which have been lengthened three feet.

The church is truly notable for its window tracery, especially in the six windows in the older part of the church, three in the north and three in the south walls of the aisles. They were rebuilt after the old design in 1855, when an architectural report said that "no church in England possesses any to equal them, and they can never be surpassed in the lightness and elegance of their tracery." The great east window, with a wheel in its tracery, is of the same time, and shows the Madonna, the Good Shepherd, and Christ with the fishermen.

From about 1280 come the sedilia and the double piscina, all of most beautiful workmanship. The piscina is divided by a round pillar into two arches. The chancel arch rests on lovely corbels carved with lilies and passion flowers, wheat, and vine. Across the chancel is a 14th-century stone screen, its five arches springing from marble pillars.

Since the middle of last century the very beautiful arcade of three lofty bays between the chancel and the spacious chapel of St Peter has become again the glory of the church; it is all that is left of a lovely 14th-century chapel and was long walled up. The capitals of its clustered pillars are daintily carved with foliage cunningly contrived to represent gnome-like faces which escape the casual eye, there being more than 40 of them. In a bay of the chancel arcade is the stone tomb of a knight in chain mail, his legs crossed, his feet on a lion, and on his shield the arms of Cantelupes. He may be Sir Nicholas who founded the chancel, dying about 1280, or his son Sir William.

Many adventures the tower has had. A lofty tower and spire came to grief in a storm in 1714; only the tower was rebuilt, and this gave place to another in 1855 on the old foundations. This was moved westward when the nave was doubled in length 25 years ago. One thing it has kept through all the changes, its 13th-century archway. Other old relics are a tiny piscina in one aisle and a founder's recess in the other. There is the base of a 13th-century font, found in the vicarage garden. An altar table in the chapel is 1622, and a 15th-century chest has two medallions, carved with a rose and a tiny head.

It is one of the few churches in which the organ is interesting, for it has built up within it one from a London church on which the great Mendelssohn is known to have played. Mournful music it must have played in memory of those Ilkeston men who did not come back, for there were 480 of them. The vestry was built in their memory, and all their names are on a cenotaph in the market-place, carved with the Sword of Sacrifice and the Wreath of Victory.

Dreaming by the Trent

INGLEBY. It comes at the end of a lovely ride, whether we ride from Repton or Ticknall or Swarkeston; the loveliest way is perhaps the charming lane from Swarkeston, in company with the winding river and the little hills.

It is only a handful of dwellings sheltered by steep wooded cliffs, dreaming by the Trent. Even its church has gone, being in such sorry plight in the 17th century that its stone and wood were given away towards the building of Foremark church a mile away. Strangely enough, it has another church it is hardly likely to lose. We come to it higher up stream at a bend of the river, where the bank is broken by deep clefts and sharp rocks out of which have been fashioned several rooms with windows and a doorway. It is called Anchor Church, for it is said to have been the cell of a hermit or an Anchorite.

The Viceroy to His Wife

K EDLESTON. It is an oasis of quiet on the edge of a glorious deer park, with groves and plantations and a stream of many waterfalls all making a lovely setting for the great house.

One of the stately homes of England is Kedleston Hall, built by the Adam brothers for the first Lord Scarsdale in classical style after the fashion of the time, with elegant Greek columns and fine statuary, and lofty rooms abounding in treasures. Its front is 360 feet long, a central block and two wings connected by corridors. On the north side a double flight of steps leads to a fine portico with six Corinthian pillars 30 feet high, supporting a pediment with sculptured figures. The entrance hall has a vaulted ceiling rising to the top of the house, supported by 20 Corinthian columns. A handsome room is the domed saloon, 63 feet to the top of the dome, and divided into lovely Grecian alcoves. Boswell tells us that Dr Johnson described the house as being more suitable for a town hall than a house, and that he found more delight in finding his Dictionary here than in all its other treasures.

On the road from Quarndon we have a splendid view of the Hall with its fine background of trees and the beautiful Adam bridge with its cascades. The village has had a great adventure, for when the great house was built the houses were all close by, and were moved some distance away to allow the land to be brought into the park. The turnpike road was given a bend, and the happy little Cutler Brook found itself filling a lake among the trees.

The story of Kedleston, which had belonged to Earl Godwin, father of the last of our Saxon kings, is one with that of an illustrious family whose home it has been for eight centuries, of father and son without a break till the 19th century, when a nephew came into this noble heritage. The first of them was Richard de Curzon, whose father came over with the Conqueror: two of his grandsons divided their estates, Richard settling at Croxall, Thomas at Kedleston.

All along the line we find distinction in their train. Robert Curzon was a 12th-century cardinal, hated by the clergy because he exposed their vices, by France because his diplomacy was always on the side of England, and by the rich because he championed the poor. He gathered great companies of Crusaders, and was present at a Council in 1215 when part of France was handed over to Simon de Montfort.

The Curzons were among the most loyal of Charles Stuart's supporters; they became baronets with John Curzon in 1641, the fifth baronet being made the first Lord Scarsdale in 1761. It was he who built the Hall.

Most distinguished of them all was George Nathaniel Curzon, known to all in the generation of the Great War. Born here, he became Viceroy of India and was leader of the House of Lords till he died as Marquess Curzon of Kedleston in 1921. Here, by his home, they laid him. He gave this church the beautiful chapel in which he lies, building it in memory of his first wife Mary Leiter. Her serene figure, very lovely, lies on an exquisite tomb of white marble, her husband beside her now, and two angels bending over them with a veiled crown. Round the parapet of the chapel are the words in Latin, *Because he loved much.*

Charming in every detail is this chapel, glowing in the soft light from windows filled with lovely glass, three of them with nine Marys, and one with St George and the Dragon. In the three bays between the chapel and the nave are iron grilles of fine design. The oak roof has fine carving and bosses, and angels supporting the tiebeams. The floor is of green marble from the Central Asia Lord Curzon knew and loved so well. Under a handsome canopy on the north wall is a carved oak seat. In the west wall are two Italian marble panels of St Catherine with her wheel, and St Michael with the Dragon, reproduced from famous sculptures in the sacristy of St Maria Maggiore in Rome. The altar covers are of old Genoa velvet. Two candlesticks and a lectern are of Spanish silver, a Portuguese silver-gilt crucifix is nearly 300 years old. There are two silver lamps, and a great pendant for electric light made by a German craftsman in the 18th century.

The whole chapel is in 15th-century style, designed by Mr G. F. Bodley, R.A. Its decorative features and furnishings were the work of Lord Curzon, who also designed the grilles. The monument is by Sir Bertram Mackennel, R.A., the windows of the nine Marys were designed by Mr F. C. Eden and are the work of Mr J. Fisher. The inscription on the tomb is by Lord Curzon himself:

> *There will I ask of Christ the Lord*
> *Thus much for Him and Me:*
> *Only to live as once on earth*
> *With love; only to be,*
> *As then awhile, for ever now:*
> *Together I and He.*

Lovely glass shines in the rest of the windows of this fine little church, which has the shape of a cross. All that is left of the 12th-century structure is the south doorway with chevrons and beak-heads and a tympanum showing traces of a man on horseback blowing a horn. Most of the church as we see it comes from about 1300, including the pointed arches supporting the central tower. The upper stage of the tower, with its embattled parapet and four pinnacles, is perhaps 15th century.

A great piece of sculptured stone about seven feet long, now making a canopy over a recess in the chancel, may have belonged to a founder's tomb; it comes from the 14th century, and has a crocketed finial and pinnacles. About 1700 the high oak pews with finely carved panels of open work were placed in the chancel. The oak ceiling of the tower and the oak roof of the nave come from 1885, the rest of the church having been restored when the memorial chapel was built. There is a Prayer Book of 1687, the gift of Lady Sarah Curzon in 1715, who gave also a lovely silver chalice 300 years old.

There are many memorials of Curzons, from the 13th century to our own time. A 13th-century coffin stone, carved with a cross, was found 50 years ago perhaps covering the skull of Thomas de Curzon. A most unusual memorial lies under the chancel floor, where two wooden lids lift up to show the heads of a knight and his lady sculptured within quatrefoils, the knight in a hood of mail and the lady in a coif and wimple. Although they appear to be separate, they are part of a great stone four feet wide and ten inches thick, sunk more than a foot below the floor, and they are 13th-century work.

Under a canopy in the chancel lies the figure of Sir John Curzon, M.P. for Derbyshire when Richard the Second was praying for a little, little grave, or to be buried in the king's highway. He is in plate armour, his head on a helmet and his feet on a lion. Another Sir John Curzon, who died about 1450, lies with his wife on an alabaster tomb with two groups of their seven boys and ten girls. The knight is in armour, his head on a helmet and his feet on a dog; his wife has a square headdress with lappets and veil, a mantle tied with a tasselled cord, and a triple chain round her neck.

The brass portraits of their son Richard who died in 1496, and his wife are in a stone on the chancel floor, with a group of eight daughters; their four sons are gone.

A 17th-century monument shows two angels unveiling the figures of Sir John Curzon and his wife; below them are four sons and three daughters all in curtained niches, the girls with ringlets like their mother, and the boys with long hair. In the north transept is a great marble monument with two 18th-century figures in flowing robes, Nathaniel Curzon and his wife Sarah; another monument with a group of four figures is to their son Nathaniel, father of the first Lord Scarsdale. In one of the transepts is a bust of Sir John Curzon who sat in Queen Anne's Parliament and lived to see the Stuarts go and the Georges come.

The most famous of the Curzons was he who lived into our own time, George Nathaniel, Lord Curzon.

The Man Who Endured Bitterness Nobly

HE was one of those men who live very near the heights yet never seem quite to reach the top. He was proud and brilliant and held high office, but the world of his day felt that his heart was broken because he could never quite have his way.

He was in public life for more than a generation, and became Viceroy of India, but it was his bitter disappointment not to be Prime Minister. He was chancellor of one university and lecturer at another, he was a Knight of the Garter and an earl, he had charge of the Foreign Office after the war, and through the war he was a member of the small War Cabinet and Government leader in the House of Lords; but he longed to be Prime Minister and he was not popular enough.

He had made his way in his early days by the power of his brain and not by his aristocratic birth, for in his youth he was poor and earned his living by writing. He was a great student of the Far East, and he wrote some poems in war time.

When he died in 1925 it became known that he had for years suffered great physical distress. It was the man who was chosen Prime Minister instead of Lord Curzon who spoke of him in the House of Commons and said that it was twice his duty to see Lord Curzon suffering bitter disappointment, and never for one moment did he show that he was dissatisfied, never did he bear a grudge, never did he fail in his duty. He felt at both these times that he had seen in Lord Curzon that, in that strange alloy we call human nature, there runs a vein of the purest gold. He died, said Mr Baldwin, in harness, a harness put on himself in youth and worn triumphantly through a long life, a harness he never cast off till his feet had entered the river.

Ilam Rock

Lion Rock

Pickering Tors and the Watch Box

IN LOVELY DOVEDALE

The Derbyshire Border, near Three Shires Head

Matlock Bath from the Heights of Abraham

The Upper Valley of the Dove

Iron Tors, Dovedale

Hanson Tor, Dovedale

Beresford Dale, a lovely reach of the Dove

It might well be, added Mr Baldwin, when we look back on that life of devoted service and of the perpetual triumph of spirit over flesh, that in some places in this Earth, early on that Friday morning, there may have been heard faint echoes of the trumpets that sounded for him on the other side.

A Little Loveliness

KILLAMARSH. It is busy with coal and steel, but it has two fine things in its church, crowned by a 15th-century tower, and keeping a few windows as old.

One is the doorway inside the porch, adorned with chevron moulding by the Normans; the other is a small window of lovely old glass showing a crowned Madonna with a sceptre, and the Holy Child, whose hands are grasping a lock of her hair. Killamarsh has lost much, but she treasures this precious bit of loveliness.

Nature's Friend John

KING'S NEWTON. A village of rare delight, it has on one side the winding valley of the Trent with Weston's spire in the trees; on the other, Breedon's church high on the hill.

Its road, with wayside lawns, is packed with charming pictures. From a great square flight of steps a fine lime grows, taking the place of the ancient cross whose richly carved head is now in Melbourne church. Near it is the old church house with round steps. A fine gabled house looks across to a charming row of brick and timber cottages with splendid trees each side. A little inn and the delightful house called Four Gables (both built of brick and timber) look over the way to the great house behind a charming garden wall patterned with ivy and lined with trimmed limes. It followed the old Hall burned down last century, long the home of the Hardinge family. It was Robert Hardinge who built the arch over the spring by the side of the old packhorse track, in 1662.

Two men who loved the outdoor world are remembered here. One was William Speechly, who early in the 19th century was gardener to the Duke of Portland. He was a noted agriculturist and wrote a useful country book. The other man was John Joseph Briggs, whose father spent 88 years on a farm close by. John, a patient naturalist and topographer, was content to farm the same fields, happy to watch the life of the country round about. What Gilbert White did for Selborne John Briggs did for King's Newton. A careful observer of every sort of life, he was the faithful chronicler of the seasons for thirty years, a student of antiquities of Derbyshire, and a contributor to many of the scientific journals of his day. When he died in 1876 he left behind him a valuable collection of notes and records which are still waiting to be given to the world.

With his deep love of the country, Briggs acquired from his schoolmaster an instructed taste for natural history in all its rural aspects; but his bent for recording in diary and journal was innate in him as in the beloved old parson at Selborne.

Day by day, year after year, Briggs set down in his manuscript volumes all that could interest the sympathetic observer of nature throughout the area over which his activities carried him. They were never published. Where he did regularly achieve print was in respect of endless notes and sketches in newspapers and periodicals, of places of interest in the Midland Counties unnoted in their triumphal progresses by the grand monarchs of antiquarian literature. Several volumes of Derbyshire history and antiquities, mainly parochial in character, were issued during his lifetime, but the bulk of his work, fruit of half a century of collecting and writing, including the biographies of nearly 700 worthies of his native county, were left in manuscript, and so remain.

Spacious Green and Rocky Gorge

K INGSTERNDALE. A mile of beauty high above the lovely Ashwood Dale, we come to it down the high road from Buxton, but there is great joy in its approach from the Dale, both for the magnificent view as we climb the rough and winding way, and for the suddenness with which we burst upon the village. All at once the road opens on to a spacious green with the broken cross in the middle and farmsteads gathered round.

Its neat church is 19th century, built by Sir Henry Hawkins who lived in the house at the top of the lovely glen of Cowdale. He built it of local stone, with a bellcot, lancet windows, and dormer lights in the high roof.

There are memorial windows to the Pickfords, who live at the great house among the trees. William Pickford, Baron Sterndale, Master of the Rolls, has been sleeping in the churchyard since 1923. In one of the windows is Peter with the keys, and a dramatic picture of St Agnes as a bound and kneeling figure at the block, with the executioner standing by.

A path opposite the church leads into the rugged gorge of Deep Dale, wild and romantic, where precipitous rocks rise on each side of the rock-strewn way, running to the Wye in Ashwood Dale by Topley Pike. It is famous for a great cavern where many Roman relics have been found.

It was here that there lay down and died, in some far-back prehistoric age, a great brown bear who in course of time was found embedded in a cave of Deep Dale. We have seen its skull in Buxton.

What Samuel Cleater Said

KIRK HALLAM. It looks across to the church-crowned hill of Ilkeston. Its own little church has a low tower and walls 500 years old, its oldest relics being two fine fragments of Norman beakhead moulding (once part of a chancel arch and now built into the porch), and the lovely bowl of a Norman font. There are three old sedilia, and a piscina niche which is rare for having a tiny niche at each side.

There are memorials to the Newdigates who have had land here for many generations and had for their ancestor a Saxon chief. A brass tablet has a rhyming epitaph to old Patrick Rice, one of the queer fellows who pop up in our village histories. He wrote his epitaph two years before his death in 1766, and at the same time had his coffin made, keeping it behind his bed and using it regularly till his death as a home for his Sunday clothes.

Samuel Cleater's epitaph on a stone in the churchyard tells of his sturdy patriotism in this doggerel;

> *True to his king, his country was his glory,*
> *When Bony won, he said it was a story.*

The Saddest Plumber Story

KIRK IRETON. Its little old church with a sturdy tower and a leaning porch and crazy stone walls inside is 700 feet above the sea. It looks over the village to miles of lovely country, its companion a cross to ten men and a boy of 19 who did not come home again.

The Normans began the tower, which was finished in the 14th century. They built the doorway through which we enter, and a pointed arch was built inside it when the porch was added six centuries ago. They raised the nave arcades with round pillars and boldly carved capitals, but their font came to a tragic end last century when, after being used for a time as a water butt by the chancel, a plumber made a fire under it to melt some lead and split it to pieces. It is one of the saddest plumber stories we know.

It is in the fine little 14th-century chancel that we find the great joy of the church, a very charming doorway under six feet high, with a slender pillar on each side, and flowers in the moulding of the pointed arch. It is an architectural gem.

It was in the neighbouring hamlet of Blackwall that Anthony Blackwall, the distinguished classical scholar, was born in 1664. He was headmaster of Derby School when only 24, and while he was headmaster at Market Bosworth Samuel Johnson was perhaps his assistant. One of Derbyshire's great schoolmasters, he had many brilliant pupils, one of whom gave him a living in Surrey. He was over 50 when he went to London for ordination, and as a young chaplain began questioning him on the Greek Testament the examination was cut short by the Bishop of London entering and saying to the examiner: "Mr Blackwall knows more of the Greek Testament than you or I."

The Parson and his Gloves

KIRK LANGLEY. We find two Langleys on the road to Ashbourne from Derby, parts of an ancient village by a Roman road, divided by a brook into Kirk Langley with the church, and Meynell Langley recalling the family who have known it for 800 years. Their Tudor home gave place to what is now Langley Hall, a handsome brick house with lovely views, built last century by Pugin.

The great stone house where the Meynells live today is seen from the Ashbourne road, its lovely park with drive and fishpond made in the first years of last century; for Meynell Langley's ancient deer park of over 500 acres was destroyed in the Civil War, when it belonged to the Royalist Duke of Newcastle, the timber being cut for charcoal.

Very pleasant is Kirk Langley with its old houses, a beautiful church, and a 17th-century rectory with a lovely garden, standing where there has been a rectory since Henry the Eighth. Against it is an old tithe barn with a 19th-century archway.

The way to the church is through a lychgate and under a fine yew like a bower. Made new 600 years ago, it is spacious and full of light. There are three beautiful stone seats with trefoiled heads and clustered shafts in the chancel, three piscinas, medieval tiles in the Twyford chapel, and an ancient font which has come into its own after being for a time in a farmyard and then used as a poor-box. The bowl has a lead lining which overlaps the rim and forms a border with a finely embossed design.

There is lovely modern glass in the east window, and a fine modern chancel screen. Screens of 50 years ago enclose two chapels, one with a fine cornice and traceried panels having some of the 15th-century screen worked into it.

The chief treasure of the church is a screen under the tower, where the light is all too dim to do justice to what is said to be the oldest timber screen in Derbyshire. It is what is left of the 14th-century chancel screen, unusual in design, with a band of trefoils above an arcade of trefoiled openings, while below is a band of quatrefoils with flowers.

One of many memorials to the Meynells is to William Meynell, who died last century on the Danube while leading the Turks against the Russians; it has his bronze portrait. On an altar tomb are the engraved figures of Henry and Dorothea Pole, he in 16th-century armour with his head on a helmet, she in a French cap and a fur-lined cloak. A stone on the north wall has the portrait of Alice Beresford of 1511 in pointed headdress and a close-fitting gown with a long girdle.

One of Kirk Langley's much-loved rectors was Henry James Feilden, who died in 1885 after being here 64 years. He used to put on a black gown and a pair of black gloves before he entered the pulpit, which in his day was an ugly two-decker near the tower.

Winding Lanes and Little Hills

KNIVETON. Tucked away in a land of winding lanes and little hills and streams are its grey stone houses, looking up to a tiny church which has seen Norman days.

It stands in a churchyard with a trickling stream and a gate shaded by a great sycamore, a little aisleless building with a low tower and a short spire. The Norman remains are in the arch of the porch, and the doorway within which has a hood adorned with a stone head in the middle and crude carvings at the ends. A round stone with a cross, let into the wall of the nave, is thought to be Norman too.

The font is 13th century, the bowl carved with an effective border round the top, and resting on clustered pillars.

Fragments of ancient glass in the chancel glow with the arms of the old family of Kniveton; it was Lady Francis who gave the altar its lovely flagon and chalice in 1572. Sir Andrew Kniveton became so impoverished through his loyalty to Charles Stuart that he had to sell most of the family estates.

The Wooden Cross

LITTLE EATON. In this village sheltered by a fine line of hills, with the little Bottlebrook running by the busy road to Derby, we came upon a poignant memory, a name and a simple wooden cross which, like Wordsworth's simplest flower that blows, can give "thoughts that do often lie too deep for tears."

We get a fine aeroplane view of Little Eaton's housetops as we drop down from Breadsall Priory, and one of the things that charmed us here was the lovely churchyard climbing as high as the church tower and making a fine lookout over the village playing-fields and the Derwent valley. There is little in the church for the pilgrim, but an odd thing we remember about it is that before it was rebuilt in 1791 it had been a blacksmith's shop. We have long known of the village blacksmith who went on Sunday to the church, but whoever heard of the blacksmith going on Monday?

It was in this churchyard that we found our memory, for among the names of the men of Little Eaton who did not come back, on the oak lychgate to their memory, is that of Theodore Percival Cameron Wilson; and at the foot of a path, between a cypress and a lilac tree, we found a wooden cross set up on three steps with his name and the words: His grave is unknown.

He was the brilliant son of the vicar here when the Great War burst upon the world. He loathed war as the hideous thing it is, and he loved this countryside, the vicarage garden in which we found still blooming the lilac of which he wrote on leaving his home:

Never again a thrush in the lilac at six o'clock, a bee droning up the sunlit silences, a poplar pointing against the stars, the village voices and cries, the faint scent of wet lavender in the night.

So from this village went out one more of those everlasting men who, not allowed to live for England, died for her instead.

He was one of two poets who lived in this vicarage, he and his sister Marjorie, both with a proud niche in our poetry.

Brother and Sister Poets

THE brother went in the first fortnight of the war, enlisting in the Guards. One spring day in the last year of the war, hearing that one of his men had been left wounded on the barbed wire, he crawled out in the face of machine-gun fire and brought him in on his back. The next day, in a moment when he was joking and laughing, a bullet struck him and he fell. The enemy was 200 yards behind. No trace of his burial has ever been found.

Among his papers they came upon letters which showed what those who knew him thought of his chances in life; and indeed he had qualified himself for a high place among the poets. He had had the great delight of seeing himself printed by Mr J. A. Spender in the old green pages of the Westminster Gazette, the best evening paper ever offered to an intellectual Englishman. He wrote for Punch. He wrote a novel which his publisher thought one of the best-reviewed books of the year.

He had been teaching at a preparatory school at Hindhead, a work to which he gave his whole heart; in his book of poems is a section called The Sentimental Schoolmaster, and in it are these lines of pity for An Exceedingly Small New Boy:

> For lo, O little cub, you are dragged forth!
> And all your hushed retreats are far away.
> And fairies wring their silver hands in wrath
> And bow their heads and weep for you today.
> They know that in a month you will unlearn
> The thousand laughing melodies of Pan,
> And unto such as me for guidance turn,
> And I, my God, what am I but a man?

The poems in his small volume Magpies in Picardy are the high-water mark of his promise. It was a magpie in Picardy that told him secret things:

> He told me that in Picardy,
> An age ago or more,
> While all his fathers still were eggs,
> These dusty highways bore
> Brown singing soldiers marching out
> Through Picardy to war.

When his body was gone they found this in one of his pockets:

> Suddenly one day
> The last ill shall fall away;
> The last little beastliness that is in our blood
> Shall drop from us as the sheath drops from the bud,
> And the great spirit of man shall struggle through,
> And spread huge branches underneath the blue.
> In any mirror, be it bright or dim,
> Man will see God staring back at him.

Perhaps most of all his friends love that fine poem of his which begins with these two verses:

> *My soul is an Inn whose guest is God.*
> *All this dark, dusty, winding stair*
> *Into the silent sunlit room He trod,*
> *And He is there.*
>
> *Hush! the great door is locked and barred:*
> *Only He and I have the key.*
> *See you the prayers that stand on guard,*
> *Watching for me?*

His sister Marjorie, who has now gone out into the Universe to join him, was a true poet, with a seeing and understanding mind which made her poems an inspiration and delight to the great multitude of readers of the Children's Newspaper. She was one of our visitors in this Grand Tour of England. She would see a small thing and make it into a great one with her words. She would sit on a seat in the park with a poor woman, and all unknowingly the poor woman would be suddenly enriched in a jewel of literature. She had the power of putting life itself into words, of moving us to laughter or to tears, and of stirring us with the solemn thoughts of life. Too modest to know it, she had the quality of genius which cannot see itself because it is so natural and so quiet.

And she was the bravest of the brave, the very spirit of pure chivalry. When, in the midst of life with all her mental powers at their best, she was told that she must die, she sat down and wrote one of the bravest letters that have ever been in the post, begging the Editor of this book that he would not be too sad for her for *it would be wonderful to go before she was old*. Then she sat down and wrote a few verses called A Memory, beginning, My wandering heart is over the fields, and ending with those dauntless lines that nothing could keep her spirit apart

> *From the days when my head was crowned with stars*
> *And a glory was in my heart.*

John Ruskin and the Fools

LITTLE LONGSTONE. Sheltering under Longstone Edge, this quiet hamlet is a joy to find, with remains of the old stocks and charming houses on its mile-long road.

One of the houses is the twin-gabled manor behind fine hedges of holly and yew, built perhaps in the 17th century by one of the

Longsdons who have kept land here through 28 generations. They have lived at Little Longstone all the time, but not always at the manor house.

At the end of the road, at Headstone Head, is a surprise in store for all who come, for with startling suddenness there opens out one of the finest natural sights in Derbyshire, a glory of rock and wood and water. It is a view of the Wye deep down in the valley, flowing at the foot of fine hills as it comes from Miller's Dale and Upper Dale, and making a glorious curve round the foot of Putwell Hill as it begins its journey through the lovely Monsal Dale. It is an enchanting river scene, where the Wye forgets its impetuous ways and flows in broad and gentle fashion, now through bright green meadow, now mirroring the lofty hills.

It is true that we see the railway bridge on its five high arches, but Nature can well hold her own. It was this bridge that vexed the spirit of John Ruskin, bringing from him these bitter words about the valley:

You might have seen the gods there morning and evening, walking in fair procession on the lawns, and to and fro among the pinnacles of its crags, but the valley is gone and the gods with it, and now every fool in Buxton can be in Bakewell in half an hour, and every fool in Bakewell at Buxton.

But the valley is by no means gone, and there are more wise folk than fools, and wise John Ruskin was extravagantly wrong once more.

The Proud Boast of the Harpurs

LITTLEOVER. Its church of many gables and its fine vicarage share a glorious prospect. At the edge of the lovely churchyard a great memorial cross towers above the road.

The church has a Norman doorway and a huge Norman font, its oldest possessions. There are 14th-century windows in the chancel and south aisle, and an unusual effect is given to the nave by the modern dormer windows.

On the chancel wall is an elaborate coloured monument to Sir Richard Harpur and his wife; they are kneeling at a desk, Sir Richard in a long gown with hanging sleeves, his wife in a hood and ruff, three sons and three daughters below with a babe in swaddling clothes. It is a typical 17th-century group. The old Hall here was built by Sir Richard's father, a judge of Elizabeth's day who lived at Swarkeston.

It was the proud boast of the Harpurs that their ancestors were of the Conqueror's days; that their women were of the proudest homes in the land, and that they have given Derbyshire more High Sheriffs than any other house in the county.

The Bad Old Days

LITTON. Nearly a thousand feet above the sea in a land of stone-walled fields, it has old stone dwellings on a road graced by little greens. On one of these are the square steps of an ancient cross with a modern pillar, and at one end of the village is a new church with just a nave and chancel. The village has little else, but its name has travelled far, for it was the home of the ancestors of the Earl of Lytton.

A farmhouse is on the site of their old home, which was in Charles Stuart's day the birthplace of William Bagshawe, the Apostle of the Peak, the great Nonconformist who sleeps at Chapel-en-le-Frith.

The rocky ravine of Litton Dale leads down from the village to Tideswell Dale, which ends at a lovely stretch of the Wye enbosomed in sheer cliffs and hanging woods. Here is Litton Mill, gladdened today with flowered cottages and gardens, but with memories of the bad old days of a century and more ago when terrible cruelty to the pauper apprentices sent many of them to an early grave in Tideswell churchyard. Cressbrook Mill, farther down the river, belonged to William Newton, the Minstrel of the Peak, and conditions there under this carpenter-poet were much better for the pathetic little ones.

A Little Town of Our Time

LONG EATON. At the end of the rich mineral valley of the Erewash, a quiet oldfashioned village in living memory, it has outstripped its neighbours and become a bright little town.

Once it belonged to Sawley; today it is making Sawley part of itself. Churches, chapels, and fine schools have come into being in this place which has set its playing-fields in gardens and its library in lawns. Near by are the biggest railway sidings in the world at Toton, while a mile away the Trent flows on through lovely meadows and under wooded hills.

At the heart of the town is a link with the past in a church the Normans and the Saxons knew. In the early days a chapel of Sawley, it was refashioned 600 years ago, when the tower and its spire were built. Now the old nave and chancel have become the aisle and chapel of a larger building; and so wisely were the additions made that the ancient stones have lost little of their simplicity and strength. There is a splendid Norman doorway in the porch, with beak-head mouldings and an unusual chain pattern. A fine round arch between the old nave and chancel, and a small deeply-splayed south window with long-and-short work, are said to be as the Saxons left them. The old chancel has a 14th-century window with flowing tracery, and in the old nave is one a century younger.

At the churchyard gate, in all the stir of the town, is a lovely lantern cross in memory of men who lie far from their home in foreign earth for ever England. In its head are sculptures of the Crucifixion, the Madonna, St George, and St Michael.

One of Long Eaton's happy playgrounds is Trent Lock, where three counties meet. Here the Soar comes into the Trent, which has only lately gathered the Derwent to itself at Wilne, and the waters leap the weir under Red Hill, a headland looking into Derbyshire and Leicestershire from Notts. A gay scene it is in summer with its pleasure boats, and the white wings of the yachts racing by.

Sir Nicholas

LONGFORD. It lies in green meadows where little streams join to drive the old millwheel. A wayside lychgate reminds us of men who died for Peace, and the top of a splendid 15th-century tower rising above the fine brick pile of the great house calls us to the ancient church.

We come to it across the spacious park, with a stream flowing in little waterfalls by the old almshouses, a beautiful church set in magnificent limes, with a great yew and a great beech. Old and new is the lovely cross in the churchyard; on one side is Christ on the Cross, and on the other St Chad, with an open Bible.

All that is left of the Norman church are three bays of the north arcade with round arches and pillars, three pillars of the south arcade, and the bowl of the font which fell from grace as a cattle trough but is now home again. The pointed arch of the north arcade and those of the south are 14th century, and it was at this time that the Norman capitals of the south arcade were given their present mouldings. There are three old oak poppyheads and graceful sedilia arches, and the nave roof has five old bosses and six heads on each side.

A great treasure of the church is the oak pulpit, on which a modern craftsman has set in canopied niches little figures carved with exquisite detail: St Aidan is with a book, St Chad with a model of Lichfield Cathedral, and Bede writing.

It is an attractive group of monuments which draws the traveller here. Under a recess in the chancel is a priest sculptured in his robes, perhaps John de Cressy, rector 600 years ago.

There are alabaster monuments of three generations of the Longfords, as well as one to the last of the family, every one a knight and every one a Nicholas. The oldest is Sir Nicholas Longford who died in 1357, lying in armour and helmet, his feet on a dog. His son, Sir Nicholas, who died in 1403, is wearing armour and helmet and has a fine belt of square medallions with a beautiful clasp. His sword is gone, but his dagger remains; his feet are on a lion, and his head is on a remarkable crest like plumes of feathers. His son is in armour with his feet on a lion; he has a richly ornamented helmet, and on his smiling lips is an odd little moustache. The last of the Longfords, dying a few years before Shakespeare, lies with his third wife, he in armour and she in a high-waisted gown of many folds.

With the passing of the Longfords the estates went to the Cokes who were here about 300 years. There are memorials to Sir Edward of 1727 and his son Edward of 1733. Under an elaborate canopy is a fine white marble bust of Thomas William Coke who died here in 1842 but sleeps in Tittleshall church in Norfolk. The bust is by Chantrey's pupil John Francis. Known as the handsome Englishman, Coke was Father of the House of Commons and famous as an agriculturist. He was made first Earl of Leicester at the beginning of the Victorian era, and married a Keppel, whose lovely marble monument is near his in the chancel. It has an angel with a child on her shoulder and a woman whom she holds by the hand.

LONGWAY BANK. Only a cottage or two and a farm, their walls of warm-tinted stone clinging to the hillside; but we come for the entrancing view of a fine gathering of hills sweeping down to a wooded valley stretching from Whatstandwell towards Matlock, with Lea Hurst's woods, full of loveliness and story, just across the vale. It is part of a charming road climbing from Whatstandwell to Wirksworth, a road which runs under woods on one hand and sees a glorious scene unfolding on the other; then goes on through a steep-banked green tunnel of trees which opens out to hilltop pastures and Wigwell Grange.

The old house is screened from the road by splendid trees, beech, elm, chestnut, and sycamore. There is a little avenue of fine beech, and a grand old chestnut by the gate of the drive.

Along this way the monks of Darley Abbey used to come, for the Grange was their summer resort 700 years ago. It is still a great house, once the property of the unhappy Anthony Babington.

What the Bell Does

LULLINGTON. A fine lime shades its tiny green in summer; a glorious daffodil carpet spreads in the grounds of its great house in spring. Its 19th-century church is at the corner of a lovely lane.

Two yews embower the church gate, and near the porch the branches of a great holly sweep the ground. The pleasant gardens of the vicarage open out beyond the tower.

The 14th-century tower and spire are all that is left of the old church. The spire is most unusual, for its eight sides rise from the edge of the tower in an almost upright line for several feet, forming a kind of lantern. It has two tiers of lights and is known as Lullington Spud. One of its bells has this inscription:

> *The fleeting hours I tell*
> *I summon all to pray;*
> *I toll the funeral knell,*
> *I hail the festal day.*

Among the treasures of the church are an ancient unused font with crude carving, said to be more than 600 years old; a reading desk of wood splendidly carved by an Italian craftsman; and two windows in the chancel. One of these windows shows Christ in white and gold and a woman in a blue dress, a little child in her arms; the other is the brilliant east window, painted in Brussels by Jean Baptiste Capronnier. It is filled with medallions on a brilliant background, showing scenes from Bible stories, the figures perfect in detail and handsome in colouring. We see Elijah being taken up to Heaven; Shadrach, Meshach, and Abednego in the fiery furnace; Daniel in the den of lions; Dives and Lazarus; the Stoning of Stephen; Mary washing Christ's feet; the Crucifixion, and the Ascension.

Carved from a Block of Alabaster

MACKWORTH. An arresting picture is the church as we see it from the highroad in a green dip of the countryside, beautiful in its trim churchyard, with a fine elm topping the tower. It comes from a rebuilding of the 14th century.

About 50 years older than the rest is the beautiful chancel, with buttresses crowned with crocketed pinnacles, and a priest's doorway with ballflowers. The tower has a spire with dormer windows, and the cross-bow loopholes, rare in a church, suggest that the tower was for defence. The little room over the porch has two peepholes for vanished altars, once at the ends of the aisles.

The interior of the chancel is a blaze of colour, with an almost overwhelming display of alabaster. It has a great alabaster reredos inlaid with coloured marbles, a richly carved canopy over a door, two lovely angels with candles like guardians of the sanctuary, and altar rails of white alabaster and blue stone. Among them all is one thing more we would not forget, the lectern magnificently carved from an alabaster block, its column encircled by an entwining vine, with leaves and clustering fruit forming the table. As the rays of the sun fall on it from a window it becomes a lovely translucent thing, warm with rosy light.

The chancel has three stone seats and a piscina, all with trefoiled arches, and in the north aisle are two 15th-century canopied niches for saints and a canopied recess known as the Abbot's Seat. The font is not yet a century old. A fine chest of 1640 has handsome clamps and hinges. Some old carved panels in the back of a seat in the porch are perhaps 15th-century bench-ends.

Under a recess is an alabaster stone with the sculptured head and finger-tips of a priest sunk in a quatrefoil; he is thought to be Thomas Touchet, a rector older than Agincourt. On an alabaster tomb lies Edward Mundy, grandson of a 16th-century Lord Mayor of London. He wears a long gown with hanging sleeves and ruffs, and in front of his tomb are tiny figures of six sons and two daughters. The window above this tomb shows the arms of the Mundys for 600 years.

Not far from the church, in a pretty switchback lane, is a great stone gateway, all that is left of a proud castle which was long the home of the Mackworths, and is said to have been destroyed in the Civil War. The old home of the Mundys, the 18th-century Markeaton Hall in a fine park, belongs now to the people of Derby for ever.

Little St Paul's

MAPLETON. In the quiet meadows of the Dove, it has houses of mellowed brick and a tiny church with a curious dome which has won for it the name of Little St Paul's. An 18th-century structure, it has only a few remains of the older church in some fragments of glass, and perhaps the five great beams supporting the roof. The oak chair is 18th century.

Five great beeches overhang the road to the one-arch bridge across the Dove, where we may stand with one foot in Derbyshire and one in Staffordshire, seeing two miles away the peak of Thorpe Cloud and the great mass of Bunster, the two splendid guardians of Dovedale. Over the river is a fine little church at the doorstep of Okeover Hall, and the deer park which we may cross to Mayfield, where Tom Moore wrote his Lalla Rookh.

One of a great Derbyshire family, Thomas Cokayne, was born at Mapleton in 1587; he is remembered as the author of a valuable English and Greek dictionary for New Testament students.

The Arch of a Thousand Years

MARSTON MONTGOMERY. We remember its lanes in springtime, glorious with damson blossom; and a charming picture of the village made by the church looking all roof from the road, the lychgate, the old pump in its shelter, and a beautiful old black-and-white house.

They were building the church a thousand years ago, and we found an old man digging in his garden who had made some of its last possessions. The Montgomerys had owned these lands 400 years when the last of them died 400 years ago, but the stones in this tiny chancel arch were old even then. They are perhaps the oldest masonry in Derbyshire. for the arch is Saxon and may have been here a thousand years. It saw the Normans come and saw them put in the small window which still gives light in the west wall. It saw them build the doorway for the people and the doorway for the priest, and it saw them bring the font. It has stood unchanged while a stripling in the churchyard has become a grand and venerable yew.

The beautiful glass of the east window has a Crucifixion showing the three Marys and the centurion, and the light falls through it on the neat, sturdy choir seats, made by the old man we found digging in his garden close by. There is fine modern wood carving in the altar rails and altar table with wheat and vine and grape; and in the lectern and the litany desk which are a peace memorial. The two figures on the pulpit were carved by a much-loved lady of the village who died in 1930.

Four Vicars for Two Centuries

MARSTON-ON-DOVE. We do not wonder that the Dove seems loth to leave its charming seclusion, encircling its meadows with winding streams.

Set in a churchyard like a lawn, looking across to the big house which has something left of the manor house of long ago, is the old church with a lovely tower and spire nearly 600 years old; proud of one of the oldest singers in Derbyshire, for one of its bells, with a prayer in beautiful Lombardic capitals, has been ringing as long as the tower has stood. Lovely things of our day are in memory of those who did not come back, the lychgate and a great cross.

We found the church returning to its old glory inside, pulling down galleries and ceilings. The chancel, with six lancets and the priest's doorway, comes from about 1200 (though the east window is new), and the lovely nave arcades are perhaps a century younger. The south aisle is 14th century, and in the 15th-century windows of the other aisle is a little old glass.

But the oldest possessions here are the top of a tiny Norman window built into an outside wall, and the massive Norman font looking like part of a round pillar. Something of its simplicity and strength has been put, by a local craftsman of our day, into the oak choir stalls, the pulpit, the prayer desk, the rails, and the solid screen across the east end of the chancel.

The most remarkable thing we found here was in the vicar's list, with a continuous run of four vicars for nearly two centuries. George Gretton was here for 65 years, from 1685 to 1750; John Edwards was here for 54 years up to the eve of Trafalgar; Frederick Anson was here 36 years, and his successor was here another 36. The first two of these vicars preached for 119 years in this place. George Gretton saw the Stuarts go and the Georges come; John Edwards saw Napoleon come and his successor saw him go. It is an astonishing record.

Beauty Gone

MATLOCK. It has sold its beauty for a mess of pottage, or for a pot of message. We remember it as one of Nature's lovely places; it has sunk to the level of a place of many hoardings, cheap houses, and mean sights.

Its glory has often been sung. One called it the most dazzlingly beautiful spot in Britain, another a romantic fragment of Switzerland set in the heart of England. Byron and Ruskin praised it, and Montgomery wrote of it;

> *Great Nature, slumbering by fair Derwent's stream,*
> *Conceived these giant mountains in a dream.*

But that was long ago, and it has spoiled itself. It has done completely what so many parts of England are doing for themselves.

The little place of ancient story which the Romans worked for lead has grown to a string of Matlocks stretching for two miles, and houses for the multitude fill the valley and climb the slopes. They reach from close by Scarthin Nick to where the valley broadens out in Darley Dale: Matlock Bath, Matlock Dale, Matlock Bridge, Matlock Town, and Matlock Bank, the first and last of them associated with the waters.

The story of Matlock Bath comes from 1698 when the first bath was built over a warm spring, with a few small rooms for visitors. Today it abounds in hotels and villas reached by startling ascents, with riverside gardens and Lovers Walks and wonderful caves; yet, though we may weary of mills and museums and shops, there are lovely paths through woods and over the hills, for it is here and along the Dale that the most beautiful scenery is found. Masson's stupendous ridge, rising 1100 feet above the sea, shuts in one side of the valley, its wooded Heights of Abraham crowned by a tower looking out from 800 feet. On the other side of the river the magnificent crag of High Tor rears its naked head from a luxuriant growth of birch and oak and mountain ash, a sheer height of more than 350 feet from head to foot. Something to remember is the magnificent panorama from the broad summit of Masson where we see the lovely valley up and down edged by woods and moors, and great hills which only end in the dim outline of the Kinder Range.

In the gardens between the road and the river is a striking monument to the Matlock men who died for us, a soldier and a sailor holding a flag between them. The wayside church of 1841 has the shape of a cross and an elegant crocketed spire. Where a path goes over Masson the tiny chapel of John the Baptist clings to the steep hillside, a charming building of 1897 built over a well, in perfect harmony with its surroundings. Its walls and roof are of local stone, great blocks forming the lower part of the wall which comes down to the road. There is a little bell turret over an oriel window in the chancel, and an oak shelter for the porch. It stands among lofty trees, one of them a splendid yew overhanging the road; it looks up to sheer cliffs that frown above it, down over the housetops to road and river in the canyon below, and across the valley to High Tor. The inside is cosy and neat; the ceiling has bands of plasterwork with painted designs of trailing flowers and leaves; and the east window glows with blue and green, gold and orange.

Near Masson Mill is Glenorchy Chapel, interesting only for its story. It was built, with the house next to it, by Sir Richard Arkwright, and when Lady Glenorchy came driving this way both chapel and house were empty. She had to wait in Matlock while her carriage was repaired, with the result that she bought them and endowed them. One of the ministers of the chapel was the father of Sir George Newnes, the famous publisher who was born here in 1851. Sir George gave Matlock Bank a cable tramway which climbed its steep slope for a generation; it was nearly a mile long and one of the steepest gradients for a tramway in the world.

Matlock Bridge, where five ways meet, is busy with shops and pleasant with riverside walks and gardens; but its joy is the fine old four-arch bridge which embodies a beautiful packhorse bridge more than 400 years old. The old bridge was widened on one side about 1800, and when the widening was rebuilt this century the narrow packhorse bridge could be seen entire.

Matlock Bank is Hydro Land, which came into being with John Smedley, a hosiery manufacturer who, having recovered from a breakdown through a visit to a spa, sought to practise the water cure on others. He made his first experiments on his workpeople at Lea Mills, and the beginning of the great Smedley Hydro was a small house on a site he bought in 1853. Out of the fortune he made with air and water John Smedley built Riber Castle, where he might catch the breezes from 850 feet above the sea; it is a great landmark from all around, but a gaunt pile which has since been a school and was empty when we called. He died at the castle in 1874: there is a hospital to his memory.

All Saints Church, high on the hillside, was built in 1884 and stands in a lovely garden of lawn and flowers and trees, with a fine view to Masson. It is lighted by lancets, three in the east wall of the chancel having lovely glass designed by Burne-Jones with figures of saints and the Four Evangelists. Above them is a rose window. The altar table is handsomely carved.

The embattled building with a tower and a tall spire facing the church was a chapel where John Smedley used to preach; now it is an engine-house for running his Hydro.

Matlock Town lies high above the river; it is the oldest of the Matlocks. Old houses line the steep and narrow cobbled Stoney Way; on a rocky ridge close by is a church with an old story, though much rebuilt; above the church by a green is a 17th-century house which has been an inn. A handsome lychgate opens to the fine church-yard, from whose upper end we see the Derwent Valley. The em-battled tower with four handsome pinnacles is 15th century, almost the only old work left in the fabric now. Some older relics are outside the church, including carved and moulded stones, and a Norman coffin stone with a cross and sword. The fine font is 13th century, now in the church after being long in the rectory garden. One of the eight bells is older than the Reformation. There is fine modern craftsman-ship in the oak stalls, the organ case, and the pulpit.

The most engaging small possession of the church is hanging on the wall of an aisle, a set of six paper garlands. Trifling to those who do not understand, they have a pathetic appeal, for these are funeral garlands, and were carried in the funeral procession of maidens who died too soon to marry. Such garlands (which we have found three times in Derbyshire) come into Shakespeare, for the poet gave them to Ophelia, and it was the protest of the priest against Ophelia's wearing them ("these crants") that stirred the anger of her brother at the graveside.

The alabaster stone of a tomb in the south aisle has engraved por-traits of Anthony Woolley and his wife, with four boys and two girls below them. Anthony has a fur-lined gown, his wife's is tied with bows down the front, and she wears a close-fitting cap of Tudor days. There is another Woolley stone on the west wall near the tomb, telling of the burial here of Adam Woolley and his Grace. They were man and wife for 76 years, Adam dying in 1657 in his hundredth year and Grace in 1669 at 110.

It is surely a record. Adam was born in the year Queen Elizabeth was crowned and died a year before Cromwell's work was done. His wife lived to talk of the Fire of London, and together they remembered the coming of the Armada, the passing of Shakespeare, and the execution of Charles Stuart. This memorial was put here in 1824 by their grandson four times removed, who has an inscription in the

187

church. He was Adam Woolley, who died in 1827, and he collected much material for a History of Derbyshire, bequeathing it to the British Museum, where it lies. The home of the Woolleys was the Old Hall at Riber, which belonged to the family for seven generations.

The Village of Queen Victoria's First Premier

MELBOURNE. We come upon its old haunts with delightful suddenness, a green corner of England proud to be the little mother of one of the Empire's capitals. And it is proud of something else, for it has one of the finest Norman churches in our countryside.

All about us here are limes, elms, and sycamores. There are two little greens, one with a shapely tree and one with a fine cross 20 feet high in memory of about 100 men who did not come home again. Here is the gabled stone vicarage nearly a century old, and the fine tithe barn 700 years old in its lower part of stone, with a doorway 500 years young, and some fine old beams.

Melbourne Hall, its Tudor walls refashioned 200 years ago, has 15 acres of lovely gardens which have been growing more beautiful since the 18th century. It is a place of endless fascination with its terraces and lawns, its noble limes, cedars, and pines, the fountains and lead statues, the summerhouse like a bird-cage of hammered iron, the fine yew hedges, and the yew tunnel a hundred yards long like an aisle of weird shapes as we walk along it. A stone urn with cupids, garlands, and wreaths is a memorial to Thomas Coke, the maker of these gardens, who was born at the Hall and lies in the chancel of the church. He was Chamberlain to Queen Anne, who gave him the lovely monument near the urn, its carvings representing the seasons. On the stone pedestal is a lead vase supported by four monkeys and crowned by a bowl of fruit and flowers; there are four heads round the edge of the vase, which has 24 figures of children at play.

It was while staying at the Hall in 1650 that Richard Baxter wrote some of his Saint's Everlasting Rest. In the 18th century the house passed to the Lambs, the family which gave the Victorian era its first Prime Minister. Today the Kerrs live here, proud to remember Lord Walter Kerr, an admiral who died at the Hall in 1927 and had among his many honours the Silver Medal of the Royal Humane Society for jumping overboard from the height of 30 feet and rescuing a man who had fallen into the Tagus.

Melbourne Pool, across the road from the Hall, is delightful with its island trees. The Pool is 20 acres, and is said to fill a quarry which gave the stone for Melbourne Castle, the vanished stronghold to which the Duke of Bourbon was brought a captive from Agincourt. Here he remained a captive for 19 years till released for a ransom of £18,000, and when set free at last, he left Melbourne for London on his way to France, but died before he could set sail. Sir Ralph Shirley, one of the commanders at Agincourt, was a Governor of the Castle, and in the church of Staunton Harold, three miles from here, are the tattered banners he captured on that glorious day, with flags taken by his relatives at Crecy and Shrewsbury. By the time of Charles Stuart the castle had fallen into ruin, and now its only remains are a fragment of a massive wall in a farmyard by the market square, and the base of a turret in a garden.

The wonderful church of Melbourne stands open to the road, built in the shape of a cross with a central tower, and two small western towers with a fine doorway between them opening into a portico with a vaulted roof. This rare kind of entrance in a village church opens at each side into a smaller portico with vaulted roof, these opening in turn to the aisles.

It is a majestic place inside, with 125 round arches built by the Normans for bays and windows. The glory here is the Norman nave with five bays each side, their fine horse-shoe arches adorned with chevrons and resting on massive pillars 15 feet high and over 12 feet round. Above the arches are the triforium arcades, opening on to the clerestory windows, the two sides of different dates. The north side is Norman, each bay having three arches divided by slender pillars and opening to a single Norman window in the outer wall. The south side has one Norman bay, the rest being 13th century.

Three tiers of Norman arcading adorn the walls of the central tower, the lowest open and the rest blind. The capitals of two of the massive pillars supporting the tower are intricately carved with grotesques, heads, birds, and animals among the foliage. The belfry is 17th century.

The chancel, divided from the nave by a medieval screen made new, is dim in contrast with the full light of the nave. Both chancel and transepts had apse east ends till the 15th century. Three chancel windows are interesting as a tribute to Colonel Gooch, who lived for a time at the Hall, and went out to Waterloo where with two soldiers he closed and held the door of a farmhouse against a strong column of the French army. There is in the chancel a tribute to John Middleton, vicar for 47 years, who was followed by Joseph Deans for 57 years of last century. A fine brass inscription to William Cantrell, who died in 1890, has on it, *God knows what his faults were; I knew them not.*

There is a fine font which is Norman or 13th century, and a tiny projecting Norman piscina in the south transept. On a bracket in the other transept is the head of a medieval cross with sculptures of the Crucifixion, the Madonna and Child, and saints; it is the head of King's Newton's village cross.

In the south transept, now used as a vestry, is a 13th-century coffin stone, and in a recess lies a battered 13th-century knight, with a jewelled bandeau round his head. Here too, against a wall, is an odd little company of stone portraits of the famous Hardinge family of King's Newton, three alabaster stones with four queer figures. One shows Henrie Hardie and his wife Elizabeth of Shakespeare's day, Henrie in armour, with hair which looks as if he had had a fright; his wife with a great ruff all round her face, and hair like a fountain playing. On the other stones are extraordinary figures of Sir Robert Hardinge and his wife, who died towards the end of the 17th century. He has a gown with many buttons and a mop of hair flowing to his shoulders; she has a gown with pointed bodice, a necklace, and her hair in ringlets.

In the busier part of the town is a group of 14 cottages and a chapel adjoining them, built and endowed by Thomas Cook whose name is known to every tourist in the world. It is odd that he should have been born in a cottage, still here, and that in the great house lived a man who carried the name of Melbourne across the world.

The Great Achievement of Thomas Cook

THE answer to the problem as to how our ancestors travelled in roadless medieval days is that as a rule "they didn't." When Thomas Cook was born a poor boy here in 1808, people were still parochial and inert, and seldom left their villages; they were still medieval in habit.

Cook, alternately gardener, wood-turner, and local missionary, travelled on foot nearly the whole of the 2700 miles of his first evangelical tour. Forty years later he compassed the earth in 222 days. His real mission as a pioneer of popular travel began in 1841 when he induced the Midland Railway to take 570 passengers, a temperance party, from Loughborough to Leicester and back for a shilling each.

Setting up in Leicester as a tourist agent, the first of his calling, Cook, aided by his son John, quickly developed his business in the United Kingdom. The son proved the chief organiser. At 17 he conveyed 165,000 people to London for the Great Exhibition, engaging a brass band to play in the streets and persuading into his trains persons who flocked out to listen.

Never since the Crusades had the world seen such hosts of travellers as Cook and Son personally conducted throughout the Old World and the New. They planned the tours, booked trains, ships and hotels, established their own banking system, and prepared every detail.

It was they who carried provisions to starving Paris after the armistice that ended the Franco-Prussian war; they who took General Gordon and his forces up to Korosko; they who transported the relief expedition. This was an enterprise of great magnitude for a private firm, involving the carriage from rail-head to Wady Halfa of 18,000 troops, 130,000 tons of stores, 70,000 tons of coal, and 800 whaling boats. The work was executed punctually and without a hitch.

Thomas Cook died in 1892, but the work continued unchecked, with headquarters in London and branches throughout the civilised world, making travellers of multitudes in many lands who had been inveterate stay-at-homes. The Cooks translated into terms of modern method and mechanism the fable of the magic carpet, and helped the world to bridge the gulfs separating nation from nation.

The Hall was the home of the Lambs, who took the name of Melbourne for their peerage, and the Prime Minister, Lord Melbourne, gave his name to the Australian city.

The Country Village and the Empire City

IT was about 100 years ago that a settlement in Australia was named Melbourne. It numbered a few hundreds of people and was much smaller than the village of Melbourne from which it took its name. The village Melbourne was in the Conqueror's Domesday Book, and had grown until it had a few thousand people; today it has still a few thousands only, but its namesake in Australia has a population of a million and a half. When we called at the Derbyshire Melbourne the Australian city was making plans to keep its centenary, and there was being drawn up in the village a message of friendliness and goodwill to send to the city far away. This is what the message said:

There is a tie between the two Melbournes like that of mother and daughter. Viscount Melbourne, who took his title from our Melbourne, his county home and estate, was Prime Minister when Queen Victoria came to the throne, and so the chief province of Australia was named Victoria, and its capital Melbourne.

Our little town (the population of which does not exceed 4000) was mentioned in Domesday Book, in which it is stated there was a priest and a church and a mill of three shillings and 24 acres of meadow land.

The church stands today as one of the finest Norman churches in England, and there is a water mill still occupying the site of the old one.

We trust that, although your city is now so great and wealthy, you may look with pride on the English town, with a hoary past, from which your city is named.

The Climb Worth While

MELLOR. A steep climb its people have, the old folk to the church and the young folk to the school, for both are perched on the edge of a ridge which looks down beyond the valley of the Goyt into Cheshire. And a fine ride anyone here may have, to New Mills by way of Mellor Moor, with magnificent views of Kinderscout.

Who would not climb any hill to stand at this church, which, though only its 15th-century tower has escaped being made new, is a shrine for two noble treasures of the past? Part of the old cross with a sundial, and remains of the old stocks are its companions in a churchyard paved with gravestones.

One of the treasures is the Norman font of the time of Stephen, round like a pillar and crudely engraved with quaint figures, one a man in a helmet riding on a bridled horse. The other treasure is one of the very oldest pulpits in England and one of the most remarkable. It is older than the old one at Fulbourne in Cambridgeshire, for it is said to be the work of a craftsman who was at work 600 years ago, and who took a single block of oak and carved this pulpit out of it. He gave it six sides, one of which he made the entrance while another he left plain; but four sides he carved with tracery and foliage. It has been restored in its six centuries, for once it was discarded here and a three-decker given pride of place, but it is a proud possession, about 5 feet high and 3 feet across, and every inch a pulpit.

The wonderful Tunnel of Yew

The lovely View from the Arbour

IN THE GROUNDS OF MELBOURNE HALL

The River Wye at Miller's Dale

The River Dove in Dovedale

Hidden in trees not far from the church is the 17th-century Hall, home of the Mellors, who have been in Derbyshire 700 years. One of them was first mayor of Derby, and died in his mayoral robes.

MIDDLETON. It is an old mining village which brings us to a lovely mountain road with a marvellous view as it winds to the foot of Nimble Jack. Deep below the cornice wall the sea of green unfolds as we draw near into the loveliness of the Via Gellia, a dell shut in by wooded cliffs. Luxuriant with all the trees that grow, with violet and primrose, forget-me-not and lily of the valley, and with a little waterfall leaping the rocks to join the rivulet, it has nothing lovelier than the view we have of it on the road from Middleton.

The Stonehenge of the Midlands

MIDDLETON. Enshrined in trees by Youlgreave, above the lovely Bradford Dale, is this charming corner of Derbyshire with something left to remind us of a sad story of the Fulwoods to whom it once belonged.

In a field of Castle Farm are remains of their 17th-century home, now but a few stones and fragments of a wall about a mound known as Fulwood's Castle. The farmhouse was built out of the ruins. Here lived Christopher Fulwood in the time of Charles Stuart, a Derbyshire justice loved for his mercy. From here he went to muster more than 1000 men of Tideswell for the service of his king, and it was here that he was surprised by a party of Roundheads when fleeing for shelter to a rock across the brook, where he was found and shot.

Fulwood's Rock is at the head of Bradford Dale within a few hundred yards of his home, a huge boulder with enough room for a man to hide between it and the cliff of which it was a part; lovely with ferns and forget-me-nots in its crevices, when we called.

It is one of the prehistoric regions of the county, and halfway between Middleton and Youlgreave is Lomberdale House, the home of William and Thomas Bateman, father and son, who gathered together a fine collection of antiquities. The result of their findings during years of excavations in the many barrows of the districts can be seen in Weston Park Museum at Sheffield. Thomas Bateman, dying young last century, is buried in a field by the roadside, two yews shading his tomb.

Two miles away on Middleton Common is the great stone circle of Arbor Low, impressive in its isolation on the brow of a hill, and looking out on a bare and lonely land from 1200 feet above the sea. Called the Stonehenge of the Midlands, it has some 40 stones lying round the edge of a round plateau 50 yards across. The stones are thought to have been upright. Between the plateau and the high earthwork, which is 260 yards round and has an entrance on each of two sides, is a wide ditch. In a large barrow near one entrance were found two urns, the shoulder blade and antlers of a deer, and many rat bones.

About 300 yards away from the circle, once connected with it by a rampart of earth, is a great tumulus known as Gib Hill, and in a barrow at Benty Grange, a mile away, has been found a leather cup with a silver edge, enamels, and a helmet.

MILFORD. It is a hamlet which grew into a flourishing village with the coming of the Strutts, sheltering under steep wooded cliffs by the Derwent. It was Jedediah Strutt who built the cotton mills, and the house where he spent the last years of his life.

They made the bridge over the river; they gave the village its school and the site for the church of 1848. Its east window is to George Herbert Strutt who was born here. He built the fine schools at Belper. Seven lancets in memory of men who died for Peace have angels, St George, and Christ crucified and crowned.

It has Sold its Charm

MILLER'S DALE. It shares the name of the dale in which it lies, once one of the loveliest in Derbyshire, a reach of the River Wye whose magnificent cliffs have been its doom, for it has sold its charm for the wealth of its stone. Yet the dale has still its glory of wildflowers in spring and surpassing scenes in winter snow.

There are old houses and water mills which still grind corn, and opposite the weir is a hamlet church of 1880. Its tiny font is carved with rocks, a Noah's ark, a dove, and a fish. It was built by Samuel Andrew, vicar of the mother church at Tideswell, where we see his finely engraved brass.

The rocky gorge of Monks Dale climbs from the middle of the village. On the hillside are foundations of a chapel of the monks, and a fine fragment of a 14th-century stone screen found here is now in Tideswell church.

Just up stream is the luxuriant Chee Dale with its magnificent Tor rising 300 feet, rent with fissures and crowned with a fringe of trees. With the Wye rushing round its foot in a grand horseshoe curve, it is one of the finest scenes on a river of great beauty.

Struck Down by a King

MONYASH. One of the gateways to Lathkill Dale, this quiet place with memories of busy days as a market town and the lead-mining centre of the High Peak has old stone houses and a 17th-century inn gathered round a number of open ponds and a small green with the shaft of the old cross. Close by is a pillar to those who did not come back.

By way of the gaunt ravine of Ricklow Dale with its old marble quarries, we come to the delightful Lathkill Dale, a deep secluded valley of wooded glen, steep cliff, and mossy paths, whose crystal stream was said by Izaak Walton's angling friend Charles Cotton to be the purest he had ever seen and to have the best trout in England.

Not far from the head of the Dale is an old farmhouse known as One Ash Grange, said to be on the site of a place of confinement for unruly monks. John Gratton, the famous Quaker who lived in Monyash for many years, used to visit the house in the time of the Bowmans, who were among the last of the Quakers here.

A rock at the head of the Dale, near where the Lathkill comes to life, has been known as Parson's Tor since Robert Lomas fell over it to his death in 1776. He was vicar of Monyash, and is said to have planted the fine limes in the churchyard, where there is also a splendid shapely yew.

The stone-roofed church has seen many changes since being built about 1200. The nave arcades are 14th century; the chancel, the spire, and much more have been made new on the eve of our time. Three fine stone seats and a piscina are as old as the church, and some of the tower is 13th century. It has something rare in our experience, a buttress pierced by a lancet window. The bowl of the medieval font rests on columns with capitals seeming to be parts of a lion and a tiger.

A great treasure of the church is a fine old chest ten feet long, with bands of wrought iron every few inches. Worm-eaten and white with age, it was used for the altar plate and the priest's robes perhaps more than 700 years ago.

There is a memorial to Thomas Cheney of 1723, a descendant of John Cheney who was struck down by Richard the Third at Bosworth Field and left for dead. His helmet being broken, he covered his head with the scalp of a bullock which lay near, and from this incident came their crest of a bull's scalp. But he was not dead; he lived to see the Tudor Dynasty and to be given a peerage and the Garter by Henry the Seventh.

The Old and the Lovely

MORLEY. We should come to it when time goes slowly, for it is rich and old, with a story going back to Roman days and a treasure house of lovely things. The church, beautiful without and within, has grown from one of Norman or Saxon times, for it is said that when the church was enlarged in the middle of the 12th century the Normans formed these fine arcades from already existing walls. The tower, with a turret and a lofty spire, comes from a great restoration of about 1400, when the walls over the Norman arches were raised for the clerestory, the aisles rebuilt and lengthened into chapels and the chancel made new.

The churchyard was lovely with crocuses and daffodils when we came; it has roses in summer and always very fine trees. The old rectory is on one side and a great house on the other, and the shaft of an old cross is crowned by a sundial. The charming approach to it is by a sunken lane and a slope which was once the village green, where the tall shaft of an ancient cross has been given a new Madonna.

The interior is of unusual charm, filled with soft light turned into sunshine by the clerestory windows. It is a place of lovely arches, low and round in the Norman arcades, lofty and narrow in the tower, wide and pointed in the chancel. It has a wonderful portrait gallery in brass and monuments in stone of folk of long ago; and the walls of the north aisle are like a marvellous picture book with glass both old and new. There are four old piscinas, a fine old oak chest, and a charming little window high up in the chancel, 600 years old and unglazed.

The story of these remarkable brasses, surely the finest and most complete in any Midland church, begins with Ralph Statham, who married Goditha, heiress of the Morley lands. With their son Richard they made the church what it became in the 14th century, and two brass plates tell of their benefactions. Much of the 15th-century alteration was the work of their grandson John Statham, in whose memory there are two brass plates asking for prayers, and a set of brasses in the north chapel which are the earliest portraits here. We see John kneeling in armour on his helmet, his hair cut close above his ears, and his wife kneeling in a loose gown and a veil. Above them is St Christopher, patron saint of the family, who appears several times on the brasses.

On an altar tomb are elaborate brass portraits of John's son Thomas of 1470, with his two wives dressed alike in fur-trimmed gowns. Thomas is in armour with a sword, his head on a tilting helmet.

Under a canopied archway which may be from Dale Abbey, is a stone with brass portraits of Henry Statham and his three wives. Henry wears elaborate armour, and two of the wives have long gowns, the other a long mantle held by a cord, a veil over her headdress. Below are five tiny figures, only one of whom grew up; she was Joan, who became sole heiress and married John Sacheverell, slain at Bosworth Field. Their portraits are in a chapel, John kneeling in armour and Joan in a close-fitting gown, and with them are eight children.

The last of this array of family portraits are those of Sir Henry Sacheverell (son of John and Joan) who died in 1558, and his wife becomingly dressed in a gown with puffed sleeves. The beautiful alabaster figure of Sir Henry's daughter Katherine lies on a tomb in the north chapel. She died in 1543, grandmother of Anthony Babington who was executed for conspiring against Elizabeth.

Jacinth Sacheverell and his wife lie side by side on an altar tomb, their figures evidently true to life. On one side of the tomb are three kneeling children and a fourth is in a cradle. Jacinth was a staunch Roman Catholic and suffered much for his faith. His brother Jonathan is said to have been the first of the family to leave the old faith, and the inscription on his painted monument, showing Jonathan and his wife holding hands, a babe in a tiny cradle and another small child on a cushion, tells us that he died a true Protestant in 1662.

Here also is the altar tomb of Henry Sacheverell of Barton, to whom Jacinth left the property instead of to Jonathan; and the tomb of Henry's son, William, who died in 1691. Speaker Onslow described him as the "ablest Parliament man" of the reign of Charles the Second. He was belaboured with abuse by the brutal Judge Jeffreys for protesting against cancelling the charters of Nottingham, and he was a bold critic of Charles Stuart and a gallant defender of the British Constitution on which he left his mark.

Among the memorials to the Wilmots and Sitwells with whom the Sacheverells married, is one of an only son who bore the three names.

It is a beautiful bronze of St George slaying the dragon, in memory of Jacinth Sacheverell Wilmot Sitwell of our own time, who went out to France and did not come home again.

One of the glories of the church is the lovely 15th-century painted glass in three north aisle windows, once in the cloister of Dale Abbey. In one window we read in seven little scenes the story of St Robert of Knaresborough who shot deer which had been eating his corn. Three of the scenes are in modern glass, but the rest are old. We see St Robert shooting the deer, the gamekeepers complaining to the king, St Robert also complaining to the king who bids him go and pen the deer; Robert driving the deer into a pen, the gamekeepers again complaining, the king giving the saint all the ground he can plough round in a day with the deer, and Robert ploughing with the deer. In another panel of this window is an erring monk, with hands manacled and a quaint expression on his face, being admonished by another monk.

The legend of the Invention of the Holy Cross is told in ten scenes in the next window, seven modern and the rest from Dale Abbey. The three scenes in the old glass are Christ on the Cross, the beheading of Chosroes after he had removed the cross on capturing Jerusalem, and the baptism of Chosroes' son. The other two windows in the lovely north wall have fine modern glass in the style of that from Dale, showing the Parables and other scenes.

The old glass of the east window of this aisle has the Madonna, Mary Magdalene, and St Ursula ascending to Heaven escorted by angels, with 11 of the virgins gathered in her mantle. At the foot of the window are three pictures illustrating Te Deum, the Church shown by nine figures led by the Pope, the glorious company of the Apostles led by Peter with the keys, and the noble army of martyrs.

There is fine old painted glass in the south aisle of St Elizabeth in a blue cloak and white robe and Peter in a red cloak, the kneeling figures of three girls and five boys suggesting that the glass is in memory of their father John Sacheverell of Bosworth Field. Especially fine is a window with Roger, a Bishop of London who died in 1241, wearing red-and-white robes and jewelled gloves; the Four Evangelists writing at desks, with their emblems; St William in the white-and-green vestments he wore 800 years ago, and a monk representing St John of Bridlington.

Charming indeed with its colour of the centuries is this noble place, and we do not forget the lovely glimpse of the grand old yew tree through the open doorway of the ancient porch.

His Own Memorial

MORTON. The coalmines have not spoiled it, for it has still its old haunts at the top of the hill, a happy place with a tiny green, a pool under lovely trees, old cottages, the rectory, and a small church with a 15th-century tower with a crown of battlements and eight pinnacles. The rest of the church was rebuilt last century, but there are a few fragments of old glass in the tower. The churchyard has a trim array of low 17th- and 18th-century gravestones, unusual for their simple inscriptions of initials and the year.

A pathetic thing is the stone lychgate in the shadow of a great sycamore and a beech. In memory of the men of Morton who gave their lives for Peace, it was designed by one of the Turbutts of Ogston Hall, three miles away. He planned it just before he fell in France in the first autumn of the war, and today it is his own memorial too.

King Charles's Hat

MUGGINTON. It has a fine lookout over a green countryside of little hills and dales, with a brook winding to Kedleston Park. Its glory is an ancient church whose life began a thousand years ago. One of two old yews in the churchyard is claimed as one of Derbyshire's oldest inhabitants; its trunk is like a three-sided shelter, and we may wonder how long it will resist the fierce winds which sweep this hillside.

But older than the tree is a tiny window in the west wall of the church, found not many years ago but probably Saxon. The tower has Norman work, including a belfry window and the corbel table below the battlements. The Norman west doorway is blocked by a buttress. A small doorway at the east end of the south aisle is 13th century. The south doorway, the nave arcade, and the font with six sides are 600 years old. Most of the windows and the arcade of two bays between the chancel and chapel, its capitals carved with flowers and shields and heads, are 15th century.

The upper part of an old oak screen between the aisle and chapel has fine 15th-century tracery. Eleven plain oak benches remain out of a number made in 1600 for William Jenkinson, who "gave to this church XXXs that made these forms." There is an old oak chest, and a stone bracket on a pillar is carved with a face. In a window of the chapel are fragments of old glass, and a very ugly head with open mouth looks down from one of the roofs. An inscription to Hugh Radcliffe of 1678 is like a 17th-century advertisement, telling us that he made hats for Charles Stuart and all the royal family.

The great treasure of the church is an altar tomb in the south chapel to one of the Knivetons, landowners in Derbyshire for 400 years, who gave all they had for the Stuarts. On the top of the tomb are splendid brass portraits of Sir Nicholas Kniveton and his first wife, with tiny figures of five children in a row. On the wife's long hair is a charming chaplet of roses. Sir Nicholas is in armour with a long sword, and a collar with the rare pendant of a portcullis. His feet are on a greyhound and his head rests on a helmet which has a great heraldic interest, for on it is a crest engraved with a fox. It is one of the rare conceptions of heraldry of which we have seen only a few examples in England. The familiar story is that a tiger (here it is a fox), pursuing the hunters who had carried off its cub, was delayed by their throwing down a mirror in which it saw itself and imagined it was looking at its lost cub.

On an outside wall of the church is the crest of the Sanders family which gave Cromwell a colonel for his Ironsides. He was the fine old Sir Thomas Sanders who has been sleeping under the chancel since 1695, having lived to see the rise and fall of the Commonwealth, the return of the Stuarts, and the coming of William and Mary.

Four Counties Meet

NETHERSEAL. Near where four counties meet, looking into Leicestershire across the River Mease, is this village where elms and limes and chestnuts grow, where thatched cottages look on to a tiny green with a cross to men who died for Peace, where a row of almshouses of 1699 and the fine gabled rectory look up to the ancient church in a trim churchyard.

Proudly the embattled tower stands among the noble limes, its stones 700 years old, and its lofty arch opening to the nave with a 13th-century arcade. In an arched recess in the modern chancel is a tomb with an engraved stone of Roger Douton in priest's robes. He was rector here and died in 1500. One of the windows has fragments of old heraldic glass.

Netherseal has lost a Jacobean house which stood near the church, but it has kept a charming 17th-century Hall built on the foundations of a Norman castle. We must like it for a window on which we can read from the road, "He that buildeth all things is God," for the peep of its garden and lake, and the sight of its splendid dovecot over the way. In it is a fine ladder which turns round like a wheel so that every one of the nesting-boxes can be reached. There is a mill grinding corn close by, as it was probably grinding corn when they put up the dovecot in 1686.

NEWBOLD. Chesterfield was once one of its hamlets; now it has just a green, a modern church, and, in a field behind an inn, a half-forgotten old chapel about 36 feet long and half as wide. It rang with praise and prayer in Norman England, but it is now a private burial-place. It has been a barn since it ceased to be a church in the 17th century, but through all its adventures it has kept the little priest's doorway the Normans built, with stone carving over it worn out by centuries of wind and rain. There is Norman masonry in its walls, the windows and the south doorway being 15th century.

Three Medieval Knights

NEWTON SOLNEY. Here the Dove comes into the Trent. Its houses are big and small, from the almshouses in the village street to the great stone house by a lovely bit of sunken road, and the house looking like a castle on a hill 150 feet above the river. From this high end of the village we look into Staffordshire and away to the distant hills of the Peak.

A charming grass-bordered road with an avenue of trimmed limes leads to a fine house and the church by the river. In the shadow of the church sleeps Thomas Gayfere, his stone telling us that his lasting monument is in Westminster Hall and Henry the Seventh's Chapel, which he helped to restore last century. In the church sleep three knights whose monuments were old when Henry's Chapel was new, three of the Solneys who were here in the 13th and 14th centuries.

The church which shelters them began to rise in Norman days, and has remains of that time in its north doorway, some stones with chevrons on the outside walls of the chancel and the tower, and perhaps the priest's doorway. Most of the rest is 600 years old, the tower and spire, the nave arcades, and most of the chancel. The clerestory is a century younger, and two windows are 13th century, one an unusual double lancet with a head carved on the middle shaft, inside and out. A carved oak flower on a beam under the tower is

500 years old, and four splendid oak benches are 17th century. The floor of the tower is paved with old tiles, and in it are two ancient stones with crosses. The corner of one of them has in it another stone with a cross, pathetic because it is only 18 inches long. They laid a little child under it eight centuries ago.

The oldest of the Solney monuments is the battered stone figure of a 13th-century knight in armour, with his hands resting on a sword. Another stone knight lies on a tapering stone, perhaps Norman de Solney of about 1275; he has a sword and wears a surcoat with some parts of his armour of banded mail visible. There are not many examples of this banded mail in England.

Exceptional for its wonderful detail is the monument of the third of these de Solney knights. Sculptured in alabaster, he lies on a tomb adorned with shields, wearing armour, and at the knees and instep, under the arms and below the surcoat, can be seen the undersuit of mail. His hip-belt is handsomely decorated, his head is on a cushion borne by angels, his feet are on a lion. He is thought to be John Solney, the last male of his line, who perhaps built the north chapel and died toward the end of the 14th century. This is said to be the only example in England where the hood-like camail is shown tied down to the shoulders.

Near these monuments, but far removed from them in dignity, is the huge marble figure of Sir Henry Every of Egginton, wearing a toga and sandals, in the manner of those who loved to look like Romans, a fashion which raged in the 18th century.

The Lady in a Bag

NORBURY. Round this meeting-place of Derbyshire and Staffordshire, her Stonyshire and Loamshire, George Eliot laid some of the scenes of Adam Bede. A mile from Norbury on the way to Ashbourne is the birthplace of her father Robert Evans and his brother, Adam and Seth Bede.

It is a delightful village in green country by the River Dove, with a deep-cut shady lane climbing to the church in company with a fine old yew, on one hand the Old Hall, with remains of the 14th-century home of the Fitzherberts, on the other the modern house whose lovely grounds spread round the churchyard. Here, built after an unusual plan, with a low embattled tower between two chapels on the south of the nave, is one of Derbyshire's most charming churches. It has a perfectly lovely chancel and a wealth of old glass equalled by few village churches in the whole country.

This superb chancel was built by Henry Kniveton, rector from 1349 to 1395, and is only three feet shorter than the nave. Its walls are all windows between the fine gabled buttresses and the wavy parapet, the windows having inside and out a double flower at the middle point of their lovely tracery. The inner walls below the side windows are filled with shallow arches, and the east wall is lined with ancient stall-work, some of which remains in the ends of the choir stalls with lovely old tracery and poppyheads. Very effective is the dark oak screen against the light background of the chancel.

It is in the chancel that we find the glory of the 14th-century glass, much of it fine interlacing patterns and scrollwork, medallions, and shields, relieved with colours of red and blue. The east window glass is chiefly 15th century, with a representation of the Trinity, the Twelve Disciples, and four saints—St Chad, St Margaret, St Fabian, and St Edward.

The east window of the south east chapel has St Winifred, St Anne teaching the Madonna to read, with a small crucifix above them, and St Agatha. Below them kneels a mother with eight boys and five girls. A south window shows John the Baptist with a lamb, a man with a staff and a book, and St Anthony with a hog; at the foot kneel Nicholas Fitzherbert with two sons and his wife with two girls. These two windows commemorate the marriages of Nicholas, who died in 1473, his tomb being in the chancel. A west window has shields of arms, and Mary Magdalene kneeling.

Splendid are the roofs, almost flat, with beautiful bosses. The chancel was roofed in the 15th century by Henry Prince, a rector seen in his priest's robes on a stone in the chancel. There are three sedilia and three piscina niches, a 13th-century font on a pillar of clustered shafts, and a mutilated cross-stone 700 years old on the chancel floor. But rarer far are two very fine fragments of Saxon crosses with interlacing and knotwork, one having a figure with a staff.

In monuments of stone and brass we read of these Fitzherberts whose glory waxed and waned at Norbury from the 12th to the 17th century; whose sufferings for their faith make one of the saddest pages of Derbyshire history. The oldest is the stone figure of Sir Henry in chain armour, with a sword and shield. He rebuilt the manor house at the beginning of the 14th century, and some of the upper windows of his time are in the old Hall still.

Very fine is the alabaster tomb in the chancel on which lies Sir Nicholas, who built the chapel where the old glass still commemorates his two marriages. He is in plate armour with a fine sword and a collar of suns and roses; his feet are on a lion with a tiny angel on its back supporting the tip of the knight's foot. At one end of the tomb are his wives, and in carved niches are their 17 children—some civilians, six women in dress of their day, one a nun with veil and rosary, another a monk with a book, one a lawyer with a scroll, one in armour, and another in a collar of roses. A very worn stone has the engraved portrait of his wife Alice.

The son and heir of the proud Sir Nicholas lies also in the chancel on another splendid alabaster tomb. He is Sir Ralph, and has plate armour and a collar of suns and roses. His lady has a mantle over her gown, and wears a lovely necklace with a pendant of the Madonna. Her hair is arranged in a beautiful netted headdress, and at her feet are two dogs. At Ralph's feet is a little monk with a rosary on a lion's back, holding up the tip of the knight's right foot. In canopied niches on the sides of the tomb are fine figures of seven sons, and eight daughters in dainty low-necked dresses. Another monument to Sir Ralph's wife, Elizabeth, is an engraved alabaster stone on the chancel floor showing her entirely enveloped in a shroud. A very queer thing is this lady tied up in a bag.

Their eldest son John, who built the tower and south-west chapel from his grandfather's design, has an alabaster tomb with a brass plate in the upper stone.

Here lies another of the sons of Ralph and his Elizabeth, Sir Anthony, who inherited the estates after his brother John. He was a great scholar and a famous judge, remembered for his fearless opposition to Wolsey when he seized the monastery lands, and he was a judge of the tribunal which tried Sir Thomas More. The splendid brass portraits of Sir Anthony and his wife are set in a stone on the chancel floor. The judge, whose head is missing, has a scroll in his hand; there is a group of five girls, but the sons are gone. An epitaph in Latin, said to be the judge's own words, tells us:

> *A lifetime's deeds are all that here I have,*
> *Who by my works am followed to the grave:*
> *Though erst a judge, now at the bar I stand,*
> *And wait the judgment of a Juster lland.*

Some of this set of brasses have been used twice, the other side of the brass of the five daughters having the fine little figure of a monk under a canopy.

Sir Anthony, who died in 1538, was born in the old manor house and it is said that the oak wainscoting in an upper room still known as his study was put in by him. Some ancient glass in the house shows the marriages of the family, and there are six 15th-century roundels of the occupations of the months from January to June. Sir Anthony was the first man to try to codify all the laws of England, and the first to raise his voice against the danger to agriculture owing to the insecurity of the tenant. He wrote two books on rural life, of great practical value. Sir Anthony's eldest son, Sir Thomas, died in the Tower after many years of persecution and imprisonment for his faith. He married the heiress of the Eyres of Padley, and was in prison when tragedy fell upon Padley Hall.

In the floor of the sanctuary is a memorial to Henry Arthur Clowes who lived at the great house, a lovely marble tablet with coloured arms and regimental badges. He died fighting in Egypt in 1916 and is buried in Cairo.

Green Fields and Smoking Chimneys

NORTH WINGFIELD. Belonging to a busy countryside of coal and iron, it has beauty at its doorstep and can turn its back on the smoking chimneys and see England's green and pleasant land, with Hardwick Park and the Nottinghamshire hills.

Where the ways meet, the base of a medieval cross and a little of its shaft have been set up on a flight of steps. It was used as a guide-post in 1702, and is carved with fingers pointing the way.

There is a lovely church with a handsome tower over 100 feet high and 500 years old, one of its bells older still. Below the embattled parapet is a cornice with shields. On the west window are heads of a bishop and one with a coronet, and a lofty arch opens to the nave.

Full of light is the interior, a blending of beautiful stone and splendid woodwork old and new. The old roofs have much original 14th-century work in their splendid beams, their trefoil tracery, their fine kingposts and bosses. There is a fine old chest and an old table, and a modern oak chancel screen with a loft reached by the ancient stairway.

The oldest thing North Wingfield has is perhaps a font which is now not used. A noble relic of the past, it was found lying in the churchyard, a round block of stone more than three feet high, the surface hollowed out in deep flutings. It is believed to be either Saxon or early Norman. The oldest masonry is a Norman archway opening into the chapel, with a lovely window above it which is probably from the end of the 12th century, the arch being slightly pointed and so marking the change from the Norman to the English. It is thought to have been a doorway, built here for preservation.

The church has a fascinating group of medieval stones and sculptures. In the porch is a small tapering coffin stone under which was probably laid a Norman child. Set in the wall of an aisle is a sculpture of St Lawrence bound to a grid, a man at each end turning him round and another looking on. On two other stones, set in the chapel wall, are kneeling and standing figures, one perhaps representing the Annunciation. In a chancel recess lies a knight in chain armour, and in a recess outside the chancel wall is a companion knight; it is thought that they are both Deincourts of the 13th century.

The nave arcades are 14th and 15th century, and a 14th-century arch opens from the chancel to the chapel. The 600-year-old east window has a glowing scene of the Ascension, and fragments of old glass. The west window of the tower has an ancient figure of a monk with a book and a rosary. In a clerestory window is glass in memory of a boy who lies in Flander's fields where poppies blow, and on his grave are these lines:

> *Though but a boy in years he paid man's price,*
> *And gladly gave his all in sacrifice.*

The churchyard has a very old sundial, and close by is an inn which was once the chantry house, and has much 15th-century work still left.

Hereabouts was born a maker of sweet music, Thomas Greatorex, who lies in the cloisters of Westminster Abbey.

His Music Filled the Abbey

IT is over a century since Thomas Greatorex played his last organ voluntary, but his name is still with us. Born near North Wingfield in 1758, he came of a family of musicians. His father was a self-taught musician, and his sister was an organist in Leicester when she was only 13. Thomas, very grave and studious, and fond of mathematics and astronomy, soon turned his attention to church music and was organist of Carlisle Cathedral when he was 12.

In his leisure hours he studied science, and at 18 he travelled in Italy and Germany. Before he was 30 he was earning as much as 80 guineas a week by giving singing lessons. Chief professor of the organ in the Royal Academy of Music, he was long regarded as one of the greatest authorities of his day, and no great performance of Handel or Haydn was thought to be complete if he were not at the organ or conducting the chorus. In the 39 years he was conductor of Ancient Concerts he is said never to have missed one performance. Keenly interested in painting and architecture, he always kept his youthful interest in science, and his invention of a new way of measuring the height of mountains won him the fellowship of the Royal Society.

For 12 years organist of Westminster Abbey, he was famous for his wonderful mastery of the instrument. He seemed to have fifty fingers, and when his hands strayed over the keys the abbey was filled with great surges of sound that rolled out magnificently like awful peals of thunder.

He sleeps in the cloisters at Westminster, not far from the choir where his music stirred all who heard it.

A Sleeper in Lincoln Cathedral

OCKBROOK. Some of it has fine peeps over the Trent and Derwent valleys into Notts and Leicestershire, some of it is in the hollow with the church. There was a Moravian settlement here in the 18th century and its school still carries on.

With a magnificent beech for company, the church is both old and new. The small tower is 12th century and the spire 100 years younger; the chancel and the nave are 19th century.

Its treasures are a Norman font, 16th-century window pictures of the Evangelists, and beautiful woodwork of about 1500 in the choir stalls and the chancel screen. The lofty screen reaches to the roof, and has a lovely upright border of vines at each end.

These fine possessions of 15th and 16th-century craft were once in Wigston Hospital in Leicestershire, having been brought here last century by one of the Pares, whose memorials are in the chancel. They lived at Hopwell Hall a mile or two away, now an institution but once the home of the Lakes, descendants of the valorous Sir Edward Lake of Edgehill. He was wounded 16 times there, and when his left hand was shot away he gripped the reins between his teeth and kept on fighting till he was taken prisoner. Then he managed to escape, and the proudest moment of his life was on the anniversary of the battle, when he was received and thanked for his valour by Charles. He has been sleeping in Lincoln Cathedral since 1674.

The Lady with a Heart

OLD BRAMPTON. Coal and iron round about have left Old Brampton its lovely green hilltop, looking out to fields and wooded valley and the moors not far away. It is charming with fine trees, trim-walled roads, old houses, and church of rust-coloured stone.

High above the road, the church is a delightful picture as we see it with a lovely peace cross silhouetted against the sky. The Norman chapel was made new in the 13th century, and we see the actual meeting of the styles when Norman was passing into English, for the south doorway has a round arch and a pointed one as well; in the niche above stands a modern St Christopher.

The sturdy 13th-century tower was altered a century later, when it was capped with the short broached spire. The stone-roofed porch is also 14th century, as is most of the rest of the church except for many 15th-century windows. In a little gallery of worn figures on the outside walls is Paul with a book and sword, Peter with a key and a book (with little birds on the pinnacles of his canopy), a draped woman and a Madonna, and a quaint corbel over the priest's doorway, with foliage coming from its mouth.

The tower arch frames very happily the figures in the west window of Faith, Hope, and Charity, and in a charming little lancet is effective glass of the Good Shepherd in a red robe.

A great treasure is a sepulchral monument against the west wall, found in the churchyard. It is one of those curious old sculptures in which we see parts of a human body below the surface of the stone, as if the lid of a coffin had been cut away. In a quatrefoil opening at the top are the head and shoulders of a woman holding a heart in her hands, while in a narrow opening below, her feet peep out from the folds of her robe. It is thought she was perhaps the heiress Matilda le Caus, who died more than 700 years ago.

The great wooden cross of Lord Gorell, who was killed in Flanders, has been brought from his grave. The book of remembrance to them all is kept in a fine little niche in the wall, with St George conquering the dragon in the spandrels, and a dainty lace-like door.

Sir Nicholas Fitzherbert's splendid Tomb

Fragment of
Saxon Cross

Fine Tracery on the
medieval choir stalls

Carving on
Saxon Cross

ANCIENT TREASURES OF NORBURY CHURCH

The Alabaster Tomb of Sir Ralph Fitzherbert

Sir Ralph Fitzherbert and the Little Monk at his feet

Sir Henry Fitzherbert in his Chain Armour

THE ANCIENT FIGURES IN NORBURY CHURCH

The Brothers

OSMASTON. We come through its lovely trees and quiet lanes to thatched cottages by a shady pool with rockery and rhododendrons. It has two fine 19th-century buildings, Osmaston Manor built in Elizabethan style but not yet a centenarian, with beautiful gardens and terraces and parkland, and a glorious grove of limes; and a church with yews among the fine trees of its lovely churchyard, where stands a great stone memorial to 13 men who did not come back.

Five brothers sing out from the lofty tower, a peal of five bells of which one says, "I and my four brothers were hung in this church in 1845." A stranger has now joined them. Beautiful arcades lead to the aisles, and lofty arches to the tower and the chancel where the east window shines red and blue and orange with ten saints and Edward the Confessor.

The modern font has a handsome band of lotus flowers and leaves, and the ancient font, the only relic of the old chapel, stands over four feet high, its bowl like part of a round pillar.

Leaping Weirs and Filling Pools

OVER HADDON. A hardy little village in upland country with endless stone-walled fields, glorying in its place above the Lathkill Dale, it sees the river, only three miles old, shining among the rocks and trees of this enchanting valley, leaping weirs and filling trout pools on its way to Conksbury Bridge, charming with its high wall and low arches. It has stone houses, a cross to four men who died for England, and a tiny church only half a centenarian, looking over the Dale to Youlgreave's fine old tower.

The village story is of Martha Taylor, a story rare enough to have found its way into many books. Born here in the 17th century, an invalid from a child, she lived for a whole year in her teens with only a few drops now and then of sugar and water, syrup of prunes, and the juice of a raisin. She was then 18 and she lived on after that another 17 years, passing away in 1684.

Where the Romans Camped

PARWICH. In the shadow of a great hill, watered by a stream, its neat stone houses, the pump in its shelter, and the church, are grouped round the little green. It is a very old place, for the Romans camped close by.

The fine church, with a tower crowned by a lofty spire and with eight of its nine bells ringing in memory of men who did not come back, is a 19th-century exchange for a Norman structure. The nave arcades are Norman in style, with round pillars and arches and square capitals carved with foliage. Fine remains of Norman work are built into the tower.

The lovely arch of the tower was the old chancel arch; the fine west doorway was in the old north wall. Both are adorned with chevrons; the tower arch has a border of stars and the doorway has beak-heads and grotesques. Over the doorway is a fine tympanum with animals long buried under plaster; among them are a stag, a holy lamb looking like a horse, a wolf with a branching tail, a bird and a boar, and two serpents intertwined.

The font is the old Norman one, shaped rather like an egg-cup, the upper part of the bowl divided into 16 faces, below which it tapers down to a round base.

The oak chancel screen has a fine cornice of vine leaves and grapes.

The Bottom of the Bottomless Pit

PEAK FOREST. Only its name reminds us that it was the hunting ground of kings; today it is a lonely stone-built village of the moors. It has one of the few churches, a modern one among fine sycamores, devoted to the memory of King Charles, with memorials to the Cavendish family who helped to build it.

In two of its windows are memorials of two tragic pages in our history, for one recalls Lord Frederick Cavendish who was murdered in Phoenix Park in Dublin in the dark days of Ireland before Home Rule, and another shows Charles Stuart in armour, with an axe, a block, and a crown beside him.

The rare dedication of the church to "St Charles" belonged also to the 17th-century chapel, built perhaps by a countess whose son died fighting for the King. It was owing to the special privilege of this chapel that the village became a kind of Gretna Green and for a time its runaway marriages averaged one a week. The act of 1753 checked the runaways, but the parsons went on marrying them another fifty years.

A mile and a half away is Eldon Hill 1500 feet high, with ancient graves at the top and the remarkable Eldon Hole at the foot. One of the Wonders of the Peak, it was known as the Bottomless Pit till 1770, when the bottom was first reached. It is a great tapering chasm about 180 feet deep, opening to a huge cavern with stalactites and stalagmites, which drops much lower still. Thomas Hobbes tells how he rolled stones into the Hole which dropped "to the depths of Hell."

He Helped to Beat Napoleon

PENTRICH. A mile from the site of a Roman camp and traces of a Roman road, this hilltop village is charming with its thatched and gabled houses, looking up to the sturdy church at the top of a picturesque flight of 48 steps.

The Normans built the lower part of the tower with walls four feet thick; their arcades still lead to the aisles, and the bowl of their font, on a 17th-century pedestal, is back in the church after being found last century in the cellar of a house at Ripley.

From the 15th century come the top of the tower, the battlements of the rest of the building, and most of the windows. Window pictures of Dorcas, the Baptism in Jordan, the Ascension, and the Last Supper, are in the fresh, unusual colours of Capronnier. Very striking is a vigorous window from the workshops of Christopher Whall, with the warrior saints of England and France and a fine figure of St Michael, in memory of a hero who fell at Ypres. Two heroes of other wars are remembered on the walls; Edmund Horne, a sea captain, who fought against the Spaniards and the French and came back to Butterley, his native place, dying in 1764; and Major Jessop of Butterley Hall. He fought with Wellington and was wounded at Waterloo, but he lived for half a century to tell the tale of how they beat Napoleon.

It was in the dark days after Waterloo that Pentrich came into history with a scene which led Shelley to forget his manners.

Shelley Forgets His Manners

IN 1817 a little company of half-starved labourers, stockingers, and weavers met at the White Horse Inn, where Pentrich post office now stands, and made wild plans for a march to London. Collecting recruits on the way, they set out to overthrow the Government. Led by Jeremiah Brandreth, who is said to have been the victim of a spy in the pay of the Government, the rebels attempted to provoke a riot. It was soon quelled, but it was made use of by the reactionary Government to show what would be the result of further attempts at reform. Nearly fifty of the men were tried by four judges at Derby, the trial lasting ten days.

In this trial the wild scheme of 46 deluded rioters, who had plundered a few farmhouses and shot a servant at Wingfield Park, was made to look like a serious revolution, and the men were accused of high treason and of levying war against the King. A few of them were pardoned, some were transported, but Brandreth and two others were sentenced to a terrible death; they were hung, drawn, and quartered at Derby.

One of those moved by their tragic end was the poet Shelley, who had not yet calmed down from his wild and rebel moods. He wrote a pamphlet giving vent to his indignation under the name of the Hermit of Marlow, in which he forgot himself so far as to use the national mourning for the Princess Charlotte, who then lay dead in a royal palace, as a peg for his essay. Shelley contrasted the deaths of the poor men and that of the Princess Charlotte the day before. The pamphlet was called by a queer title, We pity the Plumage but Forget the Dying Bird.

Wellington's Monument and Nelson's Pillar

PILSLEY. Only a mile from Chatsworth, it has a charm of its own in houses of warm-tinted stone and in wonderful views.

Down below, where the valley of the Derwent is rich in green meadows and in a wealth of trees, nestles the pretty village of Baslow; while beyond, crowning the heights on each side of the Bar Brook, are two fine landmarks 1000 feet above the sea, Wellington's Monument and Nelson's Pillar.

And as far as we can see up the valley great heights rise to sweeping moors; on one hand Longstone Edge and Eyam Moor, on the other the Edges of Baslow, Curbar, and Froggatt, carrying the eye along to Hathersage Moor, a home of early man.

PILSLEY. Six miles from Chesterfield, it has coal under its houses, and a little modern church with fine woodwork in the lectern, choir stalls, and the panelling of the chancel walls. Its splendid pulpit has figures of Barnabas, Andrew, Peter, and Paul, in canopied niches. Full of story is a small Creation window filled with vivid glass, showing in six medallions the coming of sun, moon, and stars, fishes and birds, fruit and flowers, and animal life. We noticed a lion, a lamb, an ox, and a tiny rabbit. The fine peace memorial in the nave is of Derbyshire stone, crowned with a bronze angel trumpeting, and holding a wreath of laurel.

A Legend of Fair Rosamund

PINXTON. Coal has changed this border village, but it has a legend of a lovely lady and it gave its name to a now rare china.

The fame of Pinxton china was largely due to the beautiful paintings of flowers by William Billingsley who came here from the porcelain works at Derby. Billingsley was a practical potter, too, and his recipe enabled the factory, founded in 1795, to flourish for a few years. Then he left, and the quality of Pinxton ware deteriorated so much that in 1812 the factory was closed, leaving to Pinxton the name of China House Square and to the world some lovely and some commonplace works of art.

Tradition tells us that Pinxton belonged for a time to the Cliffords, and that here was born to them a daughter who became Fair Rosamund. If there is any truth in the story their house was perhaps near the church, for when the ground was opened in 1686, during the search for coal, traces of walls and lead pipes were found. In the 15th century part of the lands belonged to Sir William Babington, the Lord Chief Justice.

The church stands high, looking out to two Derbyshire windmills shorn of their sails. A plain place made largely new in the middle of the 18th century, it has a strange plan, having a west porch, and a tower opening from a small chapel off the chancel. The oldest remains are in this chapel and tower, the chapel having 13th-century work, the lower part of the tower being 14th century. Some of the roof beams are 15th century. The old font is still in use, and on the chancel floor are remains of coffin stones perhaps 700 years old.

There are memorials of the Cokes of Brookhill Hall, a fine old house in a wealth of trees a mile away, many of its rooms still enriched with Tudor beams and panelling.

PLEASLEY. A workaday village but with some lovely ways. The little River Meden bounds it from Notts, winding through the deep and wooded Pleasley Vale to the cotton mills across the stream, and on to a charming spot where great rocks rise in fantastic shapes. Its old houses and church are on the hillside, where on a green mound are the steps of an ancient cross.

In company with a fine old yew stands the church, a long and aisleless building with 13th-century walls and some lancets among the lovely windows, all deeply splayed. The charming east window (its modern glass a bright splash of colour in the dim church) and two similar ones in the nave are 14th century. The embattled tower is a century younger, the iron clamps about the pinnacles reminding us of an earthquake shock which shook them the year after Waterloo.

There is a fragment of an old coffin stone in the floor of the porch; an unused font has a crudely carved figure of a priest perhaps 700 years old; but older than all else here is the chief pride of the church, its richly carved Norman chancel arch.

The old oak pulpit has had an adventure. Cast out from All Saints Church in Derby, it was recovered from a shop last century and brought here, its fine carving being new.

The Spring that Failed

QUARNDON. A slow drip of water in a shady lane, and a great farmhouse with splendid buildings on the lovely road to Kedleston, tell of the fame that might have come to Quarndon, for one was a spring of precious water, and the other an inn built by Lord Scarsdale who hoped this spring would make the place a busy spa.

It did not happen, for an earthquake is said to have disturbed the vigour of the spring. But Quarndon has always its charming situation among the little rolling hills, and seen from the farmhouse, is a pretty picture of a village veiled in trees, climbing to its church.

This church of the hilltop, with a fine view of Derby's towers and spires, and a fine cross in the churchyard to nine heroes of the war who did not come back and three who came back to die, is 19th century, with good woodwork in the pulpit and the stalls, splendidly carved altar rails, and a font of Derbyshire spar.

At the foot of the hill are the ivied ruins of a tower which was left when the ancient church came down to make way for the church at the top.

The Beauty About the Three Old Yews

RADBOURNE. High up in its finely timbered park is the great 18th-century house of the Poles, who have held these lands for centuries. Their old home was by Radbourne Brook at the foot of the slope, close by the little church where some of their ancestors lie.

The oldest of their monuments is a tomb with the alabaster figures of Peter de la Pole and his wife Elizabeth. The knight has long straight hair, his family arms on the hilt of his sword, and his feet on a dog. His lady's cloak is tied by a tasselled cord, and held at the hem by a dog; she has a chain round her neck three times. She was the heiress who brought the knight these lands. On an altar tomb are the engraved portraits of Peter's son Ralph, a judge shown in a long gown with hanging sleeves, a square cap on his head and his feet on a greyhound; Johanna, his wife, has a long mantle and an embroidered headdress. A low tomb adorned with angels has the engraved portraits of perhaps the judge's grandson and his wife, both under canopies; and a great marble monument reaching to the roof of the aisle has an inscription on each side of a sarcophagus to a father and son of the 17th century, both with their wives.

It is a beautiful church in which they sleep, enshrined in lovely trees with the rectory on one hand and the sound of falling water on the other. Under a wonderful bower of three old yews, whose branches sweep the ground for about 70 yards round, are stones in memory of two children of the Chandos-Poles, and one telling of a man's love for one of the family who died in 1843 before she could become his wife.

Most of the church comes from about 1300, including the nave arcade and some windows. The east window has figures of Faith, Hope, and Charity in white and gold. The embattled tower is 15th century, and the porch 18th. There is a piscina in the chancel and one in the nave. The oldest carvings in the church are the double sedilia in the chancel and a curious little carving like the top of a staff; they come from Norman days.

The splendid 14th and 15th-century woodwork in the church is said to have belonged to Dale Abbey and to have been brought here by Francis Pole of Radbourne, who bought up the fittings of the Abbey on its dissolution. In front of the Pole pew are 13 panels of linenfold vine and grapes, perhaps part of the base of a 15th-century chancel screen; one of the poppyheads of some handsomely carved bench-ends has three faces and a skull with a fallen jaw. The glory of the woodwork is an exceptionally fine font-cover which certainly came from Dale; with eight sides and two projecting rims, it is a mass of rich carving with heads and emblems of the Evangelists, the panel underneath showing the Cross and a Crown of Thorns.

The font is very old. In the tie-beams of the chancel roof are Elizabethan bosses. The oak reredos, stalls, and chancel screen are modern.

Mercia's Westminster Abbey

REPTON. We may wonder if there are more than one or two places in our Motherland where the thrill of something very old touches us as here at Repton, which lies by quiet Trent meadows dreaming of its past. It dreams of Saxon and Norman and Tudor, for here they have come in a great procession, and their story is enshrined in precious stones. There is perhaps still something left of a shrine where men worshipped when Bede was hurrying with his dictation of the Gospel of St John lest his breath should not last him to finish it; they would worship in the crypt built by the Saxons nearly 13 centuries ago when Repton was the capital of the kingdom of Mercia, the centre from which the conversion of Mercia began. It comes down to us as part of the first church of the converted Saxons in the Midlands, keeping company with great pillars the Normans set up in their priory Guest House, and with a school which has been building up a great renown since the days of the Tudors.

We feel that time lingers gracefully here, bridging the old and the new as if it did not wish to leave. Within a stone's throw of the fine old cross is Repton's splendid village group—the church with a spire like a needle in the sky, sheltering the rare old crypt where Saxon kings and princes sleep; the fine school buildings old and new, with grey walls and red walls, gables and red roofs, green carpets and lovely trees about them; delightful thatched cottages, and a wayside garden gay with flowers. Along the road to Bretby is a charming black-and-white house with a room overhanging the porch.

It was in the 7th century that a monastery was founded here, built by Saxons not many lifetimes removed from the Romans, men who were beginning the thousand years of building which has given us the noblest group of village shrines in all the world. They gave it a crypt which grew in fame till it became the Westminster Abbey of Mercia, among those buried in it being Diuma, Mercia's first bishop, Merewald the brother of King Penda, Ethelbald and Wiglaf, kings of Mercia, and Prince Wimond, son of Wiglaf. For a quarter of a century the body of the martyred Prince Wystan, son of Wimond and heir to the throne, lay in the crypt after he had been treacherously slain by his cousin, but it was removed to Evesham on the approach of the Danes in 874.

The Danes destroyed the monastery which had stood for more

than two hundred years, but the fate of the crypt is not so certain. Some say that when other Saxons built a church on the site of the old abbey they built the crypt anew, but it is more probable that they built on old foundations the chancel walls we see today. So, though the walls of the crypt may have been here while 13 centuries have rolled away, the rest of it is almost certainly 10th-century work. It has been called the most perfect specimen of Saxon architecture on a small scale that we can see; certainly it is one of the rarest corners of England. Only 17 feet square, it has a vaulted roof with small round arches resting on four spirally wreathed pillars, and eight half pillars on the walls.

Modern windows have been put in to show it up for us; there are still traces of an old altar, and an opening in the western wall is believed to have been a peephole in bygone days through which the shrine could be seen from above. Two flights of steps lead down from the church to the crypt, which was desecrated at the Dissolution and forgotten till the end of the 18th century, when a man fell into it while digging a grave. Near an entrance to it from the outside, made for the use of the priory, is a holy-water stoup.

Our great English builders of 600 years ago reshaped the Saxon church, but the chancel walls are mostly as in the 10th century, with later windows and roof. Two Saxon pillars with square capitals (which were part of the 14th-century nave arcades till last century) are in the splendid porch, company for a pathetic thing—a child's stone coffin two feet long. Above the porch door, which has been swinging here for centuries, is St Wystan in a niche, his hands on his sword; and in the room above is a grand old chest.

Crowning the lovely walls of the church is the charming tower and slender spire with three tiers of lights, rising 70 yards above the churchyard with its lychgate and shapely little yews. The tower has a band of quatrefoils below the battlements, a fine west window, and a painted clock face half as big as Big Ben.

On the ancient possessions inside the church a splendid roof looks down, 500 years old but refashioned on the eve of our time, with a fine collection of faces among 40 carved bosses. Remains of richly carved old oak pews, with varied designs, adorn a modern screen across the little transept.

Most of the windows are 600 years old, including the east of the Saxon chancel, and some have pleasing glass. In a little old lancet we see Alfrida, Abbess of Repton, and an angel holding a shield with a picture of the abbey in 697. It was Alfrida who received into the monastery Guthlac, the son of a Mercian nobleman who, after several years at Repton, decided to live as a hermit. Setting out in a boat without sail or rudder or oar, and deciding to settle where the boat should stay, he reached Croyland and lived in a hut till his death in 714. Croyland Abbey was built over his shrine.

A knight in 14th-century armour with a belt of carved medallions lies on an alabaster tomb. He has short hair, his feet are on a dog, and his head rests on a helmet. His nose has gone, and some lout of the centuries has carved initials in its place. He was probably Sir Robert Frances, lord of Foremark near by. A 17th-century wall monument has the figures of George Waklin of Bretby and his wife, kneeling.

A fine alabaster stone is engraved with the figures of Gilbert Thacker and his wife, stern-looking Tudor folk; at his feet is a quaint lion with tongue out, at hers are two boys. Their story is linked with that of the priory founded here in 1172 by Matilda, Countess of Chester, for monks who came from Calke.

The priory buildings, east of the parish church, were granted at the Dissolution to Thomas Thacker, Steward to Lord Cromwell, and he made his home among the ruins till he died. As stern as he looks in his portrait was his son Gilbert, for it was he who demolished in a single day the fine priory church. He had become alarmed at events in the terrible reign of Mary Tudor, and " destroyed the nest lest the birds should build therein again."

While still living in the ruins the Thackers sold part of them to the executors of Sir John Port whose fine tomb we see in Etwall church, and here began the school he founded which has grown great today. Friction between the boys and the Thackers led to the building of another house known as Repton Hall, now the home of the headmaster. Worked into it is what was an isolated tower, one of the best examples of medieval brickwork with turrets and battlements, built by Prior John Overton when Henry the Sixth was king. We see it well from the bridge over the old channel of the Trent.

The priory Guest House, with an old sundial over the doorway, is opposite the east end of St Wystan's church, and, though much altered, has still fine beams and massive Norman pillars. The upper part of it is now the library, where roundels of modern glass tell the story of St Guthlac; here is treasured a magnificent chest and such relics of bygone days as the Dominie's rostrum and the whipping bench. The whole of the basement of the Guest House was the cellarium, and it is said that this is the only part remaining of the 12th-century monastery. Here there were originally six Norman pillars, two of which still remain in a small room, and two in the part of it used now as the school museum, with ancient tiles in the walls found in the old tile kiln years ago.

The great tithe barn of stone and timber is now the Art School, standing by the roadside where the fine old priory gateway makes a delightful entrance to the buildings.

On the site of the old priory church, ruins of which are seen in the bases of pillars on the edge of the playing fields, a spacious hall has been raised in memory of Dr Steuart Pears, under whose rule this grammar school became in 20 years one of the great public schools of the country. The hall has a fine hammerbeam roof, oak panelled walls, and great windows filling it with light. The east window has 15 panels of heraldry set between figures of saints and patrons, Guthlac and Sir John Port among them.

The school chapel is away from the rest of the buildings. Begun in 1858 and enlarged four times, it is a fine place with an apse, arcades with clustered pillars, some lovely glass, good oak screens in the lady chapel, and a headmaster's pew handsome with golden angels with trumpets. The two saints Wystan and Guthlac keep watch over the porch.

Repton has no more charming spot than the little cloister garth of the old priory, now fragrant with the memory of the school's sacrifice. On its fine lawn stands a cross with scenes of the Crucifixion and the Resurrection carved in the head, and a great tablet on one of the grey walls has the names of about 350 Repton boys who died for England.

There had died in Repton not long before we called an old lady who remembered seeing a man sell his wife here. The poor woman had been brought from Burton-on-Trent with a halter round her neck, led like a horse for five miles, to parade three times round the village cross and be sold for half-a-crown and half-a-gallon of beer.

John Smyth of Repton School

ONE of Repton's heroes won the V.C. He was John Smyth. He went from Repton School to Sandhurst, and joined the Indian Army. His regiment of Sikhs was one of the first to arrive in France.

In May 1915 one company of Sikhs was holding part of an enemy trench, but in spite of their fire the Germans in the other part of the trench were reinforced in the night, and able to attack in the morning. The Indians held their own until their supply of bombs began to fail, and the reserves 250 yards behind made two attempts to bring them help. The space between them was so exposed, however, that both parties were practically wiped out. For a third attempt, ten Sikhs and Lieutenant Smyth were selected. They set out to take two boxes of bombs to their comrades. Smyth was 21 and full of good courage.

Wriggling through mud and between corpses, they pushed and pulled their dangerous loads; if either of the boxes were hit the men near it would be blown to pieces. Before they were halfway four men had been shot, then two more were killed and three wounded. Abandoning one box, Lieutenant Smyth and the only remaining Sikh dragged the other along, carried it across a deep stream, and reached the trench with their clothes perforated with bullet holes. The Indian was shot down at the moment of arrival, and it was considered miraculous that Smyth came through.

Far-Flung Hills and Vales

RIBER. Most of us know its name, if only for the Castle which crowns this great hill, a landmark 850 feet above the sea; but it is worth knowing for itself, for the charm of its old stone houses and its magnificent prospect, from Matlock at its feet to far-flung hills and vales.

Close at hand the pretentious 19th-century towers of Riber Castle lose whatever importance they have from afar. It is a great gaunt place built by John Smedley with the fortune he made out of his hydros at Matlock, and it was here he died in 1874. More gracious is the Elizabethan hall, with the charm of gabled roof and mullioned windows, with a stone gateway in a balustraded wall, its round steps jutting on to the wayside. It was long the home of the Wolleys.

The Romantic Story of a Little Spring

RIDDINGS. It has little enough for us to see and it is nothing on the map of beautiful England, but twice men have found treasure hidden here.

The first time was in the middle of the 18th century, when they found 800 precious Roman coins; the second time was in the middle of the 19th century, when they found a thing a hundred thousand times more precious, from which has sprung one of the greatest industries in the world, bringing with it the motor-car and the aeroplane, and all the activities depending on the internal combustion engine. It is one of the greatest romances of commerce.

In 1847 James Oakes, a colliery proprietor and ironmaster in a small way at Riddings, discovered a mysterious flow of liquid on his property and called in his brother-in-law, Lyon Playfair, a scholar and man of affairs who happened to be one of the most brilliant practical scientists of his day. He tested the flow and found it to be petroleum, then an unknown product commercially, although as naphtha, "salt of the earth," it had been known from Old Testament days.

It was found that a spring was producing 300 gallons a day, but James Oakes was too much occupied with his coal and iron to give time to it.

At Glasgow University Playfair had had a friend in a gifted carpenter named James Young, who was employed to repair instruments at the laboratory in which he afterwards became an assistant. Playfair remembered him when the petroleum came to light and wrote suggesting that Young should take over the product of the spring and manufacture useful oils from it.

Young had too much faith in his old friend to entertain any doubt of the feasibility of the proposal, and began in a small way a business which was to grow to worldwide proportions. One day soon after, he went with dismay to his friend, showing him the oil in a turbid condition and fearing that some change had occurred which would ruin the enterprise.

It was obvious to the scientist that the condition was due to the presence of paraffin, and Playfair induced Young to extract sufficient of the paraffin to make two candles. They were the first paraffin-wax candles ever produced. With one candle in his right hand and the other in his left, Playfair illumined a lecture he gave at the Royal Institution.

From this small beginning dates the enormous petroleum industry and the rich trade in paraffin and its wide range of products. Young, ever after known as Paraffin Young, made a fortune, but when the knowledge of his work spread about a worldwide search for petroleum was instituted and all the world knows what has come of it.

The Hard Years After Waterloo

RIPLEY. It gave London one of its most famous roofs and India one of its most famous men.

It began to flourish with the famous Butterley ironworks where the roof of St Pancras station was made; they were founded by Benjamin Outram, the engineer who introduced iron railways into collieries. He lived at Butterley Hall, the great house in which his famous son Sir James was born. One of Derbyshire's proudest citizens, his great career in the East earned for him the title of the Bayard of India, and a place in Westminster Abbey. The church we see was not here when he was born; it was built when he was in his teens and it has a curious little story.

It was at Pentrich close by that a little band of poor half-starved stockingers and weavers turned rebels in the hard years after Waterloo, and their insurrection, which brought three of them to the scaffold and drove some of them into exile, caused much stir throughout the country. To stem the tide of irreligion and disaffection the vicar of Pentrich set about creating enthusiasm for a church at Ripley and raised a fund from which this little place was built in 1820. It stands in the heart of the town, its tower embattled, its churchyard a trimmed lawn with flat gravestones and a few old table tombs.

Without Fear and Beyond Reproach

FROM his home at Butterley Hall Sir James Outram passed to a career in India which reads like that of a Crusader in a 19th-century setting. While still a young man he became almost a legendary figure in the East.

His first outstanding success was when, having subdued the lawless and savage Bhils, he won them to confidence and friendship, living unguarded among them, "sleeping under their swords," forming the pick of them into an efficient police force, and finally leaving them blessed with schools.

These men of the East like a man who can hunt with them, and this Outram could do; in ten years he killed 191 tigers (one after a sensational fight alone in a dark cave), 25 bears, and 15 leopards. The Afghan War called him away and he returned by perilous paths, disguised as an Afghan merchant, by a previously unknown route, bringing despatches to Sonmiani.

Although he found an unsympathetic influence in Lord Ellenborough, Outram was beloved by practically all other men on whom the safety of the Dependency hung. He was entrusted with romantic missions in which we see him navigating rivers thick with cataracts, crossing stony wastes on camels, carried through the mountains in a palanquin when a horse had shattered his leg, fighting in the hills, charging home in the plains, seizing sovereign banners, arresting refractory chiefs, here relieving an outpost, there redressing fiscal injustices, saving a rebel's life for the sake of his father who had been faithful, banishing sedition, righting wrongs, and everywhere winning the affection and confidence of native rulers and subjects alike.

"Gentlemen (said Napier at a public dinner given to Outram at Sakhar in 1842), I give you the Bayard of India, without fear and without reproach! Major James Outram of the Bombay Army," and from that hour, by that name the world has ever since acclaimed him. He cared little for command, but much for right and justice. He pleaded the native cause when he thought he detected inequity in the treatment accorded them, but when he had to defend the Residency at Hyderabad against the Baluchis, so brilliant were his tactics that Napier promised a special despatch detailing what he regarded in Outram's policy as a model for all soldiers to imitate.

He refused to accept £3000 prize money awarded to him, and in operations of great moment to India he was ready to subordinate himself, as he did during the Mutiny, when he insisted on serving under Havelock so that that brave soldier should have the glory of relieving Lucknow. Outram joined Havelock's cavalry as a volunteer, and charged victoriously at their head with a cane in his hand for weapon. Lucknow having been relieved, he took command and withstood the second siege and, with a comparative handful of men, kept at bay 100,000 enemies from November 1857 till March of 1858.

He left India a baronet and bearer of many gifts. In Bombay, where he was well known, the natives said of him, "A fox is a fool and a lion a coward compared with James Outram." He died in Paris, and his body was brought home to Westminster Abbey, where Napier's famous words are inscribed on his tomb. His statue looks out on the Thames not far away.

The Wall from Dale Abbey

RISLEY. It is an old-world stretch of a busy road, with fine trees and old buildings rich in memories of the Willoughbys who came here in the 14th century and sleep at Wilne two miles away.

The great house we see was built on the site of their old home, and has part of their terraced garden, the long stone wall enclosing the grounds being from the ruins of Dale Abbey. The church was built by Michael Willoughby in 1593 as a chapel for his house; the schools and schoolhouses close by were founded by him and his family. The church has the Willoughby arms over the doorway, and they are carved on the fine alabaster font, which, like the chancel screen adorned with cherubs, is as old as the church. Above the screen is a fine painting of Mary anointing the body of her Son.

The churchyard has a splendid yew, and by the porch is part of an old canopied niche from Dale Abbey, turned upside down and used as a flower vase. A lane between the church and the schools runs to a pretty retreat where a tiny bridge crosses a stream near a group of old cottages reached by stepping-stones.

The Sleeping Beauty

ROWSLEY. It is on the doorstep of hill and valley, rock and moorland, delightful rivers and beautiful bridges, and fine old homes of England. Round about it rise Lees Moor, the lovely stretch of Beeley Moor above fine wooded slopes, and Stanton Moor with its Nine Ladies stone circle.

Down the valleys come the Derwent and the Wye to meet below the village, the Derwent fresh from the glory of Chatsworth, and the Wye having added to its crowded life of romance the joy of flowing by Haddon Hall and gathering the waters of two lovely streams at Fillyford Bridge.

Rowsley Bridge has a charming view of the Derwent fringed by lovely trees. Twice has the bridge been widened since pack-horse days, keeping five pointed arches on the side with the ancient masonry, and round arches on the new.

The inn is a joy to see, a study of gables and mullioned windows, coming from 1652 and perhaps once a manor house. Over the embattled porch is a fine stone peacock, the crest of the Manners of Haddon. Every Peak traveller knows the Peacock; Landseer and Longfellow have been here; but the road which climbs from it is often passed by. It leads to a little church which is only 19th century, but has something worth finding both without and within.

Kedleston Hall

Longford Hall

Priory Gateway of Repton School

The old Market Cross of Bonsall

Alport Stone near Wirksworth

Adam Bede's House, Wirksworth

Hermit's Cave, Dale Abbey

A lychgate opens to a churchyard with a noble prospect and a magnificent elm whose mighty arms spread over a circle nearly 100 yards round. A fine cross with scrollwork of serpents and balls is in memory of nine men who died for Peace, and near it is a fragment of a cross which has seen about as many centuries as the other had seen years when we called, for it is said to be the head of a preaching cross set up before King Alfred's day. It is carved with braidwork and was rescued from the bed of the Wye.

The church is a pleasant place with arches and windows in the style of the Normans; its wide chancel arch has zigzag moulding and capitals with foliage. On a fine tomb in a little chapel built for her coming lies a figure as in quiet sleep, a beautiful lady who would have been a duchess had she lived. She wears a simple gown and her hands are folded on her breast. At her side on the mattress is her babe. She was Catherine, wife of Lord John Manners who became seventh Duke of Rutland, but she died when she was 23, too soon to share her lord's stately rank. In her memory the window in the chapel tells the story of St Catherine in four scenes.

The carved oak choir stalls with angel poppyheads were fashioned by the village carpenters and friends in memory of a vicar who was killed at Gloucester in 1912. The ancient bell in the gable came from the chapel at Haddon Hall.

A mile from the Peacock is Stanton Woodhouse, an Elizabethan house overlooking Darley Dale and set in a wealth of trees, among them ancient yew, chestnut, elm, and walnut. It was once the home of the Allens who had among their relatives a Lord Mayor of London and a great cardinal at Rome.

The Saxons Build on a Rock

SANDIACRE. The traffic of the world goes through it on road and rail and water. Its fields have given place to factories and workshops. Here engines of enormous power are made which work in every continent in mill and mine, making power and light in distant cities and pumping drains under London streets. Here also has grown up the first great business from the invention of a lacelike web of wire which has revolutionised the springing of our beds and the seating of our motor-cars.

Yet a place of surprising contrasts it is, for to those who look for beauty the busy street soon leads to a winding lane climbing to where a thousand years ago the Saxons found a rocky pinnacle on which to build their church. Some of their work remains in the church above the housetops, from where we see a wide view of the industrial valley, and a fine silhouette of the remarkable Hemlock Stone, a quaint geological curiosity.

It is a beautiful village church, full of years and interest. The simple 13th-century tower has Norman work in its foundations, and a spire with two tiers of lights. Its porch is not yet a centenarian, but it has a splendid Norman doorway in its keeping. The lofty nave has a 15th-century clerestory but no aisles, a 14th-century window, a Norman window on each side (lengthened to give more light), and a little Saxon window with long-and-short work above a massive Norman chancel arch of great beauty. On each side of the arch are grotesques.

The fine arch opens into what is the glory of this place, a spacious 14th-century chancel, lovely within and without. The windows are splendid with tracery; there is a charming priest's doorway, while rich buttresses carved with tracery and crowned with pinnacles, and a fine parapet pierced with quatrefoils, enhance the beauty of the outer walls. Inside, the handsome sedilia and the piscina under lofty canopies are richly pinnacled.

From the 12th century comes a remarkable gravestone on the chancel floor, engraved with a cross and a curious animal on each side of it. It was found under the pulpit and may have marked the burial-place of the builder of the Norman church. The font is 600 years old.

Four stones remain of the Charltons, who have a long story from the time when one was M.P. in 1318. Sir Richard was slain on Bosworth Field; Sir Thomas was Speaker in 1453; Edward was a Commissioner in the Civil War. They were living at Sandiacre in the 16th century, and have lived hereabouts in our own time. A pathetic floorstone tells how John Manley died in 1658, and six of his brothers and sisters all died before they were 12. In the churchyard is a stone coffin 40 inches long.

From Stony Clouds, a windswept ridge from whose side jut out great masses of rock, we see a wonderful view over the golf links to the iron furnace fires of Stanton, and over a wide countryside. A path across the links ends near an old stone quarry which the hand of man and the softening touch of Nature have transformed into a fairyland, a perfect golfing green enclosed by rock-hewn slopes over-hung with lovely trees. We knew it when it seemed a cold forbidding place; today it is a tiny natural paradise.

The Tale of a Thousand Years

SAWLEY. More than a thousand years have told their tale since a little band of monks came rowing down the Trent from Repton and brought their craft to rest by these green meadows. Something of the church they built is in the one we see between the road and the river, eloquent with the story of the years, yet with the strength that outlasts centuries and the charm of dignified simplicity. Here is work of the Saxon builders who built well enough to suit the Normans, with traces of the 13th and much of the two next building centuries. Within these walls are memories of people who have passed this way and come this way to sleep; we see their figures in stone and their portraits in enduring brass.

We come to it along an avenue of limes a century old, running through the rectory lawns like a lofty aisle not made with hands; 24 great trees we counted, making a church approach perhaps not surpassed in Derbyshire. And there, in front of us as we walk, is the fine 600-year-old north doorway with its splendid old oak door, ribbed and studded. All this time the south door has kept its old bar-fastening; all this time the priest has been going through the chancel doorway, and the children of Sawley have been baptised at this font.

Who is not stirred with the thought of all this continuity of time and this enduring heritage of our countryside? Everywhere the outside walls are strong and clean, crowned with a sturdy 15th-century tower and splendid spire with four small windows. We come inside and find it bright and light with charming windows, most of them 600 years old, with a 15th-century clerestory above the lofty 14th-century nave arcades. The Saxons built the plain round chancel arch, standing for us as it stood for them; some of the masonry above it, and some in the north wall of the chancel, is said also to be theirs. Across the east end of the chancel is another wonder of our past, a stone screen 500 years old, seven feet from the east wall. Its oak door has been here all the time, panelled and studded and with a handle of fine iron work.

This medieval treasure house is rich indeed in craftsmanship, for it has a massive 15th-century oak screen with an embattled cornice and some tracery in the Saxon chancel arch, massive ancient stalls in the choir, and some sturdy Elizabethan oak benches in the nave. It has a Jacobean pulpit with a canopy, a 17th-century altar table, an old oak chest, and remains of a 14th-century oak screen now in the aisles. The roofs of the nave and the north aisle have much of their fine 15th-century timbering, the nave with old bosses.

And it has a noble group of monuments. The 14th-century stone figure of one of the priests, thought to be Cardinal Gauselinus who often lived in the village, has suffered much through lying outside for centuries. There are two other priests in the north aisle, one perhaps Ralph de Chaddesden who died while rebuilding the church in the 13th century, the other perhaps Hugh de Scoter, who carried on his work.

Five hundred years ago the Bothes settled at Sawley in a house of which some of the timbers are still in the cellars of a farmhouse by the church. A rich and famous family, they were great benefactors of this church, and gave England two archbishops, two bishops, and two archdeacons. The first of them was Roger, and his fine brass portrait showing him in armour with his head on a helmet and his feet on a boar, is on an altar tomb under a canopy in the chancel. His wife is here, wearing a necklace with a cross, and in tiny groups are their 17 children. On another tomb are the brass portraits of Roger's son Robert, his wife, and a group of six girls; Roger a knight with a collar of suns and roses, and the wife in a widow's veil with her feet on a stag. In a handsome bay forming a recess in the chancel, built for his tomb, lies John Bothe who was buried here in 1496. He wears the dress of a canon, and his head is on a cushion held by angels.

A lady in flowing robes lies in brass on the floor of an aisle, with just the head of her husband left, showing his long hair; he was a merchant, dying in 1510.

In the lovely east window of the south aisle Christ is blessing little children, and in a small lancet is the Good Shepherd in a glowing red robe. Beautiful glass in the east window of the other aisle has a fine St George and Gabriel bringing the good news to Mary, in memory of Samuel Hey who served here for 48 years until 1893. The oak altar guarded by two golden angels is in memory of Arthur Clarke who followed till 1933.

One fine memory outside the church has Sawley, for a tablet on a little house tells us that within it John Clifford was born. He was the most famous man born in Sawley.

John Clifford of Great Fame

JOHN CLIFFORD, one of the most vital forces of modern Nonconformity, in the pulpit, on the platform, was a man of charming character, who made himself what he was, the greatest Free Churchman of his day. He was born a poor boy at Sawley in 1836, and had the slenderest form of elementary education before he was working as a boy in a lace factory. From the first, however, his love of books and thirst for knowledge were insatiable. His personality not less than this anxiety for learning marked him in early youth as suited for the ministry, and his denomination, the Baptists, welcomed him into their Academy at Leicester and College at Nottingham. When he was only 22 he was invited to accept the pastorate at Praed Street, Paddington, where (and at the larger chapel built for him at Westbourne Park) he remained for 57 years.

John Clifford was particularly attracted to London because it gave him opportunities of study. In five years he took the degrees of B.A., B.Sc., M.A., and LL.B. at London University, and built up one of the biggest and most energetic Nonconformist churches in the country, whose devotion to him was unfailing. There was no denominational organisation that did not welcome him as its president. He believed in every man taking an active part in citizenship, and as he was a convinced Liberal in politics he was as well known on the platform as in the pulpit. Education on the broadest national lines, universal, free, and unsectarian, was his special subject. He held that the teaching of creeds was the duty of the sects and not of the nation, and that revenue contributed by everybody should not be used for them. Indeed he refused to pay for such purposes, and led a movement for passive resistance against such payments. The result was that, from time to time, some of his household goods were seized and sold. In this he was the embodiment of what was called the Nonconformist Conscience.

For what he believed was right he was a doughty fighter; but it would be a great mistake to regard him as a narrow-minded demagogue. His breadth of mind and gentleness of spirit was what most impressed those who knew him best. His charity was broad enough to allow every man to believe what he must, and to respect his honesty, but he declined to be made a participant in what he regarded as other men's errors.

A great worker all his life, he worked till the moment of his death, which came one day as he sat among his friends at Baptist House in Kingsway. His long brave life ended (at 80) as he would have wished it to end, on the platform where he had spent so much of it, fighting for every good cause and all downtrodden people.

The Lady Constantia

SCARCLIFFE. It has the memory of a gracious lady for whom it rings its curfew every year for three weeks on each side of Christmas. It is said that the lady and her little one were lost in a forest hereabouts, overcome with weariness and cold when the curfew bell of Scarcliffe led them safely home; and she left five acres of land to the church for the ringing of curfew for ever.

She was the Lady Constantia, probably one of the Frechevilles who held the manor in the 13th century; it was one of their ancestors who gave the church to the monks of Darley. The doorway through which the monks came is here to this day, with a tympanum over it carved with geometrical patterns of a design so varied that it seems as if the sculptor had been practising his art. Here also are four round arches and three pillars of varying shapes set up by the Normans; one of the three pillars is round, one octagonal, and one is four-clustered.

The fine little priest's doorway is Norman too, buried in plaster until last century, and the tiny piscina in the corner of the chancel is the old one used by the monks.

In this fascinating little place lie the mother and her child who were lost in the forest 700 years ago. They lie in marble, the babe in the mother's arms, one of its hands up to her face. With her right arm the mother gathers up the graceful folds of the mantle she is wearing over her simple gown, which is fastened at the throat with a round brooch. Her hair is in plaited braids and on her head, which rests on a lion for a pillow, is a lovely coronet telling of her high estate. It is a lovely memorial, one of the finest for its time.

The tower of this old place is hardly yet a centenarian; the roofs are fine and old, and there is an enormous chest about ten feet long made out of four huge planks.

The Shipload of Slaves

SCROPTON. It has a charming bit of road between two lych-gates, one gate leading to the churchyard, the other, lovely with carving of vine and grapes, opening to a burial ground close by; it is a memorial to 16 men who did not come back. Their memory will not fade, for in the chancel of the church they are remembered by four things; a window of the Crucifixion, a marble floor, oak stalls with a prayer desk splendidly carved, and a white tablet bearing their names with figures of three angels.

The church was made new last century, and all that remains of the older one are two memorials now under the tower which has a pyramid roof. One is a fine alabaster stone with the engraved portrait of William Schower, a London merchant of Dick Whittington's day, his feet on a greyhound. On an altar tomb adorned with angels lie Nicholas Agard and his two wives, he in armour with a double chain round his neck, they with mantles tied with cords, little dogs touching the hems of their garments. They lived in early Tudor days at Foston, a mile or so away.

Very unusual are the altar and the reredos, with 12 fine little paintings of the Disciples set in a framework of wood, all from Vienna. A small window in the nave has lovely glass showing St George.

Another window shows an angel and a kneeling figure on a ship at sea, a fitting memorial to one who was happiest when pacing the deck of his ship. He was Admiral Sir Arthur Cumming, who spent his last years at Foston and was buried in this church in 1893 after a life of much adventure. He distinguished himself at the storming of Sidon when he was 23, and he did something when he was 26 that was as wonderful as anything we have read in romances of the sea. Cruising off South America, he fell in with a pirate ship with a cargo of slaves. He gave chase, shot the captain, leaped on board with seven other men and fought against 30. He drove the pirates below hatches, chained them all, and had complete control of the vessel till his own ship came up.

There is a peep of bygone days where a fine half-timbered house with gables sees the Foston Brook make ready to meet the Dove.

SHARDLOW. Road and river run through it side by side till the Trent swings under Cavendish Bridge to its meeting with the Derwent at Wilne.

Busy days began for Shardlow when this fine bridge, with its three lofty arches, was built in 1771, for it robbed the ancient Swarkeston Bridge of the stream of coaches and became itself the main highway from London to Carlisle. It is busy with waterways, too, for at Wilne Ferry close by the Grand Trunk Canal takes boats from the Trent to the Mersey.

It has a fine stone Hall of 1684 which is now a school, and among its old houses is one 300 years old, whose lead pipes have quaint figures of birds and animals. The church is 19th century.

A Kiss From a King

SHIRLAND. The busy road to Chesterfield runs between its little green and the fine old church which has seen five centuries go by. It is adorned with battlements and pinnacles, eight of them crowning the splendid tower. The porch, with a vaulted roof, has a niche over the door in which stands a modern St Leonard.

A beautiful recess in the chancel comes with its carved finials from the older church, where it sheltered the figure of a knight. The front stone of its alabaster tomb still remains, carved with 21 shields of the Greys, who held the lands in the time of King John. The vanished knight was perhaps Sir Henry Grey, who was summoned to Parliament about 1377.

An alabaster stone on the chancel wall has the headless figures of two men and two women wearing mantles and kneeling at desks; they are perhaps Reginald Grey with his wife and two children, and are over 600 years old. His father was kissed by Henry the Third for his willingness to go with him to Holy Land in 1252, when very few men were ready to go.

On the top of an alabaster tomb in an aisle are engraved the portraits of John Revell with his wife and eight children. He is in 16th-century armour with his sword and a dog; his wife has a flowing gown with close-fitting sleeves and wide cuffs. The Revells of Ogston founded a chantry here in the 15th century.

Two windows have fragments of ancient glass, and there is a chained folio copy of Jewell's Apology (1609), an ancient Bible, and a pitch pipe used by the leader of the choir until 1767.

How Are the Mighty Fallen

SHIRLEY. Two veterans have fallen on hard times in this small place in so pretty a setting among the little hills. They are the old yew and the old cross in the churchyard, and both are past their glory, for, though the yew stands proudly high, with a trunk measuring 17 feet round, its branches were sadly broken in a gale, and the cross has only two feet of its shaft on its base and three steps.

The tower of the tiny church is 19th century, as is the north aisle and the arcade leading to it. The rest of the church is chiefly 14th century, with a font 500 years old. Its oldest possession is a stone in an outside wall, once part of the tympanum of a Norman doorway, crudely carved with animals and foliage. On a floorstone near the altar rails is the worn portrait of a priest, Nicholas Bentley, who was vicar here till 1515. He would know the tiny silver paten of Henry the Seventh's day which is still in use.

Two 19th-century memorials are of the Shirleys, an ancient family which took its name from the village 800 years ago, and were its lords till the 19th century. One of them is immortalised by Shakespeare as valiant Shirley, having perished in the Battle of Shrewsbury. A farmhouse near the church has part of their old homestead in a gable, some oak panelling, and the moat.

A brass cross is in memory of Canon Shirley of Christ Church, Oxford, where he was buried in 1873. A stone monument with three canopied niches is to Walter Augustus Shirley of 1847, a vicar here who became a bishop, greatly esteemed for his wide reading and scholarship, and much beloved for his kindly humour. Here his son Walter was born, one of Dr Arnold's most brilliant scholars at Rugby.

The Weathercock at the Inn

SMALLEY. It has a fine view of little rolling hills, a great house by a lovely bit of trim grass-bordered road, and Stainsby Hall on the hillside, home of the Sitwells since 1785.

But it has nothing more pleasing than its church garden (as we would like to call all our churchyards). A veritable garden of flowers, it has tree-lined walks, roses and rhododendrons, cypress and yew on every hand, the king of all being a magnificent old yew with stately trunk and spreading branches which lost two arms in a storm of 70 years ago.

The church has seen much change in its short life of 140 years. At first just a nave and chancel, it had transepts added in 1844 but lost them 20 years after, when the aisles and a bigger chancel were built. The tower, like a pagoda, was built the year before the war.

The old turret it replaced had what was perhaps the only weathercock in England which has been held as hostage at an inn. When the church was being built messengers were sent to bring the weathercock from Derby, but returned without it, having had so good a time at an inn there that the landlord kept it till they paid his bill.

One relic of the older church is here still, a stone with an engraved cross perhaps 800 years old.

The Heiress Under the Pews

SMISBY. Its church looks over the housetops into Leicestershire. It has monuments of the Kendalls who lived at the old Hall which is now a farmhouse near the church.

Three monuments has this small church, of which one has not been without adventure in its six centuries here. Once on a raised tomb, it was long hidden under the pews, but we found it saved from this humility and set against the wall.

It is an alabaster stone sculptured with the figure of a woman in a long mantle, her hands clasped on her breast. She was Joan Comyn, who died about 1350, heiress of the lord of the manor. Her face is much worn and one of her shields is gone, but the heiress found under the pews was for long the most important lady of Smisby, for it was through marrying her descendant that the Kendalls came to the Hall. Here is William Kendall, his portrait engraved in stone when he died in 1500; he is worn away though his wife can still be seen. Here, too, is Henry Kendall, kneeling with his wife on a great monument against the chancel wall, their 16 children with them, two sons and one daughter in shrouds.

The low tower is 15th century, the oldest work in the church being a 13th-century lancet and a buttress. The nave arcade, the east window, and the font bowl are 14th century. Seven old tie-beams support the roof. The fine linenfold panelling in the chancel and the tower was once part of the glory of the castle of Ashby-de-la-Zouch.

The village still keeps its old lock-up, a tiny octagonal building with a studded door and a roof like a spire. It is believed that here, in the fields behind the school, was fought the famous tournament described by Scott in Ivanhoe, less than two miles from the castle round which some of the scenes in the story were laid.

SNELSTON. The River Dove dividing it from Staffordshire, it is sheltered by wooded hills, and has delightful lanes. In one of them is a tiny church and a great house, and a lodge which is a fine little study of stone-roofed gables overhanging brick-and-timber walls. The handsome Hall, a century old, stands at the head of terraced lawns, looking rather like a church with its embattled turret.

The 19th century took most of the old church away, except for the low 15th-century tower with pinnacles, gargoyles, and heads on the dripstones of the windows. The font is 600 years old; the bright interior has fine woodwork, the chancel screen being extended to make a canopy over the pulpit. On the richly carved and gilded reredos, with figures in wood and alabaster, is a panel of Christ giving Peter the keys. A beautiful memorial of delicate Moorish carving, with arcades and lattice windows in red, blue, and gold, is in memory of eight heroes, their names on each side of a tiny Crucifix.

700 Years in a Hollow of the Hills

SOMERSAL HERBERT. It nestles in a hollow of little hills at the end of winding lanes, with a tiny church by a charming old house, the half-timbered and many-gabled home of the Fitzherberts who have lived in this place for 700 years. Much of it is Elizabethan, and in the entrance hall are two oak tablets to John Fitzherbert and his wife which have been here since 1564, odd for being in two halves, one unreadable without the other.

An oak lychgate to men who did not come back opens to a delightful churchyard of lawn and flowers, set among fine trees and orchards, where a rose-lined path leads to a fine cross with a tapering shaft. It stands on three steps and is perhaps 13th century, almost the oldest occupant of the village.

The church with its sturdy exterior and low embattled tower, and its pleasing interior with black-and-white roof, has little left of the old work since the rebuilding of last century, but its treasure is a very fine Norman font, shaped like a tub and carved with 26 interlaced arches below a lattice border.

In a chancel recess is the battered figure of a priest with a chalice, perhaps Robert By-the-Broke, who became rector here when Joan of Arc was fighting the English in Orleans.

The Boy Who Made the Wheels Go Round

SOUTH NORMANTON. Here, it is said, was born in 1726 Jedediah Strutt, who rose to wealth and fame by inventing the ribbed stocking frame, and lies buried in the lovely cemetery above the Derwent which turned his wheels at Belper.

A busy village has grown round a church begun in Norman days, made new in the 14th century, and much refashioned since. Of the 14th century there are left the north arcade of the nave, the font, and a piscina. One or two windows and the embattled tower with modern pinnacles are 15th century. The oldest relic is a splendid Norman coffin stone engraved with a cross, now in the floor of the porch; and the most beautiful relic is the charming 13th-century carved arch of the doorway leading to the vestry. It was originally the priest's doorway, and was hidden till last century.

There is a monument with weeping cherubs to Robert Revel, lord of the manor in Queen Anne's day, one of a family who lived at the old gabled Carnfield Hall near by.

The Ruin Splendid

SOUTH WINGFIELD. It takes to itself the church of its neighbouring hamlet Oakerthorpe, lying on the old Roman road; but it is for its fine pile of ruins that we come. They crown a low hilltop and are the stones of Wingfield Manor, among the finest remains in our land of a great house of the 15th century. It was built by one Cromwell and destroyed by another, and in the two centuries between them it had a remarkable history as a stately house, a prison, and a fortress.

It was in 1441 that Ralph Lord Cromwell began building the house, and it was still unfinished when he died in 1455. A man of great wealth, he was Lord Treasurer of England, and is said to have built the castle and church at Tattershall in Lincolnshire where he lies. The house was completed by the 2nd Earl of Shrewsbury, and became a favourite seat of the family. George Talbot, 6th earl and husband of Bess of Hardwick, had the custody of Mary Queen of Scots for nearly 16 years, and she was here in his care for a short time in 1569.

She was at Wingfield again in 1584 with 250 people as guards and retinue, and it was during this time that the plot was hatched which cost Anthony Babington his head and brought Mary to Fotheringay. Young, handsome, and an ardent Roman Catholic, Babington had been a page to the Queen in his boyhood, and had remained devoted to her cause. He lived only a few miles away at Dethick, and it is said that in spite of the strong guard placed over the Queen, he managed to visit her frequently disguised as a gipsy. The story is that the great walnut tree near Mary's apartments grew from a walnut he dropped. News of the conspiracy leaked out through Walsingham's spies, and in September of 1586 Babington was executed at Lincoln's Inn.

The house was garrisoned for Parliament in the Civil War, and after falling for the King was taken by Sir John Gell and dismantled. After the Restoration Immanuel Halton, an astronomer, settled here, turning the Banqueting Hall into a two-storeyed dwelling and allowing the rest to fall into decay. A century later his descendants used the ruins as a quarry for stone to build the house at the foot of the hill, as plain as the other was lovely. But in spite of the ravages of time, and of the vandals, there is still enough dignity left in walls and gables, entrances and windows, to suggest its ancient splendour, and what we see today is to be preserved for all time.

The ruins spread over a space of a quarter of a mile round, 416 feet long and 250 feet wide; the inner court devoted to state and dwelling apartments, the outer to accommodation for guards and retainers. The Banqueting Hall has still a projecting bay window of rare beauty, with exquisite tracery. The fine porch leading to the Hall has a lovely archway and a small traceried window of most beautiful design; and there is a charming round window in a gable of the state apartments. Under the Hall is a remarkable room with four entrances and a vaulted roof enriched with great bosses carved with tracery, resting on arches which spring from the walls and from pillars between two aisles.

In the range of buildings between the two courts is the great inner gateway with a turret on each side. The buildings east of the gateway have been modernised into a farmhouse, and at the other end stands the watch tower, 72 feet high, with fine steps leading to the summit. Often must Mary Queen of Scots have climbed these steps to reach her rooms, desolate now with only fragments of the walls which held her captive. Little is left of the outer court, but near the entrance gateway stands the grand old barn, 70 feet long and with massive timbers.

The church, just within Oakerthorpe, is set in pleasant meadows with the Amber flowing by one side of the churchyard. Made new in Georgian days, it has still the 15th-century tower with worn heraldry on the buttresses, and nave arcades of the same time. From the 14th century come the priest's doorway with its crude little figure. The bowl of the font is Norman, oldest possession of all. In the churchyard, below the east window, is a coffin stone with a battered 13th-century knight in a tunic of mail, his hands folded on his breast. Long after his day the old coaches came lumbering along the Roman road through Oakerthorpe, and there is still a platform at the old inn where 16 coaches changed horses every day.

Arabi Pasha Gives Up His Sword

SPONDON. The pressure of the Artificial Silk Age has left it still a few quiet ways about its church, and still we may all take a walk among the deer of the beautiful Locko Park with its great lake and its charming waterfall sheltered by yews. Locko is said to come from the days when this stately Hall began its career as a leper hospital.

Here was born in 1830 Sir Drury Drury-Lowe, the famous soldier who served in the Crimea and the Mutiny and made a moonlight charge at Tel-el-Kebir. He received the surrender of Arabi Pasha, who gave up his sword to him. It was Henry Gilbert, whose family were here from the time of Elizabeth, who built the chapel to the house; we see his wife with her pretty ringlets in Spondon church. She died in 1665.

The church, with a spire as a landmark on the hilltop, was made new after a fire in 1340, except for part of the tower. Fine and lofty, with wide arches and great windows, it is a splendid example of a 14th-century church, with porches and north aisle new built a hundred years ago. There are three sedilia, a fine little piscina, and a stone lectern on the chancel wall.

In the churchyard is a noble elm and something centuries older, a massive fragment of a Saxon cross with knotwork carving almost worn away.

War Upon War

STANLEY. It has a great house, a glorious cedar, a cottage with a fine thatched roof, and a tiny church with a double bell-turret.

All that is left of the chapel that was here 800 years ago is a Norman priest's doorway now in the wall. A small lancet and some buttresses are from the 13th-century building. The chancel is not yet a century old, but its 14th-century east window was in the old chapel.

The font was made 600 years ago, and the pulpit 300. In the nave is a small piscina.

In the floor by the pulpit is a brass tablet to Sir John Bentley of Breadsall, who came to sleep here 20 years before the Civil War was to darken the countryside. The timbered porch is in memory of the men who gave their lives in the War to End War 300 years after.

The Bridge of Kneeling Children

STANTON-BY-BRIDGE. With a fine view from its windblown hilltop of the great Trent meadows, this tiny place is at one end of the beautiful bridge which stretches nearly a mile over the low-lying land and links it up with Swarkeston. There the graceful span of five arches over the river was rebuilt in 1796, but there are 13th-century remains in the raised causeway of weathered stone, fine buttresses, and group of six splendid arches which lies for the most part in Stanton.

Full of years is its little towerless church, for its plain round chancel arch, a tiny west window with a deep splay, and much masonry of the west wall are said to be a thousand years old. Within the porch is a lofty Norman doorway with chevron, the little cross over it being perhaps the consecration cross of the Norman church, where the bishop put his hand 800 years ago.

From the 14th century come a beautiful window and the priest's doorway in the chancel, the nave arcade, a piscina, and the font. There is a lovely old oak chest. In the west wall of the aisle are fragments of 12th-century coffin stones, one very rare with a little animal carved by the cross.

Under an arch in the aisle lies the stone figure of a priest who rebuilt the old church; it is perhaps Geoffrey or Thomas de Stanton, who followed each other here in the 14th century.

On the wall of the chancel is a stone with the engraved portraits of William Sacheverell of 1558 and his wife; above it is another stone with their seven sons and seven daughters, a fine effect as of a bridge of kneeling children. Another alabaster stone against the chancel wall has the engraved figures of Katherine Francis and her husband Richard, in Tudor dress; six boys and seven girls at their feet are hidden by the stalls.

A mile from the village is a farmhouse known as St Bride's, with some remains of a chapel of 800 years ago.

The Rare Little Sundial

STANTON-BY-DALE. It looks one way to the wide industrial Erewash Valley beyond the glowing fires of the great iron-works, and the other way to Leicestershire with Charnwood Forest, while at its doorstep is the rocky ridge of Stony Clouds, with a quarry which has become a little fairyland. Its roads are up and down, with low stone walls crowned by hedges, and by the green where three ways meet is a village cross with a weatherworn shaft and a later head.

A row of almshouses 200 years old, trim with lawn and flower-beds, brings us to the church with flowers creeping up its walls, in a churchyard like a garden. Lighted by fine windows of deep splay, it has grown from a Norman church made new in the 14th century. There are fragments of Norman cross-stones built in the outside walls, and a tympanum of much interest over the south doorway. In the middle of it is a raised round boss believed to be a crude sundial of Norman or Saxon days, with lines cut out to mark the hours of 6, 9, noon, 3, and 6; round the boss has been cut at a later time a circle containing a cross outlined in relief. The stone-roofed porch which shelters it, with two tiny lancets, is 13th century, and another old lancet is in the aisle. The nave arcade and the font are 14th century, and the tower is a century younger. Three windows glowing with rich colour show the Nativity, with figures of Luke and John, the Crucifixion, and Our Lord appearing to the Disciples.

We read here of Edward Holt who was 100 when he died in 1606, and among the Pilkingtons of the old manor house who lie here is Matthew, the last of them, who died in 1765. He is remembered because he made an index of the Bible, a remarkable piece of work which appears to have passed into oblivion.

The Storied Moor

STANTON-IN-THE-PEAK. Climbing the steep hillside to Stanton Moor, this village of gabled stone houses has a wonderful view of the lovely valley where the waters of the Lathkill and Bradford dales run together to meet the Wye, fresh from its journey by Haddon Hall. Youlgreave's splendid tower and Bakewell's elegant spire are landmarks in the scene.

Its old Hall is a farmhouse, with some remains of the ancient home of the Foljambes and the Plumptons. The Stanton Hall still here, in

Peak Forest

Chapel-en-le-Frith

An Industrial Scene at Staveley

A Pastoral Scene at Parwich

a deer park with a drive nearly two miles long, was built in the 18th century by the Thornhills whose memorials are in the church they built.

It is proud of its moor, a high plateau about a square mile in extent, for, though it has lost much of the oak, fir, larch, and chestnut with which it was planted years ago, and has quarries now, it is full of interest for its ancient remains of monoliths, barrows, and stone circles. Skeletons and calcined bones have been found in some of the barrows. Among the detached stones about the moor are the Andle Stone (a massive block 15 feet high), the tower-like Gorse Stone, the huge Heart Stone, and the curiously shaped rock called the Cat Stone almost on the edge of the precipice overlooking Darley Dale. The small Stone Circle called the Nine Ladies, about 33 yards round, and with all but one stone upright, has its pointer (the King Stone) 100 feet away.

Not far from this circle is a square tower, a landmark from far around, with the inscription "Earl Grey 1832," a tribute to the man who carried the great Reform Bill through Parliament.

Thankful the whole country should be for its share (through the National Trust) of this moor, for Stanton Moor Edge, a natural terrace 900 feet above the sea, about a mile long and comprising 28 acres, is ours for all time; ours with all the glory of its magnificent views of encircling heather-clad moorlands, and of the winding Derwent valley from Chatsworth to Oaker Hill in Darley Dale.

The Miner's Lamp is Lit

STAVELEY. One thing we remember here which we have not come upon elsewhere. We have seen lamps for ever burning by the altar in memory of some great figure, but here a lamp is burning for ever, not in memory of any hero of war, not to mark the memory of some one gone, but as a tribute to men who go in peril for us every day to keep our home fires burning.

It is a miner's lamp burning for ever
near a piece of coal in Staveley church.

Famous for its coal and iron, it has pleasant ways by the church, with the ancient cross restored in the churchyard, and the great house close by. The house is now the rectory, much changed since the Frechevilles put their arms over the door and enriched its walls with splendid woodwork. They were here six centuries ago. Margaret founded the school at Netherthorpe in 1572, Peter built the little stone almshouses at Woodthorpe 300 years ago. John lies in the great sarcophagus in their chapel in the church, the last of his line and its first and only peer. He garrisoned his house for the King and fought for it till the Parliament men took it. He filled a window in this chapel with glowing heraldry surrounded by cherubs and wreaths of flowers, the glass said to have been brought from France. His daughter Christian lies in the chapel, finely sculptured in white marble, a baby in her arms.

In the chancel where he sleeps, we see an earlier Peter Frecheville in brass, without his head, but still with sword and dagger, wearing armour adorned with his arms, and all his ancient dignities upon his tomb. He set it up here at the death of his wife in 1482, and when he died after 21 years more they put another brass on the chancel wall, where he kneels, facing the wife who left him, with their eight boys and seven girls kneeling in fur-trimmed gowns. His oldest boy John died a few years after him, and he lies between the chancel and the chapel, his hands clasped, his sword at his side.

The church with something of all our great building centuries, from Saxon days to 500 years ago, was made a large and stately place by 19th-century restoration, which gave it a new porch, and a north aisle with a splendid arcade dividing it from the nave. Its oldest possessions are monuments of birth and death. Fragments of engraved coffin stones in the sills of two windows are thought to belong to the church the Normans put in their Domesday Book. A long tapering stone with a cross and a sword, and a splendid font with a man's head on it, bearded and crowned, are both 12th century.

The base of the tower with lancet windows and corner turret is 13th century, its 15th-century upper storey was crowned with battlements and pinnacles 200 years later. The sides of the south doorway and their foliage capitals are also 13th century. From the 14th century come the beautiful south arcade, the two low arches and the pillar between the chancel and chapel, and the row of small clerestory windows above them, rare in a chancel. A handsome recess of this time, built into the new aisle, has crude little carvings on the pinnacle at each side, of a man with folded hands, one with a crown, a woman with a crown, and one in long gown. Within the recess a wall painting is fading away.

The old chancel screen has been sacrificed to give the church more light, and the finely carved screen in its place is in memory of a rector of our own time. A sanctus bell still rings in its old place between the nave and the chancel.

Here we remember the miner's lamp, and here we remember the odd old man with his hurdy-gurdy, almost all that is left of a fine array of ancient glass. He is one of two roundels in the east window, and is a comical figure with his toes turned in as he turns the handle of his funny little organ.

The Rodes of Woodthorpe Hall were neighbours of the Freche-villes, and at the old Hall, of which fragments remain in the farmhouse on the site, was born about 1530 Francis Rodes, a judge of Eliza-beth's day; and there he died after beginning the building of the fine Barlborough Hall which became the home of his son Sir John. Judge Rodes took part in the trial of Mary Queen of Scots.

The Wonder Unsurpassed

STEETLEY. It is a tiny hamlet sheltering one of Derbyshire's gems, hiding it with a veil of trees even from the narrow way that brings us to it.

It is a Norman chapel of the time of Stephen, a temple of loveliness all alone except for a farm. It has only a nave and a chancel ending in an apse, 56 feet from east to west and less than 16 feet wide, but it is so rich in ancient beauty that it has been said to be "a gem of early architectural art, one of the most complete and beautiful specimens of Norman work on a small scale to be found in this country or in Normandy."

Less than 60 years ago it was a roofless ruin, except for the roof of the apse, and cattle wandered in and out of the ivied walls through doors made for them. In 1875, for the first time for 300 years, people met within the ruins to make plans for their restoration, and five years later it stood in its glory as we see it.

The south doorway has been given two new pillars and mouldings. The old part of the arch has three orders of moulding, one plain on plain pillars, the second ornamented with beak-heads and resting on pillars with deep-cut interlacing foliage, the third with chevrons, on pillars carved with medallions.

The interior is all too dimly lighted to show its loveliness. The glorious chancel arch has triple mouldings, the first a scalloped border with a cone in every scallop, the second embattled, the third with chevrons. The capitals on which they rest are quaintly carved; one with a double-bodied lion, another with St George coming to the rescue of a prostrate figure under a winged dragon whose long sweeping tail curls round the next capital and branches into foliage.

A fine frame is the chancel arch for the charming apse, which opens with an arch resting on capitals handsomely carved. The four ribs of its vaulted roof are carved with beak-heads, with a holy lamb in a medallion where they meet. The capitals of the pilasters on which the ribs rest are elaborately carved with interesting designs, one showing the temptation of Adam and Eve with the serpent curled round a tree loaded with fruit, and another with two doves. It is lighted by three exquisite lancets filled with glass like patch-work in the colours of the rainbow.

Below these windows on the outside wall the apse is encircled by a beautiful string-course carved with foliage, and it has a cornice under the roof, continued round the rest of the chapel, resting on brackets with grotesque heads and other devices.

An ancient stone in the churchyard is carved with an altar, a chalice, and a hand held out in blessing. Under this stone was found a skull, thought to be that of a rector at the time of the Black Death.

The Judge and His Pigs

STONEY MIDDLETON. It is a little singular and well named, for its houses rise tier on tier on ledges of rock and under hanging cliffs; it is all so steep in places that when a sheriff was asked by a judge why he had no coach he answered that the town where he lived stood on end.

But it has little crooked ways and sudden turns with unexpected bits of charm, one of them by the church in company with gay gardens and a little brook on its way to the grounds of the old Hall, the home of the Denmans.

Here lived Joseph Denman of Bakewell and his famous nephew Thomas, one of the greatest reformers of the Victorian era. He was an upright judge, a man of high moral character, and one of the most persistent advocates of the abolition of slavery. His sons rose to high positions, one an admiral, another a judge. The son Thomas who succeeded him lived to be 89, and is still remembered in the village for his queer hobby of keeping black pigs and taking them in his carriage as presents to his friends.

An odd little building is the church, the nave and chancel being an octagon added to the low 15th-century tower in 1759. There is a tribute to Urban Smith, for 54 years vicar last century, and when we called, John Riddlesden had just retired after 47 years, the second vicar in over a century of continuous service.

Near the church are the old stone buildings of the baths fitted up by Lord Denman on the site of what is believed to have been a Roman bath, no longer used though the warm spring still flows.

At the doorstep of the village is Middleton Dale to take us on to Tideswell, a gorge of wild scenery of grassy slopes and stupendous rocks stretching in weird shapes along a mile of the road, with Lover's Leap and the mighty Castle Rock's projecting towers, a cave which kept for many years the secret of the murder of an old Scotch pedlar, and the charming rocky glen which goes uphill to Eyam.

Three Little Ones

SUDBURY. It is in the rich meadows of the Dove, with old houses, old inn, old stocks, and a wayside green. Through it two busy highways join for a spell so that none shall miss its beauty, bringing us to the open lawns of the stately Hall. A house of warm red walls, it is full of treasure within and beauty without; on one side it looks to fair parklands; on the other to gardens and lake, river valley, and Needwood Forest.

Since the 17th century it has been the home of the Vernons to whom the Montgomerys brought the lands in the time of Henry the Eighth. The Montgomerys held the manor soon after the conquest, though they lived at Cubley a few miles away. In the beautiful church close by, set in a garden of wonderful yews, lie two of the Montgomery ladies of 700 years ago, carved in stone with wimples under their chins and hearts in their hands. They would come through the doorway which lets us in, for it is Norman, part of the church which was rebuilt about 1300—the time of the nave arcades, the chancel arch, and most of the tower. Among the old carved stones built into the outside walls is the head of a lovely floral cross, and an angel with a shield which belonged to a 14th-century roof.

The splendid roofs of nave and chancel, one with winged angels and one with fine bosses, are modern, as are the fine oak chancel screen, the sanctuary panelling, the stalls and the prayer desks. Among fragments of old woodwork fixed on to an old oak chest are two from a 14th-century chancel screen. The fine font with ball-flowers is modern.

The church is rich in memorials of the Vernons, from Sir John of 1600 to two who fell in the Great War, one the 8th baron. Sir John lies under a heraldic arch, looking stately in his armour, wearing a ruff and a beard. His wife lies on the tomb below, her head on an embroidered cushion. It was she who built the Hall and died in 1622.

There is a monument to the first Lord Vernon and his three wives, the third being the daughter of Sir Simon Harcourt who became Lord Chancellor. An epitaph to Lord Vernon's daughter Catherine, who died when she was 25, was written by the poet laureate William Whitehead, and says:

> This fair example to the world was lent
> As the short lesson of a life well spent.

There are sculptured heads of the fourth lord and his wife; he died at Gibraltar in 1835, and they sleep under a magnificent old yew in the churchyard, a spot he chose himself. Another monument is to the fifth lord who died in 1866, having changed his surname to Warren. His son Augustus Henry is remembered by a window and the handsome alabaster reredos; but it is a tiny monument to his three children that we remember best in this great array, a sculpture in white marble set in a black frame, showing two lovely boys asleep in each other's arms. They fell asleep within nine days of each other, little Two-Year-Old and Four-Year-Old, and their small sister followed them the next year.

Over the Norman doorway stands St George in memory of eight men who did not come back, and near the pulpit is a wooden cross rescued from a hut outside Armentieres after a night of shell-fire.

No longer do the deer roam in Sudbury's beautiful park, and the little Shetlands are no more; but they had just laid to rest here, when we called, an old man who loved to tell how he took four ponies from this place as a wedding gift for Edward the Seventh and his Queen.

The Story Of An Amazing Book

ONE of the most illustrious of the Vernons who have known Sudbury was the 5th lord, born at Stapleford in Notts.

He was only a boy when he visited Italy for the first time, but he fell in love with it the moment he saw it. He afterwards lived much in

Morley: Sacheverell family, 1525

Tideswell
Robert Pursglove,
1579

Morley
John Statham and his wife, 1454

Sawley: Roger Bothe
and family, 1467

Morley
Henry Sacheverell and his wife, 1558

Ashover
James Rolleston and
his family, 1507

Walton-on-Trent
Robert Morley, 1492

Morley
Sir Thomas Statham and his wives, 1470

Ashover
Philip Eyre, 15 c.

Florence, where he was a great student of Italian literature and history. As a young man he dedicated himself to the worship of Dante, and from that time till his death in 1866 he devoted a great part of his time and fortune to the making of a wonderful book.

With the help of his Italian friends, he prepared a remarkable work about Dante, published in three of the handsomest volumes the book world has ever seen. It was an astonishing piece of scholarship, and has been described as a book which, for utility of purpose, comprehensiveness of design, and costly execution, has never been equalled in any country. It has illustrations by the greatest Italian artists of the 19th century, many of whom were employed for twenty years. It has Dante's great poem, The Inferno, together with a sort of encyclopedia of the poet's Italy and a masterly account of his life. The third volume, with 112 engravings and a marvellous collection of facts about 14th-century Italy, was not finished till after Vernon's death at Sudbury in 1866. In acknowledgment of his great tribute to their national poet, the Italians made him a member of one of their most distinguished orders of merit, but he was even then slowly dying in his lovely house here. Only a few copies of the book were issued and they are highly valuable today.

Sir Samuel's Wives

SUTTON-ON-THE-HILL. The village is in a hollow but the church is on a hill, a fine landmark with a wide view of the countryside from Tutbury Castle to the hills of the Peak.

A lychgate and little avenue of fine yews brings us to the church made partly new, though a merry boy with his tongue out greets us, as we come inside, as he greeted people in the days of Agincourt and long before. He is 14th century, as old as the tower with rebuilt spire, the priest's doorway and two windows in the chancel, and the nave arcade, which he adorns in company with a king and a bishop among other heads.

Fine corbel heads adorn the dripstones of the windows; the fine reredos, desk, and pulpit were made from the alabaster of the old chancel floor. During the rebuilding 13 silver coins of Henry the Third's day were found in the north aisle.

On the sanctuary floor are alabaster stones to Sir Samuel Sleigh and his three wives: Judith of 1634, Margaret of 1647, and Elizabeth who died in 1738 aged 82, *there being 104 years between the deaths of the first and last.* The great marble monument in the chancel was erected by Sir Samuel, the last of his line, to Judith. Unusual and very striking in its suggestion of death, it has a simple black coffin under an elaborate canopy with coloured arms. An inscription to Gervase Sleigh, Sir Samuel's brother, has been added to the monument.

It is recorded in the registers that 200 years ago a man was paid five shillings a year for driving dogs out of this church with a whip, and for waking sleepers with a white wand.

The village, half a mile below the church, is a group of farms and houses with the Sutton Brook meandering through the fields. Here a charming bit of road sets off to Etwall, between a fine house embattled like a castle and stately trees; a riot of daffodils and primroses we found it in the springtime.

After the Death of the King

SUTTON SCARSDALE. So secluded is it that we forget it lies so near the great industrial world. All about it are memories of lost splendour, for it looks out to the ruins of Bolsover Castle and to a gabled house which has taken the place of Oldcotes (one of the three great houses in Derbyshire built by Bess of Hardwick), while its own great house was in pitiable ruins when we called.

It was built in Grecian style by an Earl of Scarsdale on the site of the old home of his family, the Leakes, who came here in the 15th century. One of them was made Earl Scarsdale for his services to Charles Stuart. He fortified the old house and defended it against 500 men, and when he was eventually taken prisoner he was set free on giving his word to submit to Parliament at Derby. He broke his word, and the house was plundered and his estates seized. It is said that after the death of the King the earl went about in sackcloth, had a grave dug, and lay down in it every Friday. He was buried in the church in 1655.

Long before him there came here John Foljambe, a boy who died in 1499, and is here engraved on a floor stone, wearing armour with his head on a helmet. Here also is a bust of Samuel Pierrepont, in a long curled wig; he died in 1707, the last of a branch of the family which acquired the famous Derbyshire house of Oldcotes by marriage with Bess of Hardwick's daughter.

A few fragments of old glass are all that are left of that which a

15th-century John Leake put in the church. The nave, porch, and most of the chancel are 14th century; the tower is 15th. An old bracket in the aisle is carved with a human face, and in a roof are bosses with the arms of the Leakes and their marriages.

The Bridge of the Broken Heart

SWARKESTON. It has meadows in spring like the Field of the Cloth of Gold, and over them winds in and out, up and down, the famous Swarkeston Bridge.

Five arches span the Trent, built at the end of the 18th century, the rest runs as a raised causeway with low parapets full of nooks and curves, while arches here and there, ending in a fine group by Stanton-by-Bridge, accommodate the floods. The long causeway has 15 ancient arches, and some of the stones are believed to be from the 13th century, when two broken-hearted daughters of the great house set up this bridge.

The merry-making at their betrothal was interrupted by the calling of their lovers to an assembly of the Barons, and during their absence heavy rains flooded the meadows. In trying to ford the stream on their return both men were drowned, and the sorrowful sisters built Swarkeston Bridge as a memorial. We like to think of it as one of the favourite haunts of Derbyshire's great philosopher Herbert Spencer, who walked here one morning when the world was asleep and began fishing by moonlight. Here Sir John Gell routed the Royalists in 1643 when they were trying to hold this key to the north, and here the advance guard of the Young Pretender's disconsolate army turned back for their retreat in 1745.

Here is a fine farmhouse built from the ruins of the home of one of Queen Elizabeth's judges, Sir Richard Harpur; a barn, a gateway, and a stone building with a domed tower at each end are still left. The domed building was perhaps a banqueting hall or a summer house; it stands in a walled enclosure which may have been a playing-ground, and is known in the village as the Balcony Field or the Bowling Green.

It is the monuments of the Harpurs that are the pride of the little church, made new in the 19th century except for its 15th-century tower and the chapel with the Harpur tombs. Built into the wall are fragments of the Norman chancel arch, and Swarkeston children are still baptised at the Norman font.

Sir Richard Harpur lies with his wife Jane, the last of the Finderns, on a fine alabaster tomb, he in his judge's gown with a cap, ruff, and collar, and three rings on his fingers. Charming is Jane, in a gown with many bows and a girdle from which hangs a pomander box, with a French cap and ruffs, a chain three times round her neck, and a posy of primroses in her bodice. At her feet kneel two children. On the brass inscription round the tomb are tiny figures of dogs, boars, stags, dragons, lions, an elephant, a fish, a mermaid looking at her reflection in a mirror, and a dog running off with a duck. Above the tomb hangs a helmet with the Harpur crest of a boar.

It is an engaging monument, and yet for richness of detail it is surpassed by the fine tomb of their eldest son John, who lies in armour with a fine head of hair and portrayed in detail true to life; there is even a wart on his cheek. His wife has a French cap on her lovely hair, a ruff, and a long gown opened to show her embroidered petticoat. Their 12 children kneel at prayer on the front of the tomb, the sons in cloaks and kilts, the girls in tight bodices with wide sleeves, little caps, and ruffs.

Under a canopy in the chancel is a raised tomb with the engraved portraits of a 15th-century knight and his lady; he is John Rolleston and is in armour. On the front of the tomb are two angels and two fine groups of seven sons and seven daughters. Their family were the great people here before the Finderns and the Harpurs.

A Chambered Barrow of the Stone Age

TADDINGTON. Charming is its approach from Ashford, with changing scene of woodland glen and towering hill as the road winds with the Wye as far as Brushfield Hough and Fin Cop, the splendid guardians of the lovely Monsal Dale. Here the road climbs through Taddington Dale by dense plantation, and leaves with surprising suddenness the beauty of the valley for the bare uplands. Here the old grey village, one of the highest in England and 1000 feet above the sea, looks up to heights all round. On Taddington Moor is the famous Five Wells chambered barrow of the Stone Age, where many remains of skeletons have been found.

In the churchyard is a stone whose wonder is its age, the slender tapering shaft of a cross six feet high. Three of its four sides have chevrons and patterns like the designs on Celtic jewellery and pottery. It is thought it was set up in the 7th century, either by Celtic

Missionaries from Lindisfarne, or to mark the place where the first Bishop of the Mercians preached in the wilds of Derbyshire.

From the 14th century come the lovely south doorway of the church, the chancel arch on corbels carved with heads, the nave arcades with tall and slender pillars, and two piscina niches. Many lovely 14th-century windows fill the place with light; the clerestory is 15th century.

The 14th-century tower and spire were made new last century from the old design and with the old masonry.

Projecting from the north wall of the chancel is one of the few stone reading desks in Derbyshire. The eight-sided font is 15th century, bowl and base tapering in unusual fashion towards the middle. An old and well carved oak pulpit has lately come into its own. An old wall painting which has recently come to light is said to represent David playing the harp and Time standing by his side with his scythe; but older still, perhaps the oldest thing in the church, is a floorstone with a Latin cross.

Set in a marble stone once part of a tomb are the brass portraits of Richard Blackwall and his wife, with groups of five daughters and six sons. Richard wears civilian dress of the 15th century, a long gown thrown open to show the fur lining, and a pouch hangs from his girdle. His hair falls on his shoulders. His wife is in the dress of a widow, with a close-fitting hood and long mourning mantle held by a tasselled cord.

The Blackwalls held their lands at Blackwall, close by, from the 12th century, and lost them through loyalty to Charles Stuart. It is said that Sir Thomas Blackwall's debts amounted to more than £130,000. A floorstone in the south aisle has the engraved portrait of a man thought to be Wendesley Blackwall, father of Sir Thomas.

Gateway to Our Loveliest Dale

THORPE. It brings us to hidden glories at the foot of the hills all round, but it has joys of its own for the wise. Its houses and gardens are scattered at random on the hillside above the meeting of the rivers, the Manifold at the end of a romantic journey over and under ground, the Dove fresh from Derbyshire's most beautiful dale. The proudest possession of the village is a little church which looks all tower and was built in the days of King Stephen.

The tower is as the Normans left it, except for an altered doorway, with a plain round arch to the nave. Its parapet is thought to be Norman, and is rare for its age in having small battlements; it rests on a corbel table with heads worn by eight centuries of weather.

The bowl of the font is Norman, round and slightly tapering; it is said that it was used last century as a trough for cattle, and that bands of animals covering its surface crumbled out of doors.

The chancel was made new last century. A window of 15th-century masonry has been set in its south wall, filled with beautiful modern glass of children bringing flowers to the Child on Mary's lap. A window in the nave shows the raising of Lazarus, with Martha and Mary in robes of green and blue. Both windows are the work of Mr F. C. Eden, and are of delicate colour and design.

All that is left of the 17th-century tomb of John Milward projects a foot from the chancel wall. In front are tiny figures of two daughters in gowns with embroidered bodices, and two sons in cloaks and wide-topped boots. Both the boys were soldiers, one a colonel for Charles Stuart.

For 200 years and more the church has had two magnificent sycamores to keep it company in the churchyard; for all its long life it has looked out to the hills that call us to beauty beyond. Fine guardian heights are the great mass of Bunster rising 1000 feet on the Staffordshire side of the river, and Thorpe Cloud like a cone on the Derbyshire side, holding in the stepping-stones between them the key to Dovedale which we come here to find. The road brings us to the Dale from the Staffordshire side of the stream, where the Izaak Walton Inn reminds us of one who loved these haunts.

TIBSHELF. Its miners look up, on their way to the pit, to an embattled tower which has been standing here 500 years, its narrow archway reaching to the new roof of the nave.

The church, a light and spacious place with splendid arcades, is mostly modern. The east window has a picture of the Resurrection morning. A window in the south aisle was given by a teacher who taught four generations of children here, being 35 years at the school, and wished that in her gift she might still be speaking to them. Her window shows the mothers bringing their children to Jesus. The fine marble font, its white bowl on coloured pillars, is 19th century. In a niche on the porch stands John the Baptist, the patron saint.

Blowing Up the Old Walls

TICKNALL. It wanders pleasantly haphazard, a charming picture as we come to it from Stanton-by-Bridge. In one of its pretty scenes a stone bridge like a horseshoe crosses the road to Calke Abbey Park, in which an 18th-century house lies hid in trees on the foundations of a medieval priory. Further on is the village lock-up, with a pointed roof and a studded door, and by the church gate are the almshouses built in the 18th century, when the old cross was taken into the churchyard.

As if to lend the dignity of age to a church not a century old, two fragments of the ancient shrine remain in the churchyard, kindly creeper and a fine beech softening the sadness of the ruin when we called. They are a corner of the tower and the east end of the old north aisle, with a window of intersecting mullions, all standing since the 14th century, when the church to Thomas Becket was rebuilt. Of such great strength were its walls, especially in the tower, that they had to be blown up with gunpowder when the new church took its place.

The new church has a fine embattled tower and lofty spire, fine windows filling the place with light, a hammerbeam roof, and lofty arcades. The font has splendid carving and a fine oak cover with bands of foliage. One window is in memory of a vicar whose 47 years here ended in 1885, and the sturdy oak seats are in memory of the vicar who followed him for half as long.

Some of the old monuments have happily found shelter here. In a 14th-century recess lies the stone figure of a civilian in a close-fitting hood, holding a heart in his hands and with his feet on a dog. He was perhaps William Frances, rebuilder of the old church 600 years ago. Against the north wall is a marble stone with the engraved portrait of John Frances in 14th-century armour with a pointed helmet and a sword. Part of their old home is in the vicarage.

Cathedral of the Peak

TIDESWELL. Between bleak moors and a chain of lovely dales is this lonely little town 900 feet above the sea, with houses old and new, a peace memorial cross 24 feet high, and a treasure house known as the Cathedral of the Peak. A stately place without and within, built in the shape of a cross, it has seen six centuries come and go, its builders disturbed by the Black Death.

The handsome west tower was the last to be built, rising 100 feet with a rather overpowering array of pinnacles like turrets with slender spires. It has a vaulted roof below the ringing chamber, and a lofty arch to the nave. The porch with a lovely modern door has an upper room panelled with 17th-century pews, and on each side of the south doorway is a consecration cross.

The crowning glory of the interior, where lovely windows and the unusual 14th-century clerestory shed light on the mellowed charm of lofty arcades, on monuments of brass and stone and on splendid wood-work old and new, is the glorious chancel, a gallery of light and beauty. It has handsome sedilia and a charming piscina, and a fine embattled stone screen with two great canopied niches and a door to the vestry beyond.

The oak chancel screen is old and new, the lower part almost as old as the church.

It was on the top of the old screen that Samuel Eccles would sit proudly with his family in the pew he was allowed to erect in the form of a loft. It had two rows of seats, and up there Mr and Mrs Eccles with all the little Eccles would march every Sunday morning. Their pew was there for 100 years till 1824; now Samuel's proud seat has gone, but there is a tablet to him on the chancel wall and his paten is used on the altar.

One of the transepts has ten stalls with miserere seats nearly 600 years old, once the original chancel stalls. Two tables have ancient tracery, some of it from Lichfield Cathedral. There is a fine little old north door, and much medieval timber in the roofs.

The splendid array of modern woodwork, some of it by a local craftsman, Advent Hunston, is exceedingly effective. There are screens in both transepts and across the tower arch, and two oak porches. The choir seats in front of the chancel arch have ends carved to suggest Confirmation, Ordination, Baptism, Prayer, and Praise. The beautiful chancel stalls have St Chad with a model of Lichfield Cathedral at his feet, John Baptist, angels, a bishop, birds feeding their young, and a charming Annunciation. Two have miserere seats, one with a queen holding a heart in her hands, the other with a human between grotesques.

Here lie the Foljambes, the great folk of Tideswell from soon after the Conquest to the 15th century. John, a 14th-century benefactor, has his brass portrait on the chancel floor, showing him in chain armour; the brass is a copy of the old one, given by Cecil Foljambe last century. He also gave the lovely glass of the east window in memory of his ancestors buried here, and of his wife whose little white figure we see at the top. Below her are scenes from John the Baptist's life, each side of a Jesse tree.

In the floor of the south aisle are brass portraits of a 16th-century ancestor of Bulwer Lytton, Sir Robert Lytton, and his wife, both in gowns trimmed with ermine. The Lyttons lived at Litton near by before they went to Knebworth.

There is in the chancel floor a splendid brass portrait of Robert Pursglove, Tideswell's Vicar of Bray, who was born here, and has been sleeping in the church since 1579. He wears the pre-Reformation robes of a bishop and has his pastoral staff; at the corners of the stone are symbols of the Evangelists, and there is a rhyming inscription. A brass plate tells of his life and how he founded Tideswell Grammar School, the old building being still near the church, though a school no longer. In 1539 he received a pension for surrendering the Priory of Guisborough; he was a Protestant bishop under Edward the Sixth and a strong Papist under Mary. In 1559 he lost all his appointments for refusing to take the oath of supremacy to Elizabeth, and lived his last 20 years at Tideswell, where his bequests still help the poor. The original brass plate was used for the tomb of a later vicar, and is now on the wall.

On the chancel wall is a beautiful brass in memory of Samuel Andrew, a much-loved vicar who ended the 19th century here and was buried near the church. We see his engraved portrait as he lies at rest after restoring the dignity of this church during his service here since 1864. The work was carried on by Canon Fletcher who followed him, and who gave the lovely glass of the west window in memory of his own and his wife's mother. It is a Te Deum window, with saints and angels, prophets, martyrs, and apostles in adoration of Our Lord enthroned.

In the north transept, restored as a peace memorial, lie the oldest monuments in the church: two stone figures of women, one perhaps 13th century, the other 14th, both unknown. On a table tomb in the other transept lie the alabaster figures of a knight and his lady, much battered through being moved about, but with 14th-century armour and dress of splendid workmanship. Though an inscription says they are the de Bowers, it is thought they may belong to the Foljambes or

Tideswell   The Road through the Dale

Castleton   The Castle of the Peak

Tissington   The Ancient Church

Tissington   The Elizabethan Hall

Lyttons. To the 15th century belongs the fine alabaster tomb in the middle of the chancel in memory of Sir Sampson Meverell, lord of the manor and Knight Constable of England, one of a family here for 400 years. His long story is told in a brass ribbon, of his birth, his christening and marriage—how he was page to a lord and lady, served the Archbishop of Canterbury, and how he fought in 11 great battles against Joan of Arc. How he ended we all may see by peeping through the open tracery of the tomb, where he lies a corpse, carved in stone and in a winding sheet. On the top of the tomb are brass symbols of the Evangelists, heraldic shields, and the Trinity, God seated with a crucifix and a dove.

The 14th-century font has come back to its own after some adventures, for it has been used for mixing paint and has been long in the churchyard. A small coffin stone in the south transept is perhaps 12th century. Part of a stone altar with two consecration crosses, some tiles with heraldic devices and symbols, and a fine bell now pensioned on a transept floor, are all from medieval England. A 17th-century sanctus bell hangs in a gabled turret, and on a transept gable is a 14th-century crucifix. An old Dutch almsdish of brass shows the temptation of Adam and Eve.

Here in the churchyard are two graves of much interest to travellers. One is of Samuel Black who died in 1822, once a chorister here and summoned to sing before the King. His great bass voice brought him celebrity but did not help him to lose his uncouth ways. The other is near the picturesque sundial on the ancient steps of the churchyard cross, and is of the carpenter poet who was much loved hereabouts. Prosperity made him owner of the Cressbrook Mills at a time when the hard life of the pauper apprentices at Litton Mills brought many of them to untimely graves in this churchyard, and he was greatly beloved for his humanity.

He was William Newton, still remembered as the Minstrel of the Peak.

The Little Poet and His Mill

THE Minstrel of the Peak, William Newton, born near Abney in 1750, received his title from Anna Seward, the Lichfield poet. Son of a carpenter, he had little education, but improved himself by reading the books he found at houses where he worked.

He was able to buy a few volumes, chiefly poetry, to read in the little home he set up with a village girl as his wife. He was a born poet of limited range, with a parson-poet, Peter Cunningham, as his patron, and Anna Seward as his ideal. To her he addressed flattering verses, and so began a correspondence and friendship ended only by her death.

Very little of his work survives, and that little we owe to the woman whose vanity was flattered by the tuneful praise of her rustic adorer. Eventually she was able to help him materially by assisting a fund which gave him the opportunity to acquire a minor partnership in a cotton-spinning firm. This became famous as the Cressbrook Dale mill, where, thanks to the poet, the horrible factory system, with apprentice children housed at the mill, was conducted on model lines, the children well fed and clothed, with proper rest and instruction, and with methods resembling those of a good modern boarding school as part of the day's work.

In course of time Newton, happy with his little workpeople and their elders, his own family at home, and the delights of excursions into verse, attained prosperity and some reputation as a poet. He died in 1830, a fortnight before his wife. One of his sons gave Tideswell a water supply at his own cost.

All Roads Lead Here on Holy Thursday

TISSINGTON. If ever roads lead to sheer delight they are surely the roads to Tissington, where a splendid lime avenue, half a mile long, brings us to little stone houses in gay gardens, gathered in haphazard array about a spacious road with wayside lawns, a fine old Hall of Elizabeth's day, and a tiny church as old again keeping them company.

All roads seem to lead to Tissington when Holy Thursday dawns, bringing the world to see the celebration of a custom as full of beauty as of years, a floral festival going back perhaps to pagan days. It is the great day of Tissington's wells.

They have never failed in time of need. They kept the village from the desolation of the Black Death when all around were stricken, and again from a terrible drought in the 17th century, giving abundantly to help the neighbouring countryside. All this Tissington remembers, and, though other places have their Well-Dressing in one form or another, it is here that the custom is kept up with all its ancient pride.

The five wells are by the road which makes a circular tour of the village: Hands Well, taking its name from folk who once lived near; the Hall Well under a stone canopy opposite the great house; the Town Well; the pretty Yew Tree Well; and the Coffin Well named from the shape of its trough, in a cottage garden. For days the folk who love their wells are gathering moss and flowers and leaves in hedge and field and garden, pressing them into beds of salted clay in designs worthy of a painter and his brush, or in living pictures of Bible scenes, the story of a parable, the picture of a church, often with a text to speak its message in this charming fragrant way.

On the morning of Ascension Day, when the wells are literally flowering, comes service in the church and a visit to every well in turn, a hymn or psalm being sung at each, a prayer offered, and the water blessed by the vicar.

For more than 400 years the Fitzherberts, one of the oldest of Derbyshire's families, have lived here. They built the charming house which lends its beauty to the road and is full of treasures within; its fine gates are said to be the work of the famous Derby craftsman Robert Bakewell.

In the church across the way are many of their memorials, one of them an elaborate monument reaching nearly to the roof, and unhappily cutting off one side of the lovely chancel arch which has been the glory of the church for 800 years. The arch is, in spite of the tomb, a piece of Norman splendour. The tomb itself is charming in spite of its intrusiveness, divided into two compartments with kneeling figures of two generations of Fitzherberts, Sir Francis and his wife and Sir John and his wife who followed them. The older figures are in the Tudor fashion and convention; the younger are from Stuart days, and delightful in their grace and freedom, John's wife being daintily dressed, with white sleeves that are very neat. There is an inscription to Alleyne Fitzherbert, Baron St Helens, the famous diplomat who spent his life making treaties.

Tiny still, though it was enlarged last century with a north aisle and arcade in Norman style, the church is high above the road in company with majestic sycamores and fine old yews, and remains of the old churchyard cross. The sturdy tower is mainly Norman, and its buttresses are 13th century. The modern porch shelters a Norman doorway, over which is a tympanum having a quaint little figure on each side with arms akimbo. Other Norman remains are the fine font, its round bowl with crude carvings of strange figures, among them a man, a wolf, a bird, and a bear.

A notable possession of this small place is its great two-decker oak pulpit, with a canopy; and the oddest of its treasures is a clarionet used to lead the singing in olden days, now kept in the porch. On the chancel wall is one of the rare modern brasses, on which is a portrait of Wilhelmina Fitzherbert, of 1862, kneeling at a cross.

Thomas Gray's "Little Fitzherbert" was born here in the year 1753.

Little Fitzherbert

IN Alleyne Fitzherbert lived again the qualities of his father and mother, described in immortal language by Dr Johnson. Arriving at Cambridge University at 17, he charmed the solitary Gray into visiting him, so that he wrote to his friend Mason, "Little Fitzherbert has come to St John's and seems to have all his wits about him."

For a generation those wits were devoted to promoting the peace of Europe, beginning with his appointment, at 24, as British Minister at Brussels. At 30 he acted as peacemaker between France and Spain and the Netherlands, then going as ambassador to Russia, where he accompanied Catherine the Great on her tour of the Crimea, fortified by her gift of a fur pelisse, cap, and muff, for a great sledge journey, with huge bonfires burning along the route and horses waiting in relays.

He passed to Ireland as Chief Secretary and to The Hague as ambassador; effected a treaty as a substitute for war between England and Spain; and, while in St Petersburg again for the accession of the new Emperor, concluded a treaty with Russia, following this with equally happy results in Denmark and Sweden.

Trusted by all parties, and a first favourite at Court, he retired on a pension to nurse his broken health and cultivate friendships.

The Garlands and the Altar Cloth

TRUSLEY. The winding lanes bring us to a small place of unsuspected interest, a plain brick church little more than 200 years old; just a nave and a chancel and a bell-tower with a bell perhaps 500 years old, but with beautiful modern glass and fine old craftsmanship, and with something we have found in only a few other places.

The sanctuary is panelled in oak, the very fine three-decker pulpit towers with its canopy over the box pews, and an oak eagle sits proudly above the alabaster font. The three richly coloured windows are memorials to the Cokes with pictures of Calvary, of Christ rising from the tomb while soldiers sleep, and of His appearing to the disciples.

Among other memorials to the Coke family, who have known this village from the 15th century, is a stone to Sir Francis Coke of 1639. One of his brothers, Sir John, born here in 1563, was for many years Secretary of State to Charles Stuart, and his brother George became Bishop of Hereford. On an alabaster stone is the engraved portrait of Bridget Curzon, who died in the happy days of Charles Stuart. Her sister was the wife of Sir Francis. The old home of the Cokes has gone, but the massive stone doorway of the church and the fine old lead waterpipes embossed with their arms and crest, are said to have come from it. Trusley's great house now is a fine brick gabled building not far from the church.

Something that will interest every woman here is what remains of the blue altar cloth worked by Catherine Coke while her husband was building the church. It was on the altar on the opening day in 1713 and was used for 150 years, and its three fragments are now under glass.

But more interesting still is the pathetic relic kept in a glass case in the vestry, one of the paper garlands of white flowers that were sometimes carried in the funeral procession of a maiden betrothed. It was the mark of a pure life cut off in youth, and it was usual for a handkerchief or a glove of the girl to be left with the garland, perhaps with her name and age. We have come upon such garlands at Ashford and Matlock; they are the things which roused the indignation of the priest at Ophelia's funeral, where the priest was angered that Ophelia was allowed to wear them.

TURNDITCH. It lines a lovely hilly road, rich in wonderful views of the charming valley of the Ecclesbourne. The simple wayside church, with fine limes in the churchyard, and one bell in the turret, has little left that is old except some 13th-century buttresses and a 15th-century font. Some of the stones in the north wall are three feet long, unusual in so small a place. The west window is in memory of Francis Lambert Cursham, who was vicar here for 40 years and died at the end of our long peace in 1914. It has the

Madonna and a Nunc Dimittis, with Simeon with the Child in the Temple, Mary and Joseph attending with doves.

Little Church by the River

TWYFORD. The Trent flows in beautiful calm reaches a few yards from the tiny church, with a low tower and spire and little outside to tell of the beauty within. Unexpectedly charming it is, with a fine low Norman arch enriched with chevrons, framing the 14th-century chancel; and a pointed arch opening to the 13th-century base of the tower with three lovely lancet windows. The rest of the tower and spire are 14th century.

Here sleep some of the Harpurs, descendants of Richard Harpur of Swarkeston, one of Queen Elizabeth's judges. George Harpur of 1672 and his wife have a monument with arms and crest. Some of the Bristowes lie in the church, but Simon Bristowe, who fought in the Civil War and lived almost to see his century out, dying in 1699, sleeps in the churchyard.

We pass a truly magnificent cedar as we come from Willington.

From Kinder Low to River Noe

UPPER BOOTH. It is on a pathway over Kinder, a charming upland dell looking out to wild heights which rise like waves of the sea, a tiny Peakland hamlet in a haunt where the only sound is the music of mountain streams. Near a tiny one-arch bridge the wild Crowden Brook comes rushing to meet the little River Noe from the lofty height of Kinder Low, both eager for the fair Vale ahead.

UPPER LANGWITH. Through it flows the River Poulter, on its way to Welbeck and Clumber.

Its little aisleless church has seen many changes since its birth 800 years ago. The chancel lost a Norman arch last century but kept a 13th-century lancet, and the 14th-century east window is in the nave. The fine porch, with its stone roof and crocketed pinnacles, is 14th century, and so perhaps are the beams of the roof, with kingposts and struts carved with tracery. There is an old piscina and a medallion of old glass in a window. The handsome font is modern.

Out in the sun and rain, under the east window, is an old coffin, and a coffin stone with an engraved cross, a chalice, and an open book fading away. Until 1878 the stone was in a chancel recess, and may have marked the grave of the builder of the chancel 700 years ago.

How Three Men Died

UPPER PADLEY. It is a charming spot where the Burbage Brook comes down a lovely dell with many cascades, hurrying from its moorland home to join the Derwent before it runs under Grindleford Bridge.

The little church, lately come into its own again, has had its adventures, for it was long an old grey ruin used as a cowshed and a barn. Once it was part of one of the most important houses in the county, and through all its desecration it has kept a quaint piscina and four carved hammerbeams in an upper room which was the private chapel of the great Hall.

Romance and tragedy these old stones have known. The romance brought the Eyres to Padley, when Joan Padley married Robert Eyre home from Agincourt, where he took prisoner a marshal of France; the portraits of Robert and Joan are in brass in Hathersage Church. The tragedy came to them through their faith, and it was because of it that the ruins of Padley have been a place of pilgrimage.

The Eyres were staunch to the faith of their fathers, and so were the family of Sir Thomas Fitzherbert, who came to Padley when he married Anne Eyre. He was the eldest son of the famous judge Sir Anthony Fitzherbert, and suffered terribly for his faith, dying in the Tower in 1591 after 20 years in prison. While Sir Thomas was in prison two priests were found hiding in the chimney buttresses of his house. They were Nicholas Garlick and Robert Ludlam, and were imprisoned at Derby, where they came upon a third priest named Richard Sympson who had escaped death by recanting his faith. They persuaded him to be true, and the three were hanged in Derby in 1588. It is said that Sympson, who was first to approach the scaffold, seemed to lose courage, whereupon Nicholas Garlick went before him, kissed the ladder, and ascended it with ecstasy to encourage him.

John Fitzherbert, who had been looking after his captive brother's estates, was condemned for harbouring the priests, and died in prison even as did Sir Thomas.

The dignity of this old place had just come back when we called, and there had been made the discovery of the ancient altar stone, lying in a cowshed for centuries, hidden away perhaps at the Reformation in the hope that it would come to light in safer days. Often must the two priests, who died for their faith, have served at this old altar stone.

It is still a church in a farmyard, and in the east gable we still can see the pigeon holes, now blocked. Simple within, it has a gallery at the east end with a flight of steps each side.

One window shows the finding of the old stone altar, with a bishop, a companion, and a man with a spade, and the date August 24, 1933. The altar is now set up. Another window shows the arrest of the two priests at Padley Chapel on July 12, 1588, and scenes of their martyrdom on St Mary's bridge in Derby. A tiny window has Richard Sympson holding a scroll and palm.

On the north side of the chapel are the ruins of Padley Hall, shaded by three sycamores growing from the bank. Remains of walling show the outline of the rooms, and there are a few steps of a spiral stairway. The kitchen has a great open fireplace and hearthstones black with the smoke of centuries ago. On one side of it is the crude kitchen sink cut out of a solid block of stone, and on the other a tiny oven as it was when the bread was taken out of it long ago. Many old stones and shields are lying among the relics, among them a small arch.

Robert Morley in Brass

WALTON-ON-TRENT. It seemed to us that nothing could have disturbed the peace of its lovely Trent meadows since Edward the Second came riding hotly by, chasing the Duke of Lancaster and the rebellious barons. Church and rectory, flowered cottages and gardens, are all by the wayside, and looking over the river to Staffordshire is the great plain house which was built by one of the few men who grew rich out of the South Sea Bubble. Part of the old Hall which it replaced survives in cottages.

The church is among lovely trees, with a shapely yew near the chancel and a fine silver birch shading the beautiful lychgate in memory of a 19th-century rector who did much to restore the glory of his church. Its few remains of the one begun by the terrible Hugh Lupus, a friend of the Conqueror, are a doorway to the vestry, a little moulding on the outside wall near the porch, some carved stones on a window sill, a fragment of a window over a pillar of the arcade, and perhaps the pillars themselves, supporting pointed arches.

The chancel takes up the story with three lancet windows, the sedilia, and the piscina, all 13th century. The chantry, charming with its windows, piscina, and three stone seats with clustered pillars, was built in the next century by Richard Waleys, who was rector for 59 years. He lies under a low arch in the wall, battered and headless but still in his robes, his stone figure having been cut when he was used under the floor as a resting-place for the joists.

The fine tower was built about 1400, and has a lovely arch under which stands the old font. In the floor of the chancel is the fine brass portrait of Robert Morley, a 15th-century rector, in his robes, blessing the chalice and wafer. It is a rare brass, for it is said to be one of only two known of a priest in this attitude. Over the priest's doorway is the bust of Thomas Bearcroft, a 17th-century rector.

Modern days have given of their best in the woodwork here, in the screenwork of the chantry, the traceried chancel screen with fan-vaulting supporting a gallery of 18 small figures in niches, the stalls and reredos, the pulpit with a panel of the martyrdom of St Lawrence, and the lectern with two doors opening to show three carved Bible scenes, an engaging piece of work. Lovely glass fills the modern lancets of the east window; and in the glass of the north aisle is a vivid little gallery of illustrious familiar folk—Wilberforce the friend of slaves, the great talker Dr Johnson, Izaak Walton the fisherman, and Sir Thomas More who loved honour more than life.

The Hiding-Place for Priests

WEST HALLAM. It stands on a hilltop with little to suggest the great coalfield round it. A lovely avenue of limes brings us from its peace memorial, with two soldiers standing at a gun, to the church set between the great house and the rectory. The rector's garden has a glorious lime tree, and looks out over the valley to a great windmill with its arms still working as the monks of old Dale Abbey saw them.

The massive tower was made new in the 15th century, and it is said that four stunted trees once grew at the top of it. The legend has found its way into verse, of which one verse says:

> At each corner right over the battlements high
>   There grew a tufted tree:
> An elder, and ash, and a gloomy yew,
>   Of the four were surely three.
> The name of that other we never knew,
> But its leaves had a mystic blood-red hue.

Beautiful is some of the stone inside the church, its amber colour veined with purple tints. The north arcade is 13th century, and the south a century younger, as are the chancel arch and the great font. Old glass in the chancel shows two small figures under canopies, and tiny birds in quaint attitudes; and high up in a clerestory window is a figure of James the Less, holding a book and the club with which he was martyred. One window is in memory of John Scargill who founded the village school.

On a stone on the chancel floor is engraved the portrait of Thomas Powtrell in armour of the 15th century. On a magnificent canopied tomb lie Walter Powtrell of 1598 and his wife Cassandra, both with ruffs; he wears richly decorated armour, and with her gown of many folds, the lady wears a French cap with falling lappet. Round the tomb are seven children.

It was the Powtrells who rebuilt the tower. Their old home is gone, and the last of their men died in the year of London's Great Fire. Their home was a famous hiding-place for fugitive priests, and Father Campion is said to have often sheltered there. One priest taken at the house was condemned to death, but was banished after long imprisonment. Another sentenced for celebrating mass at West Hallam Hall died during his imprisonment.

Twists and Turns and Little Bridges

WESTON-ON-TRENT. It seems all twists and turns and little bridges, with cottages finely thatched in gardens ablaze with colour, and church and rectory in lovely isolation, looking down on meadows where the Trent flows under overhanging woods of the Leicestershire border.

Well worth finding are two gems of river scenery. Where the ferry crosses to King's Mills at the foot of Donington Park, the swiftly-flowing river plays hide and seek among the islands, making music as it falls over a great weir, and running today as it ran when the Civil War came by and some of the soldiers were laid in Weston's churchyard. From the cliffs not far from the church is a glorious view of valley and hills, with Breedon church silhouetted against the sky.

The church is lovely without and within. The low sturdy tower and slender spire are chiefly 14th century with younger battlements. Fine battlements adorn the continuous roof of nave and aisles, and the 17th-century brick-and-timber porch shelters a doorway of about 1300.

A fine effect is given to the nave by the exceptional height of the 14th-century arcades, their pointed arches resting on tall graceful pillars which show up the warm tints of amber and purple in the stonework. The chancel is mainly 13th century, though the east lancets are new. Many of the windows, a charming feature of the church, are 14th century. The east window of the north aisle is especially fine, and the east window of the south aisle, said to be unique in Derbyshire, has geometric tracery. There is a fine piscina in this aisle, and one in the chancel with the sedilia. There is a good Jacobean pulpit, and a plain oak chest of 1662.

A delightful group of painted figures in the south aisle shows a rector's family of Shakespeare's day, Richard Sale and his wife Dorothy, their six girls and two boys, and two babes in bonnets tucked up in their cots. Proud and quaint they look, the father with his beard, the mother with almost a flush of life on her lovely face, all but the babes in ruffs and kneeling at prayer.

One pathetic thing we found here, a wooden cross from Flanders, with a brass plate on which has been stamped one of the names that live for evermore. It seemed to us that the little brass was made at the front, the letters being lightly stamped in.

Our Village—By its Children

WHATSTANDWELL. It has little but its place in the world, but that would be hard to beat. It lies in a land where Nature is at her loveliest in vale and hill, where the earth is strewn with exquisite flowers that only wait for their season.

When the Children's Newspaper offered a prize for the best description of a village by its children it was Whatstandwell that won the prize, with this account of itself by its Teacher and his School.

WE look out from no hilltop; we nestle in the valley, and that the loveliest valley in England.

We lift up our eyes unto the hills, and the highest of all is crowned with a tower whose beacon shines over Nottinghamshire and Derbyshire to remind all who behold how, of 140,000 men of Sherwood, 11,400 died in the Great War. We look up, again, across the valley of the Derwent and see Shining Cliff, beautiful name for a glorious hill, rosy in June with masses of rhododendrons. We climb steep lanes to our own cottages and farmhouses, and still look up to the heights beyond.

Florence Nightingale knew and loved our tiny village. We cherish the memory of the goodwill message she sent to our school and the practical interest she took in the social activities of the community. But, though Whatstandwell lies within strolling distance of buildings crowded with history, it has itself passed a remote and peaceful existence. Once it belonged to Darley Abbey, and saw the monks and their servants riding through to the great tithe barns at Wigwell.

Since the monks lost their lands the road over the bridge has seen many changes, and the inn near at hand has seen very varied fortune. A bustling place the inn and forge must have been when the Champion coach drew up at its doors before labouring up the steep hill, horses all a-lather. But the 19th-century road along the valley has relieved the village of the heaviest modern traffic and left us in a quiet backwater.

The grey stone cottages, built from the stone of our own quarries, merge quietly into the background of wood and cliff. Here is a little home with a waterfall in its own domain, there a gay cottage garden, unfenced, on the roadside. There are most lovely gardens in our village.

Best of all is the lovely wild-flower garden in which we glory. If you promise to respect our flowers we can show you our daffodil fields and primrose banks; our acres of cowslips and purple and meadow orchises; later our butterfly orchises and huge foxgloves, standing like hillside sentinels, heartease and milkwort, and hundreds of other flowers in season. If you come in May no one need lead you to the bluebells, for they cover every hillside, creeping from woodlands into the open spaces, making patches of rich purple almost to the riverside.

To know Whatstandwell properly you must love it the whole year round, but no season will fail you: the loveliness of the English countryside is always here.

The Wayside Cross

WHESTON. In this home of very few people, where the old Hall has long been a farmhouse, is one of the most interesting medieval survivals in the Peak, a wayside cross which marked the road to the Forest 600 years ago. Proudly it stands in a walled-round group of trees, its tapering shaft on a great stone and a flight of three steps; its head showing the Crucifixion on one side and the Madonna and Child on the other.

At the Tideswell end of the village is the stone of another wayside cross, known in the neighbourhood as the Wishing Well.

Dutch William for the Throne

WHITTINGTON. It has an exciting little story, and a surprising little gallery of famous people.

The story is of a band of men who planned to overthrow a king and change a dynasty. It was in 1688, when Protestant England was incensed with the policy of James the Second and his attempt to change their faith, that William Cavendish, Earl of Devonshire, the Earl of Danby and a few honest friends met on Whittington Moor to arrange to bring Dutch William to the throne. They were driven by a storm, it is said, to find shelter at the village inn, then a busy calling place for packhorse and travellers on the old road from Chesterfield to Sheffield.

A new Whittington has grown up since then, but what is left of the inn still stands in the quiet haunts of the old village. Restored and altered, and the Plotting Parlour gone, it is now a little stone house with a thatched roof, and has a tablet on the wall telling the story of how it came to be called Revolution House.

The gallery of famous people is in the church which was twice made new last century, on the site of the older one where Dr Pegge, the famous antiquary, was buried in 1796, after preaching here 45 years. It is at a quiet end of the village in a churchyard clothed with trees, and the portrait gallery is in the windows of the north aisle. Here we found the great Earl of Shaftesbury, the great Liberal leader Mr Gladstone, heroic Hugh Latimer and Thomas Cranmer, and Bishop Ridding of Southwell. Milton and John Wesley are in the window given in memory of an old lady whose charming face is in a medallion.

In the east window, a memorial to 172 men who did not come back, are figures of St Margaret and the Black Prince with those two heroic men, King Alfred and St George. We liked the brief inscription on the modern font, "The Children's Gift."

Little Tobie

WHITWELL. Its great possession, adding to the glory of its view of Welbeck Park and Sherwood Forest, and its own wood of over 400 acres, is a proud church high above the busy village. It is a fine monument to the builders of eight centuries ago, and to the local quarries from which they took their stone; and is much as the Normans left it, except for the transepts which gave it the shape of a cross in the 14th century, the chancel then rebuilt, and the aisle windows added in the 15th century.

It is an impressive sight, its round arches and round pillars a joy to see. The Normans built the tower except for the 15th-century belfry, and set in the little window above the lovely west doorway with chevron moulding round the arch; they set up the great chancel arch and the nave arcades, made the massive bowl of the font, put in the west window of the south aisle, and carved the corbel table of quaint heads along the side walls of the nave; and they did what Norman builders rarely did in building the clerestory windows.

From the 14th century come the fine windows of the chancel, the exceptionally beautiful sedilia with lofty canopies and pinnacles, two piscinas, and three old brackets on which are set modern figures of St Lawrence with a gridiron, the Madonna, and Paulinus. A 14th-century recess in a transept is adorned with tracery under a hood with a woman's head in square headdress and a man's head with a beard and curls. Here and in the chancel are old fragments of glass.

On a pretentious alabaster monument lies Sir Roger Manners, son of Dorothy Vernon of Haddon Hall; he lived at the gabled manor house near the church. We liked better than his monument that simple memorial in brass with a little heraldry and a quaint inscription to Tobie Waterhouse who died a few years after Shakespeare, aged four years, but even then "full of grace and truth."

WILLINGTON. It looks from the banks of the Trent across the meadows to Repton's slender spire, and we remember that in Repton church porch is kept the old toll board of Willington's five-arch bridge, one of the last main road bridges in the country to be freed from tolls. The church, with a tower only a century old, has three 13th-century lancets in the chancel, a worn coffin stone in the porch, and a Norman doorway with a tympanum crudely carved with squares and lines.

The Wonderful Font the Saxons Made

WILNE. A lane with lofty trees brings us to this small village in the meadows, where a toll-bridge crosses the stream and the Derwent says Goodbye to its last mill-wheel. Here it joins the

Trent, being the most important of all that river's tributaries. It has come from the lovely peaty moors through a run of sustained beauty such as no other English river has, for 45 of its 60 miles are attractive to various tastes in scenery.

Surprising it is to find a church in so remote a spot, but winter floods have driven the folk to higher ground at Draycott, now a busy little town.

Yet more surprising still it is to find in this small church so great a treasure, perhaps the second oldest font in the land, fashioned from a solid stone by a Saxon craftsman of the 7th, 8th, or 9th century. Said to be part of a round column or the shaft of a cross, and hollowed out to make a font in early days, its beauty was unimpaired till fire swept through the church in our own time. It has been restored, and a great part of its old surface, carved with interlaced knotwork and other intricate designs, can still be seen.

The ancient church was made new in the 14th century, but the lower stage of the sturdy tower is 13th century with three lancets in deep splays; its upper part is a century younger, with battlements later still. The fine stone-roofed porch is 14th century.

Bright with lovely windows of the three medieval centuries, the church has its old piscina and two brackets close by, and an Elizabethan chest six feet long, elaborately carved. A great treasure is a lovely silver chalice older than the Armada. When the church was restored after the fire, the pillars and arches of the arcade were rebuilt, and the nave re-roofed in oak. Plain oak screens, strong enough to stand a thousand years, took the place of the simple 15th-century chancel screen and of a most elaborate Jacobean screen which led to the Willoughby chapel.

For centuries the church was the burial place of the Willoughbys of Risley. An alabaster floorstone in the chancel has the engraved figures of Hugh Willoughby of 1491 and his wife; on a wall are tiny brass portraits of Hugh of 1514, his wife and their five children.

Old glazed tiles are in the floor of the Willoughby chapel which was built in 1622, and the brilliant glass of its windows, brought from abroad and restored after the Civil War, shows the Nativity, the Crucifixion, and the Ascension. Here, on a tomb with a canopy like a triumphal arch, lies Sir John Willoughby of 1605 in armour, with his wife in a gown with finely pleated bodice, their four children kneeling on the front of the tomb. It was their son Henry who erected this monument, and to his daughter Ann is a monument with two weeping children.

It is worth while walking to the old toll bridge, by the cotton mill and the pleasant house standing out so bravely into the stream where the waters make a mighty roar rushing through the sluice gates in the mill's leisure hours.

Moving the Milestone

WINGERWORTH. Into its wide view come the crooked spire of Chesterfield and Bolsover Castle on its high ridge.

In a churchyard with fine yews and the base of an old cross, stands the little embattled church, whose glory is in what is left of early Norman days. A Norman doorway is sheltered by a 19th-century porch, the Norman arcade of three arches is on massive round pillars, the tiny archway into the chancel, under nine feet high and seven feet wide, is one of the smallest the Normans left in the county, and theirs also is the great font bowl, which was found on a farm.

The fine tower, with two gargoyles on every side below the embattled parapet, is about 1500; two of the gargoyles are an ape and a muzzled bear.

A fine relic, unique in Derbyshire, is the timber structure on which the rood was raised about 1500. It projects two feet from the wall above the chancel arch and is 15 feet long. The upper edge is embattled, while the front is panelled and adorned with leaves. The rood stairway to the platform is still here.

In the chancel lies the stone figure of a priest with a narrow fringe of hair round his head; he is about 1200, and is probably the priest who was here when the chancel was first built.

In a north aisle window are fragments of old glass patterned with crowns and diamonds. The neat oak seats were made 30 years ago from wood grown on the estate.

In the chancel floor are stones to the Hunlokes, who in 1783 built the ugly mausoleum on to its north wall, open on one side save for an iron gate through which we see the rows of compartments in the walls for the dead.

A quaint story of Sir Thomas Hunloke who died a year after Waterloo tells how he invited French prisoners at Chesterfield to his private chapel at Wingerworth, and, finding that the Hall was out of bounds, overcame the difficulty by moving the tell-tale milestone to a

Matlock   High Tor

Grindleford   The Burbage Brook

Longford
Sir Nicholas Longford

Longford
Medieval carving

Longford
Ancient Sedilia

Longford   Sir Nicholas Longford of the 14th and 17th centuries

Youlgreave
Norman Font

Ashover
Babington Tomb

Ashover
Norman Lead Font

Winster
Norman Font

more convenient place. A few years ago the church lost its old companion, the great house which was long the home of the Hunlokes, who garrisoned it for Charles Stuart.

Llewellyn Jewitt

WINSTER. It hides itself from the world among lovely hills, finding a wealth of interest all around in rocks and dales, and lovely views at the end of delightful walks to the moors with ancient graves.

Old houses tell of its prosperity in lead-mining days, and though its market is no more, the quaint old market-house still has its stone walls perhaps 500 years old, though the round arches are filled in; its upper part, which came from Jacobean days, has been made new. Close by is the old Hall with pilasters and a balustraded parapet, its stone brought by packhorse from Darley Dale 300 years ago. It was for a time the home of Llewellyn Jewitt, the 19th-century antiquary to whom Derbyshire owes so much.

He sleeps near the church, sharing a gravestone with a brother who was buried at sea. He was a skilled engraver, and illustrated a famous book on Architecture. He is best remembered for his scholarly book on Ceramic Art and his History of Derbyshire, a great work he did not live to finish. Llewellyn Jewitt was an expert in many subjects, founding and editing an antiquarian magazine, and writing handbooks on coins and tokens, burial mounds, historic buildings, and the stories and ballads of the county he served so well. He was a practical man, too, helping in the scheme to bring pure water to Winster.

The church was made new last century except for its 18th-century tower. An arcade of pointed arches on very slender clustered pillars divides the nave, so that the chancel has two arches between it and the nave. Nothing is left of the Norman chapel unless it is the fine font with cable moulding round the top, vigorously carved with quaint and varied figures. It has two children with an open book, a lily in a pot, the Madonna and Child, and a figure in a font which is said to represent the dedication of the church to John the Baptist.

Forty Figures on a Stone

WIRKSWORTH. As we come to it the moorland way from Whatstandwell it is a delightful picture of brick and stone in a green valley almost surrounded by hills, some richly wooded, some riddled with old lead workings and scarred with quarries echoing with the thunder of falling stone. Its lead mines were worked by the Romans and the Saxons, and it was long the centre of the lead-mining district known as the King's Field, in which any man might search for lead, subject to the quaint laws and customs which governed the mining. At the time of Domesday Book Wirksworth was prosperous both with the mining and smelting of lead, the ore being smelted in the tops of the hills around. The name of these hilltop hearths still survives in Bole Hill a mile away, where Olive Schreiner lived for a time while writing her Story of a South African Farm. It is said that the lead coffin sent to Croyland in 714 for the body of St Guthlac was from the Wirksworth mines.

In the little 19th-century Moot Hall, with the miner's arms, his scales, pick, and trough carved on the front, is kept the massive brass dish once used as the standard measure for lead ore. Said to be the only old one left in the country, it has an inscription telling us that it was made in the time of Henry the Eighth. In a lead mine a mile away, known as the Dream Cave, was found the almost perfect skeleton of a rhinoceros.

It has sentiment enough to keep up at Whitsuntide the old custom of Well-Dressing, decorating water-taps instead of wells with flowers. There is a charming little Cottage Hospital on Greenhill, with gables and dormers and an old sundial on the wall. In the market-place is an old inn with a new front and a fine Elizabethan chimney-piece carved with fleur-de-lys, unicorns, and Tudor rose. At a pretty corner is the little 15th-century priest's house, now an outhouse in a trim garden; and close by are the almshouses and the grammar school, both looking on to the ancient church, where sleeps the man who founded them in the 16th century.

A treasure house indeed is Wirksworth church of a thousand years, for it has a marvellous Saxon relic which would be considered a treasure even in the British Museum. It seems to us a veritable Saxon masterpiece. Set in a north wall, it is a sculptured stone slightly coped and measuring five feet long and about three wide. It was found near the altar, upside down over a vault in which lay a perfect skeleton.

Was ever a more amazing coffin lid than this in a village church? It has about 40 figures, all seeming to be part of scenes in the life of Christ, carved above and below a ridge along the middle of the

stone. Along the top we see Christ washing the feet of the disciples;
next comes a sturdy cross with a lamb in the middle, figures thought
to be Peter and John above the arms, and below the arms two
extraordinary birds. Then is what appears to be a quaint entombment scene, with Joseph of Arimathea and a companion carrying
Christ on a bier, under which lies a figure perhaps symbolising
Victory over Death; while above the bier are six head like birds in a
nest, representing the guard placed over the body. Three standing
figures, one with a palm branch, complete the top row. The lower
half has one of the most captivating Saxon processions we have seen.
It begins with a representation of the Nativity; in the middle is an
enchanting sculpture of angels with stately wings bearing Our Lord,
who holds a cross, to Heaven; and this impressive piece of pageantry
ends with a row of figures returning to Jerusalem after the Ascension.

An expert has said of this stone that it differs from all other work
of early Christian times, and has the distinction of Roman work with
traces of Byzantine influence, and that perhaps some craftsman from
a Roman town in Britain, or some sculptor who had seen the marvellous work of the Romans on similar stones, here tried to introduce
the spirit of something he had seen. It is older than Alfred, coming
from the beginning of the 8th century or even earlier.

It is a lovely church which shelters it, built in the shape of a cross,
with a 13th and 14th-century central tower crowned by a modern
spirelet. The charm of the interior is in lovely arches on clustered
pillars; they are everywhere, for the nave, the chancel, and the transepts all have aisles. The nave arcades are 14th-century, and eight
fine lancets are a century older.

As if all this richness were not enough, the walls inside have been
made captivating with many carved stones of Saxon and Norman
days, fragments of moulding, heads of shafts, quaint faces and figures
peeping out unexpectedly here and there. Among a medley in one
transept is a pair of legs without a man, in the other is a tiny impish
figure above a head with a bearded face. A Saxon stone has on it a
crowned king and a lady almost covered by a heart; she has one
hand raised and a book in the other, and they look like a king and his
queen of hearts. A Saxon fragment in the north aisle seems to show
the Temptation of Eve, with a serpent coiling round a tree with an
apple in its mouth, and our ancestors on each side rather worse for
wear. Another stone has the quaint figure of a miner with his pick

T 2

and bucket. A large coffin stone in the wall of a transept was engraved perhaps by a Norman craftsman with a fine cross, a sword, and a bugle.

There is a lovely font with a bowl 700 years old. There is a fine modern oak pulpit with the four Evangelists and their symbols under canopies. Rich glass fills some of the windows, and a reredos in a chancel aisle is a mass of carving, coloured and gilded, by the peasants of Oberammergau. It shows the Crucifixion with Mary and John at the Cross, and six figures in niches.

There is a fine group of 16th-century monuments. Set in the wall of a chancel aisle are brass portraits from two different monuments of the Blackwalls. There are 29 portraits in all, with 18 tiny figures of children above Thomas Blackwall and his wife, and seven children with another Blackwall and his wife below, the groups of children having found the wrong parents when being moved. An alabaster tomb has the engraved portraits of Ralph Gell and his two wives, and figures of their children round the tomb. Ralph, who was one of the Gells of Hopton and died in 1564, is bareheaded and has a long gown, and his wives have round caps and dresses tied with bows. Ralph's son Anthony is a fine figure as he lies on a handsome tomb, with moustache and beard, and a long gown with ruffs at his neck and wrists. He died in 1583 after founding the almshouses and grammar school. There is an inscription to Sir John Gell, the notorious general, and a monument to Sir Philip, the last baronet, who died in 1719. Very proud is Anthony Lowe of Alderwasley as he lies on a fine tomb in his armour and helmet, a skull under his feet; he was servant to four monarchs, dying in 1555.

Many come to Wirksworth, not for the glory of the church or the beauty of the monuments, but for an unknown grave in the churchyard where there is still the massive shaft of the old cross ten feet high. In this unknown grave lies a very well-known lady, Elizabeth Evans. She was George Eliot's aunt, and Wirksworth claims that their town was the Snowfield of Adam Bede, and that Elizabeth Evans was Dinah Morris, Adam's bride.

Those who love this great story will find much interest here, for there is still standing the little Methodist chapel where Elizabeth Evans would preach sometimes. In it is this inscription:

To the memory of Elizabeth Evans, known to the world as Dinah Bede, who during many years proclaimed alike in the open air, the sanctuary, and from house to house, the love of Christ; also of Samuel Evans her husband, a faithful local preacher.

The cottage where they lived and ended their days still stands a mile out of Wirksworth, opposite the Tape Mills where Samuel was manager; it is a two-storeyed house with tiles where once was thatch.

Tax Collector for King Charles

SIR JOHN GELL, who was born at Hopton in 1593, married at 16, left Oxford without a degree, and from an early age took a prominent part in county affairs. As Sheriff he had to collect Ship Money from Sir John Stanhope of Elvaston, who refused payment, and died defying authority, whereupon Gell, a widower, married the victim's widow.

The pictures of Gell and his conduct during the Civil War are drawn by Royalist pencils, and represent him as a man without ardent convictions leading men whose delight was plunder; but both sides plundered, and the fact stands out that Gell was a military commander of skill and courage, who successfully led his forces to the overthrow of every fortified place he attacked, kept his own county loyal to Parliament, and helped to preserve Nottingham and Leicester as Commonwealth strongholds.

After the Royalist rout at Naseby he was accused of neglecting to destroy the fugitives, but nothing came of the charge. Five years later, however, he was held guilty of plotting against the State, and committed to the Tower, with forfeiture of his estate. He was released after two years, and was given a full pardon.

A Cottage Lad

WORMHILL. It lies in an upland hollow, sheltered from the coldest winds by a line of high hills. At one end of the village is a lovely grove of trees, and at the other an old gabled stone Hall, an Elizabethan house restored by the Bagshawes who have known this village for centuries.

The prettiest corner is by the church, where the churchyard and vicarage grounds make a charming garden of lawn and evergreens.

Its oldest stones are in the tower, which has looked down on the churchyard for 700 years, except that it has changed its gabled cap for a copy of the steep-pitched cap of the famous Saxon tower at Sompting in Sussex. In the tower hangs one of the smallest peal of bells that rings out anywhere in our countryside. There are six of them, and they were made as models at the famous Loughborough foundry. The lovely churchyard has the foundations and a little of the shaft of the old cross, and an extraordinary tomb with five huge layers of stone like a pyramid.

The joy of the interior is the fine little oak sanctuary with panelled walls, an altar table carved with wheat and vines, and a reredos with a scene of the Last Supper and figures of the Good Shepherd, Dorcas, and two saints. In keeping with this fine work are the pulpit, litany desk, and choir stalls.

The Ascension in the east window and some of this woodwork is in memory of the Bagshawes, and it was here that William Bagshawe, the Apostle of the Peak, preached his first sermon.

Of his family no doubt, was that Nicholas Bagshawe of whom we read in the registers here that in 1674 he was clerk and schoolmaster "for want of a better."

By the wayside is a drinking fountain in memory of a man born about a mile away, a generation after this poor schoolmaster, another poor son of Derbyshire, who could hardly read or write yet became the greatest canal engineer of his time. He was James Brindley, born in a cottage at Tunstead, where is still an ash known as Brindley's tree. It began to grow through the floor of the cottage where he was born, and grew until the cottage was sacrificed because of it. Tunstead has but a farm or two, yet is rich in the memory of this famous man. It knows that Carlyle said this of its distinguished son:

The English are a dumb people. They can do great acts but not describe them. Whatsoever of strength the man had in him will be written in the work he does. The rugged Brindley has little to say for himself. He has chained seas together. His ships do visibly float over valleys, and invisibly through the hearts of mountains; the Mersey and the Thames, the Humber and the Severn, have shaken hands.

We found our way down a precipitous path lovely with trees and flowers to the beautiful gorge of Chee Dale, where the River Wye is at its loveliest in a wild romantic setting, making a horseshoe curve between the mighty Chee Tor and the crescent rocks of the other side.

All But One Came Back

YEAVELEY. It offered 24 men for England and almost became one of the 30 Thankful Villages where all the men came back— almost but not quite, for, though 24 were living till October 11, 1918, on that day one fell and only 23 came back. There is a tablet to the one in the little brick church (not yet a century old), and the east window has been filled with glass in memory of them all. In it are St George of England glowing in red and purple and Joan of France in blue and gold. The oldest possession here is an ancient font of unusual shape set on a modern base.

A mile away, in a delightful green hollow reached by a field path, which we found fringed with primroses and violets, are the scanty ruins of a chapel of the crusading knights of the time of Richard the First, a fragment of wall with two graceful lancets, a curious font with a tapering bowl, and a coffin stone on the grass carved with a cross and a sword.

In company with the ruins is another relic of the past, the fine red brick house called Stydd Hall. With embattled stone parapet and embattled stone windows, it comes in part from Tudor England, but is now a farmhouse.

Between the Enchanting Valleys

YOULGREAVE. It lies between the enchanting valleys of Lathkill River and Bradford Brook, whose waters meet at winsome little Alport a mile away. It looks out to the ancient Stone Circles of Stanton Moor and Harthill Moor, while only three miles away is Arbor Low, the most important Stone Circle in the county, all three a happy hunting ground for Thomas Bateman. At Lomberdale House, where he lived between Youlgreave and Middleton, he built up a magnificent museum, now in Sheffield. We come upon this antiquary at Middleton.

Long before we reach the village we see the splendid 15th-century tower of one of the most delightful of all the Peakland churches, lovely in its structure and rich in the treasures it shelters. Of its Norman days there still remain the fine south arcade of three bays with round arches, sturdy pillars, and capitals, and the pillars and capitals of the north arcade supporting the graceful arches of the 14th century.

The chancel was rebuilt 500 years ago, keeping its 14th-century arch. The east window has been filled with lovely glass by Burne-Jones and William Morris, in radiant colouring of orange and yellow, silver and gold; it shows Christ blessing the world, a globe in His Hand, with figures of the Four Evangelists. The fine oak roofs are 15th century. The north aisle has the remains of an ancient piscina and one in the south aisle has its drain carved into a face.

The tower is one of the chief joys of the church, and one of the finest in the county. Square and massive, with stepped buttresses rising to the embattled summit, it has eight crocketed pinnacles, eight belfry windows, a window over the fine west doorway, and a charming little stair turret with battlements of its own.

The splendid font is very unusual and has a story, its round bowl resting on a central column and four small shafts. From the side of the bowl projects a tiny bowl seeming to be held by the mouth of a strange animal carved upside down on the font itself. Its purpose is not certain, but it was perhaps a holy water stoup. It is unique in our experience, for, though we have come upon other fonts with projecting brackets, they are not hollowed out as this is. Coming from the 12th century, it is said to have belonged originally to Elton church, and to have been thrown into the churchyard there last century. It was taken into the vicarage garden at Youlgreave, and later brought into the church, the squire of Elton having a reproduction of it made for his village when it pleaded in vain for its return.

In the north wall of the nave is a stone 17 inches long with the figure of a draped woman, her hair parted in the middle, and holding a staff. It is not known what it represents, but it is probably much older than the 15th-century wall in which it is set.

In the middle of the chancel is one of the loveliest things in the church, an exquisite alabaster tomb only three and a half feet long, whose workmanship is a joy to see. Its sides and ends are adorned with angels holding painted shields, and on it lies a knight in plate armour. Round his neck is a collar of suns and roses; his feet are on a lion and his head is on a helmet with a cock's head, the crest of the great Derbyshire family of Cokayne. He is Thomas Cokayne, who lived at Harthill Hall close by and died in 1488. The oldest monument is a cross-legged knight in the chancel, wearing a quilted coat of 700 years ago; he has a sword and holds a heart in his hands. He is perhaps Sir John Rossington, who married with the Cokaynes and the Gilberts.

The Gilberts were at Youlgreave for ten generations, and the north aisle has a remarkable monument with 21 little alabaster figures sculptured in alabaster, showing Robert Gilbert of 1492 with seven sons, his wife with ten daughters, and the Madonna with the Child among them all. Near the monument is the small brass portrait of Fridswide Gilbert in a long-sleeved gown with the skirt open to show the patterned petticoat. She was a descendant of Robert and died in Shakespeare's day, when

> *Her soul to God that first it gave*
> *On angel wings went with her heart.*

Another monument in the north aisle shows Roger Rowe of Alport and his wife kneeling at a desk, he bare-headed and in armour, she with a curious tall hat, and below them tiny figures of six boys and two girls, all wearing Tudor ruffs. Roger died in 1613.

It is pleasant to find the modern woodwork well worthy of its place in this light and spacious church; the pulpit is finely carved, a fine tower screen has panels of linenfold, and the benches have linenfold ends.

A monument of marble and alabaster is in memory of 23 men who died for Peace; to one who fell at Gallipoli a window is filled with glass which stirs us as we look at it, for it has a medley of fragments within green wreaths which were once in Ypres Cathedral and other Belgian churches destroyed in the war.

Youlgreave keeps the steps and massive base-stone of its old cross, and we were told that its registers and parish books are the most complete and interesting local records in Derbyshire.

DERBYSHIRE TOWNS & VILLAGES

In this key to our map of Derbyshire are all the towns and villages treated in this book. If a place is not on the map by name, its square is given here, so that the way to it is easily found, each square being five miles. One or two hamlets are in the book with their neighbouring villages; for these see Index.

DERBYSHIRE TOWNS AND VILLAGES

INDEX

This index includes all notable subjects and people likely to be sought for. The special index of pictures is at the beginning of the volume.

INDEX

286

INDEX

INDEX

INDEX